# Only Fools and Stories

# DAVID JASON

CENTURY

7 9 10 8 6

Century
20 Vauxhall Bridge Road
London SW1V 2SA

Century is part of the Penguin Random House group of companies
whose addresses can be found at global.penguinrandomhouse.com.

Penguin
Random House
UK

First published in 2017 by Century

www.penguin.co.uk

A CIP catalogue record for this book is available from the British Library.

Hardback ISBN 9781780897950
Trade Paperback ISBN 9781780897967

Typeset in 13.25/17.5 pt Goudy Old Style by Jouve (UK), Milton Keynes
Printed and bound in Great Britain by Clays Ltd, St Ives plc

Penguin Random House is committed to a sustainable future
for our business, our readers and our planet. This book is made from
Forest Stewardship Council® certified paper.

MIX
Paper from
responsible sources
FSC
www.fsc.org    FSC® C018179

*For all the brilliant writers past and present who have created so many wonderful characters for me to portray*

# INTRODUCTION

## *Your mission, should you choose to accept it*

The giant Hercules banks heavily and then rights itself in the black night sky over Afghanistan. Inside the plane the nerves are biting deep. We are well into our descent now – dropping down below five thousand feet. This, we know from the briefing, is the zone of maximum vulnerability, the point where this massive flying troopship and its human cargo become one huge, low-slung, slow-moving target for the torpedo-touting rebel forces in the mountains.

I'm strapped tight in a cramped row of hard seats, with my back to the fuselage – just one of the hundreds of us, in our helmets and our flak jackets, with our kitbags wedged between our knees. The plane banks again and slowly twists, fumbling blindly for the runway in the blackness.

Seeking comfort, but not wishing to show my own terror, I glance at the face of the soldier beside me in the dim, green glow of the darkened interior. He stares unflinchingly ahead, his jaw set. What's in his mind? Is he calculating his chances of being blown out of the sky? Is he longing as strongly as I am for the safety of home and the arms of loved ones? Conversation is impossible above the constant, gnawing thunder of the engines. But if I could make myself audible, I know the words I want to say to him – my unknown neighbour, twinned with me by fate and duty, my comrade on this mission into the fathomless desert night.

I would say, 'This is a hell of a lot of trouble to be going to, just to present a "Pride of Britain" Award for ITV.'

Look, they asked me and, obviously, I said yes, didn't I? This was back in 2010. 'Would you present a Special Recognition Award to the British Army's Counter IED Task Force?' they said – somehow not mentioning where and how.

'Of course!' I replied, straight away. Honour the armed forces? Couldn't be happier to do so. If you grew up, as I did, in the aftermath of a world war, playing on north London bomb sites, romping around in the holes where people's houses used to be, respect for the military comes as naturally to you as breathing.

And even if you never played on a bomb site in your life, how could you not respect the work of the Counter IED Task Force? An IED is an improvised explosive device – which might be a landmine or a roadside bomb, something deviously placed in a trap by your enemies to cause carnage. It's the job of the Counter IED Task Force to go out and sweep for these devices – isolate them and annihilate them before they can do any damage to troops and innocent civilians alike.

In other words, these soldiers head out every day and feel around on the ground for bombs in order to save lives. Talk about bravery.

So, an award for people who do this work, and who have been doing it in extraordinarily dangerous circumstances during the seemingly interminable conflict in Afghanistan? I'm right behind that. Frankly, it's the least an actor like me, with no military experience, can do.

And let's face it: it's not really a hardship. I've been around a while – I know how these televised awards ceremonies go. They're not my favourite thing in the world, as will become clear a little later in our story. They're certainly not my favourite thing in the world when it's me who's up for an award. But this is different. This is doing the handing-over. Step out onstage, bit of a smile, bit of a wave, quick kiss for Carol Vorderman, say your piece, hand over the silverware, step back out of the way – a doddle.

My agent, Meg, says: 'No, ITV want to do it as a pre-filmed thing, and insert it into the live show.'

'Oh,' I say. 'Well, that's fine, too, obviously. Maybe better, actually. Where do I have to go?'

'Afghanistan.'

'Afghanistan?'

'Afghanistan.'

3

Picture me, if you will, pausing a moment to digest this tiny detail.

'What, you mean the actual Afghanistan?'

'Yes, that's right.'

Another pause.

'The Afghanistan that's in Afghanistan?'

'Exactly.'

Now, I hope you'll understand me when I say: this put a slightly different coat of paint on things. Jumping onto the stage under the chandeliers at the Grosvenor Hotel, or, as may be, driving over to some suitable external location one afternoon for a spot of light filming: that was one thing. Flying into an actual war zone, on the other hand . . . well, that was definitely another thing. Another, very different, thing.

The problem was, there wasn't exactly room for negotiation here, was there? Either I was in, or I was out. I could hardly say, 'All right, I'll hand over the award to those unutterably brave Counter IED Task Force people in honour of their selfless duty on behalf of the country – but they'll have to come to me.' That wouldn't have seemed altogether in the spirit of it, somehow.

Anyway, setting all that aside and reflecting on it for a moment, there were plenty of positives in this Afghanistan offer, weren't there? Well, one or two positives. It would mean, for one thing, that I could tick Afghanistan off my list of 'places visited'. Work, by this point, had taken me to many far-flung and exotic places, but never taken me there. Australia? Yes. Singapore? Yes again. The Pier Theatre at Bournemouth? Indeed. Afghanistan? No. And it wasn't somewhere that had come up all that much when we were planning family holidays, either, because mostly we like to go to Florida.

So, purely from the point of view of new travel experiences, this trip to a dangerously violent desert state with a long history as a centre for irresolvable conflicts would have to go down as an opportunity. Be honest: how often, in the general run of things, as a civilian, do you get the chance to fly into a war zone? And I'm not counting Aylesbury in the rush hour here (although, don't get me wrong, I know how rough that can get). Accordingly, I would certainly come back from this little adventure with a tale to tell. Assuming I came back.

In any case, we were only going to be there for one night. How bad, actually, could it be? It was only a . . . war zone.

So I pledged myself to the cause, and tried not to think too hard about it in the meantime, which proved quite difficult, as it happened. It proved especially difficult when, a week or so before setting off, I had to attend a briefing regarding the trip with the Ministry of Defence. There was me and the members of the production team that would also be flying out: the cameraman, the soundman and a couple of others. The talk, we were told, was to give us the key information we would need before departure on our journey. I suppose it was like the obligatory safety speech on an aeroplane, really. Except I don't recall the cabin crew on Virgin Atlantic ever having very much to say about waterboarding.

The briefing started out cheerfully enough. Our man from the ministry stood in front of us with one of those big pads of white paper on an easel where you flip the pages up over the top. The first page, as I recall, was about the weather we could expect over there in Helmand Province: sunny and warm in the day, fairly cold at night. It sounded quite pleasant, actually. Then there was some stuff about food – how and when we'd be fed in the camp. That sounded OK, too. I've always had fairly simple tastes with regard to food,

However, from there onwards, each time the ministry man turned a page, the overall picture seemed to darken slightly. For instance, the page concerning the logistics of the journey was ostensibly harmless enough. We would be taking a Boeing 747 from RAF Benson in south Oxfordshire to a military base in Cyprus, where we would pause before heading down to Helmand Province, in the south of Afghanistan. Once there, we would transfer onto the Hercules troop carrier for the remainder of the flight into our destination at Camp Bastion, as it was then known. (It later became Camp Shorabak.) But here was where our man, with very little emotion in his voice, stressed the importance of flying in under the cover of darkness and mentioned the mild but definitely disconcerting possibility of ground-launched enemy torpedoes. Then he turned the page again and there was some more troubling stuff about the military and political situation in the region. Pretty soon after that, and with no particular change in his tone, he was talking about emergency first aid in the event of a wounding and instructing us on the making of a rudimentary tourniquet.

By this time, me and the members of the production team were shooting each other looks. Emergency first aid? A rudimentary tourniquet? I was thinking, 'I bet Carol Vorderman isn't going through any of this.'

But our friend at the easel had already moved on. Now we were into the section of his talk entitled 'What to expect if captured'. I'm not making this up. Each of us was issued with a small piece of white paper which we were told to keep about our persons. Not much bigger than a till receipt, this little sheet explained in the tiniest grey print our rights as prisoners of war. These were helpfully repeated underneath in what I was told was Pashto, or Afghan Persian, for the benefit of any non-English speakers among your hostage-takers. Clearly, the traditional English tactic for getting understood while abroad (say it again, only louder) wasn't automatically going to cut the mustard here.

'Civilians must be treated humanely,' it said on my little bit of paper. That was good news. I suppose it was also quite reassuring to know that your captors had an obligation to make 'adequate provision of food and shelter' for you – and that you could remind them of that obligation by waving this piece of paper at them, in the event that they forgot. However, that's assuming you were in a position to be able to wave your piece of paper, or anything else for that matter. 'There is a possibility that they will put a sack, or similar, over your head and force you to kneel,' explained the man from the MoD.

This was no longer sounding like much of a holiday.

Too late now, of course. I had to sit there, swallow hard and compose my face into an expression of benign interest, for all the world as if getting lectured on the possibility of being taken prisoner and tortured behind enemy lines was just part and parcel of another Thursday morning as far as I was concerned. Anyway, what was I going to say? 'Listen, I've done farce in the West End, love. I was in a touring production of *Look, No Hans*. I was in *Crossroads* when you were a mere slip of a lad, my friend. Nothing you can teach ME about war zones.'

Hardly. I just sat there and tried to encourage my lower lip to stop trembling.

After these words from the ministry man – and still pale and numb from the effect of them – we were issued with our kit for the trip. What can I tell you? It turns out that a bulletproof vest is actually quite heavy. Then there were the desert fatigues and a helmet which was far too big for me and which pushed down on my ears, folding the tops of them outwards at an unflattering ninety-degree angle. A pair of sand goggles completed the outfit. I tried everything on when I got home later and went to look at myself in the mirror. Did I resemble a dashing military hero, poised on the brink of great acts ahead of the bravest day in his life? No. I looked like Dopey from the Seven Dwarves starring in an unfinished remake of *The Bridge on the River Kwai*.

I was also given a fawn-coloured ID card in a protective plastic envelope – a handy, waterproof guide to my vital statistics.

> Name: David Jason
> Date of birth: 02/02/1940
> Height: 5ft 6
> Place of birth: Edmonton, London
> Blood type: O

Good to have these things on the record, I guess.

Eventually, after a few more sleepless nights, the day of the mission dawned. Me, my kitbag and my oversized helmet solemnly reported to RAF Benson at the appointed hour, and boarded the promised Boeing 747. Which turned out to be not too bad, actually – maybe slightly more basic in its fittings than a commercial plane, but otherwise not that different. I almost began to relax at that point.

It was when we were on the ground in Helmand Province and transferring to the Hercules that reality began to bite again. Other troops were joining us at this point, so the numbers had grown massively. You walk onto a Hercules through a giant door at the back, so we all lined up across the tarmac in our uniforms. Queuing for that plane in that horde of soldiers was the point where I really and properly thought: what the hell am I getting myself into here?

Onto the plane we trudged. These were clearly not the circumstances in which to start insisting on an aisle seat. I parked up in the first place that was available and, on a nervous reflex, was about to ask the soldier next to me, 'Do you come here often?' But that was when the engines started up, immediately deafening everyone. We then rattled and juddered out onto the runway. What a piece of kit that Hercules plane is. It's like a town with wings. It doesn't so much soar into the skies as stagger into the air, breathing heavily amid the noise of a million vibrating rivets.

The terrors of the descent negotiated (and without a single torpedo fired, blessedly), we landed at Camp Bastion. I was shown to my quarters – a little room in a stack of Portakabins, with a separate shower and toilet block up at the far end. This was officer-standard accommodation, apparently, so I'm not going to complain about it. I slept and then, in the morning, got my first proper look at the camp. What a scene! The place is four miles long and two miles wide – a dusty, tented, pop-up city, criss-crossed by roads built wide enough, literally, to get tanks down. Here were Brits, Americans, Danes, all mixing in together. There seemed to be a lot of *Only Fools and Horses* fans among them, but then I guess I learned long ago that *Only Fools* fans are everywhere. However, I can guarantee that I was more impressed by these troops than they were impressed by me. If you want to feel that what you do for a living is trivial in the great big scheme of things, go and visit some soldiers in a place of conflict. That will do it for you every time. And then observe the matter-of-fact way in which they set about the job. The atmosphere was strangely mundane in a way, with people calmly going about their daily business. Except that every now and again a Chinook helicopter would clatter by – patrolling the camp's borders, I learned, and ensuring the Taliban weren't digging their way in.

Also, periodically you would hear a succession of sizzles: schf, schf, schf. 'What's that?' I eventually asked. 'Oh, that's Americans launching missiles,' I was told. 'They're trying to take a few out in the mountains.' So much for mundane. Not even in Aylesbury at rush hour is the sizzle of missiles a routine part of the soundtrack.

That said, on the subject of Buckinghamshire, a soldier came up to me in Camp Bastion at one point while I was looking around and said, 'You don't recognise me, do you?' And it was true, the uniform and the context did throw me for a moment – but I did recognise him, in fact. He was the bloke who used to live in a house at the end of my lane. Honestly, you travel all the way to Afghanistan and run into your old neighbour. Small world.

11

Eventually we got around to filming. I interviewed Lt Col. Mark Davis who was in charge of the Counter IED Task Force and who very smoothly explained the work of his unit. I was taken to see the mocked-up village where they do their training, and shown the dogs and the robots that help them with their work, and given the chance to pull myself into the gunner's seat on an armoured vehicle, which I accepted with glee, mostly for the opportunity to point the gun in the direction of the producer. At the end of the day, in a huge circle of servicemen and -women, I handed over the Pride of Britain's silver winged figurine which had travelled out in the producer's kitbag, and then, in perhaps the most surreal moment of them all, I looked into the camera with my best broadcaster's face on and handed back to Carol Vorderman, presenting the show three and a half thousand miles away (and a number of days later) in London. Ah, television.

That evening, after supper and sunset, we were out of there on board another Hercules, heading back to Cyprus. It might have been something to do with the relief of turning for home, and the particular relief when the lights in the cabin went back on at 30,000 feet. But the sight of the sky above us as we took off has remained printed on my memory to this day. It was a blanket of silver – the starriest night sky I have ever seen outside of the movies.

At the time of writing, and subject to further unforeseen developments, this remains the only occasion when what I do for a living has caused me to descend into a war zone. However, it's by no means the only time that what I do for a living has had completely surprising, totally unlooked-for consequences, utterly unimagined by me. That's pretty much the theme of the book you're holding.

In my previous volume of memoirs, *My Life* (still available from reputable booksellers, the publishers have asked me to point out, and possibly from one or two disreputable ones as well), I told the story of my journey from north London electrician with his own van, to television actor with his own car. In this volume, I intend to dwell largely on a bunch of other people whose life stories I think I know pretty well – the characters I've played during that journey. The chances are you know some of these characters, too. Derek Edward Trotter, maybe. Or William Edward Frost. (Funny how those two shared a middle name. They didn't share an awful lot else.) Or Sidney Larkin, perhaps. Or the lad Granville, who, it pains me to say, is not so much of a lad any longer – and possibly wasn't much of a lad to begin with, if we're being honest. I've been fortunate enough to get some parts which seem to have gone over quite well, and to have been in some television shows which have proved to be quite popular – to a degree which none of us involved in them remotely expected or even dared to dream about. A few of those parts, it's fair to say, took on a life of their own, to my delight at times, and much to my alarm at others. That's the story I'm going to tell.

So, in these pages, I'll write about creating the characters I was lucky enough to be introduced to in my career, and about fleshing those characters out – their voices, their clothes, their walks, their mannerisms, the things that made them who they were. I'll go into detail about life on the set during the making of the programmes those characters appeared in. I'll talk about the reactions people had to those characters when they were broadcast. I'll try and explain, for instance, what it was like to make a Christmas special edition of a certain comedy show and discover that more than 24 million people watched it, putting the nation's electricity grid under threat. And I'll talk about what it was like for me to play the people who, ironically, made my name, and about the things, both good and bad – and some-times plain ridiculous – that happened in my life as a consequence of playing them. Like flying to Afghanistan on a mission for the Pride of Britain Awards, for instance.

Also, because I always find it endearing when people make the effort to share the wisdom and expertise that they have gleaned down the years, and because I would like this book to have, if nothing else, a small practical application, you will learn along the way how to fall sideways through the hole where a pub's bar hatch used to be. Apparently I'm quite renowned for that. There may be a few other tricks of the trade thrown in as well, depending how we go.

Strap yourself in, then, as our second journey begins. There are, to the best of my knowledge, no torpedo-touting rebels in the surrounding hillsides. At the same time, it might be wise to keep a watchful eye out at all times.

But first, take, if you will, a look at the photograph on the next page. It may hold the key to everything.

# CHAPTER ONE

## *Just getting away from it all*

What a picture. This beautifully composed and subtly lit piece of photographic art is an out-take from an award-winning session that I did with Annie Leibovitz for a cover story in *Vanity Fair* magazine at the point where my career was really beginning to take off in America.

Oh, all right, then: no it isn't. It's a blurry snap taken in the late 1970s by hands unknown, with a Kodak Instamatic most probably, and then delivered, in all likelihood, to the local chemist's for processing, prior to collection from that chemist's in a glossy folder a fortnight later, if you were lucky. (Kids: there's simply too much out-of-date stuff to explain here. Ask an adult who has got a free hour or seven.)

However, since then, this photograph has lived with me in various boxes and trays and drawers, growing no sharper or better lit with the passing years, but somehow accumulating meaning, at least from my personal point of view. Every time I come across it, it seems to strike me anew. It's just a quick picture, grabbed behind the scenes in a theatre. Yet there's something about it which seems to get to the heart of the matter and sum a few things up.

A few details about this noble image. We are backstage at the Arts Theatre in Cambridge, a decent, 600-seater provincial venue, and the date would have to be at some point in October 1978. That makes me a willowy thirty-eight years of age – a veritable infant, I would argue, in thespian terms. Certainly the most prominent points of my life in the business are all ahead of me.

The play I am appearing in is called *The Relapse – or, Virtue in Danger* – a Restoration comedy, written in the late seventeenth century by Sir John Vanbrugh. This was only my second appearance in a piece from that period; as a member of the Bromley Theatre repertory company, in my first proper job as an actor, I appeared as Bob Acres in Richard Brinsley Sheridan's *The Rivals*. These were perhaps not the kinds of roles you would expect an actor with my background to land. I had come out of amateur dramatics and hadn't been to drama school or done a course in acting in which Restoration plays and their customs and techniques might have been part of your studies. So I was going on intuition, direction and what I could pick up from reading a bit around the subject. Which is why I'm in a position to tell you that, when he wasn't busy writing plays, John Vanbrugh practised as an architect, during the course of which work (on, I like to think, an idle Sunday), he designed Blenheim Palace, the massive pad in Oxfordshire which has provided a stately home down the years to various Dukes of Marlborough. So Vanbrugh was no slouch, clearly. And on the subject of people who aren't slouches, the director of this 1978 production of *The Relapse* was Jonathan Lynn, who was the artistic director of the Cambridge Theatre Company at this point in his career, but who is probably better known to you as the co-creator of the comedy series *Yes, Minister* and, later, *Yes, Prime Minister*. OK, *Yes, Minister* wasn't exactly Blenheim Palace but it was pretty good, too, and for a decent portion of the 1980s, it was getting many more viewers than Blenheim Palace on a weekly basis.

I know that Jonathan Lynn directed *The Relapse* because, as well as the photograph reproduced above, I also have to hand a programme from the production – one of quite a number of programmes that I seem to have tucked away over the course of time, because a blend of sentiment and pride stopped me from parting with them. That said, it's always a bitter-sweet experience to look back at the programme from a show that you were in and run your eye down the cast list. On the one hand, there are the actors who went on to have careers and whose names remain familiar to you. For example, in the case of this 1978 production of *The Relapse*, there's Louise Jameson, who was very famously Doctor Who's leather-wearing assistant during the 1970s, had big roles in *Tenko* and *Bergerac*, and later spent two and a half years playing Rosa di Marco in *EastEnders*. And there's also Guy Siner, the comic actor who landed the nice part of Lieutenant Hubert Gruber in *'Allo 'Allo!*.

But then there are the names that you never saw again. What happened to those people? They seemed so talented and capable at the time – as talented and capable as anybody else in the cast. Why didn't it work out for them? Did they mind that it didn't? Did they get happy doing something else? It's a very fine line, is the sobering lesson here.

On a slightly less melancholy note, there's another vivid memory which, for some reason, rises unbidden with great clarity as I gaze at the pages of this ancient theatre programme: namely, that someone at some stage threw the cast and crew a candlelit party, at somebody or other's abode in Cambridge. And at this candlelit party in all of our honours, a stage assistant, perhaps in search of attention that wasn't otherwise coming his way, devoted himself to going round the room eating all the candles.

Now, it's beholden upon me at this point in the narrative

to issue a brief but important lesson in human biology: candle wax does not sit terribly well in the digestive system. Moreover, I must stress that, if you are looking for something to ease the passage of candle wax through said digestive system, alcohol, in the form of beers, wines and spirits, will be of precious little use to you as a solvent. As a matter of fact – and as was amply proven that night – your predicament will only worsen. Indeed, there was a moment in the evening where, with the wax and the alcohol in this bloke's body reaching saturation point, he would probably have burned at both ends. Which would have redefined the term 'lit up'.

Nobody tried, fortunately. Suffice it to say, though, that I have never seen anybody so ill, who was still standing up and breathing unassisted, as that stage assistant the following day. But at least he survived. More or less.

Anyway, to return to the play: my part in *The Relapse* was Lord Foppington, who was (and you may be ahead of me here) a fop – a trivial dandy, all manners and affectations. Names that functioned as large-scale clues about the sort of people you were dealing with were always a big number for these Restoration comedy writers. Also in *The Relapse* are characters called Sir Tunbelly Clumsey, Sir John Friendly and Serringe, a surgeon. Lord Foppington, it turns out in the course of the play, was formerly known as Sir Novelty Fashion but then managed to buy himself a title. Scandalous. Would never happen nowadays, of course.

In the photograph, I'm not yet in costume, but I'm presumably just about to climb into it. I have just had my make-up done. It has been applied using a version of the Japanese kabuki method, where you slather the face completely in a thick white undercoat and then paint in the features over the top. It's a bit like decorating a sitting room, I suppose, except on a slightly smaller scale and with less furniture to shift. On top of the white face mask, I have been given thickly blackened eyes and brows, and heart-shaped, ruby-red, permanently puckered lips. My hair, you will observe – which was still capable of providing an all-over covering for my head in those wondrous but, alas, far-off days – has been carefully trapped and flattened inside a net, from which there will be no escape for it, barring an explosion in the vicinity large enough to blow the pins out.

This use of a hairnet is in order to provide a suitably flat platform for Lord Foppington's wigs which, in this production, were absolute works of art. The production was rather lavish altogether, as I recall. *The Relapse* was the last play in that year's season at the Arts Theatre and there seemed to be money in the kitty – money which needed spending, or else the theatre would simply have its Arts Council budget cut the following year. So the production was an extremely well-furnished one, with Lord Foppington's wigs in particular feeling the benefit. There were three of these in total, each more elaborate and foppish and ridiculous than the last, and culminating in a long, flowing cloud of ginger curls, which resembled nothing so much as a skinned and blow-dried poodle, or possibly two skinned and blow-dried poodles, glued together. When I say long, I mean long – and when I say flowing, I also mean flowing. When not in use, this big, final wig had to be hung up to stop it getting tangled, and when it was suspended from its hanger in the dressing room it was as tall as I am. Which – before you make the point yourself – is not all that tall.

But this wig was almost big enough, and agile enough, to have its own part in the play. I only had to walk on in it to bring the house down, and I don't mind confessing that I used to milk the moment mercilessly, taking a moment or two to give the audience an affronted eye, as if to ask them what, exactly, they thought they were laughing at. As far as I could tell from my research, contemporary Restoration players were perfectly willing to involve and interact with their audiences, who were very vocal in those days. So I wasn't being hammy, you understand; I was being authentic. Well, that's my story.

Anyway, look at me in this picture, thrusting upward from the hips, cocking my head for the camera. I stare at this photo now and I'm thinking: 'Who is this bloke? Where has he come from and what does he want? What is that pose he is already unthinkingly striking?' Even before strapping on the absurd buckled orange boots, shaped like twin gondolas, and climbing into the orange brocaded frock coat with its floppy lace cuffs and equally floppy lace neck-piece, and then clambering underneath that ridiculous pile of wig, I seem to have turned into Lord Foppington – albeit Lord Foppington in his underwear. The truth is, when I look at the person in this photo, I don't see myself at all, or anything that I think of as resembling myself. That bloke – the bloke that I'm obliged to live with the rest of the time, when I am not, as rule, wearing Japanese kabuki-style face paint – has gone. He has already done a runner. He has vanished under the make-up. He has disappeared through a side door and into the theatre.

That, I reckon, is why this arbitrary, casual snapshot is such a weirdly compelling image for me, why it exercises such a lasting fascination. It seems somehow to contain the essence of the thing that drew me in the first place – the thing that lured me into amateur dramatics as a shy teenager from a terraced house in north London, that persuaded me to dump the work as an electrician that I had trained for and which seemed to be my destined course in life, and, instead, give myself five years to try and make the grade as a repertory actor. That thing was the chance acting offered to be other people, people who weren't me or anything like me – the possibility, however momentary, of absolute escape into other characters and other lives, of absolute escape from yourself, which sometimes, looking back now, the job has delivered, and in spades, and which sometimes it hasn't.

# CHAPTER TWO

## *The things some people keep*

It's an early spring afternoon in March 2017, and I am in a lock-up unit in a storage depot on an industrial estate on the outskirts of Milton Keynes, staring in wonderment at a life-size ceramic statue of a collie dog.

'Blimey, is that the actual one?'

It is, indeed, the actual one – the actual mock-porcelain mutt that, for many episodes of *Only Fools and Horses* in the 1980s, sat looking a bit gormless in the sitting room of the Trotters' flat on the twelfth floor of the Nelson Mandela House tower block in Peckham, which was, of course, a set in a BBC studio, but you know what I mean. That ceramic dog wasn't the only thing that sat looking a bit gormless in that flat, it has to be said, because Rodney and Grandad also had their moments. But, unlike them, perhaps, the dog had a decent excuse.

And now here I am, three decades and more later, in this chilly storage depot, eye to eye with that extraordinary beast again, this absurd, ornamental Lassie lookalike – man's best friend, only in very shiny and very still form. Who seems to be in quite good shape, I am pleased to see, after all this time: bright-eyed, no more chipped than he was back when the two of us enjoyed each other's company on a regular basis. OK, he's not much livelier than he was back then, either; he's still just sitting there, just as gormless, and not saying much. Probably just as cheap to feed, too. And as I reach forward and run my hand over the smooth, cold surface of this ridiculously naff, waist-high piece of sitting-room statuary, memories, as absurd as it may seem, come flooding back that are almost painful in their poignancy.

But before we get into all that, perhaps I should explain why, in the seventy-seventh year of my life, I am spending a midweek afternoon stroking a pottery dog in a Milton Keynes storage facility. Not for an episode of *Antiques Roadshow*, let me immediately tell you – although no doubt you and me both would be surprised, and possibly even stunned, to learn how much a mock-china collie that had regularly appeared in *Only Fools and Horses* would be worth these days, were those numbers available to us.

But I'm not here to get anything valued by Fiona Bruce. I'm here because I've agreed to film a sequence for a documentary programme that UKTV is doing about the making of *Only Fools*. UKTV is a cable channel that devotes a lot of its airtime to reruns of *Only Fools* and has, in a sense, become the show's second home during its prolonged and seemingly ceaseless afterlife. Now they want to make six one-hour programmes about the series, going back to the locations where the show was shot and talking to the key people – the ones of us who are still alive, at any rate. Those members of our family who have sadly passed since the making of the programme get a free pass. And, on the grounds that this sounds like it isn't going to turn into one of those cheap and cheerful 'tribute' shows, where they show you clips from the programme in question and then get a familiar-looking talking head (who is frequently a comedian, for some reason) to say something about the clip that is less funny than the clip was, I'm on board.

So, on the appointed afternoon in March, I drive from my home in Buckinghamshire to Milton Keynes, pausing only to consume, by way of luncheon, a dead sandwich from a service station on the ring road, for such is the non-stop, 24/7, five-star glamour of the television actor's life. Then, carefully following the instructions, I nudge the car down a bumpy and gradually narrowing road past the recycling centre and the cement works to the self-storage warehouse. Here, a dab of powder is tenderly applied to my face in the little side office which has been temporarily requisitioned as a make-up room for the day; and, after that, the plan is to lead me to a numbered unit in the main warehouse, not a million miles dissimilar from Derek Trotter's old lock-up and storage space in the old strip of garages near the

Peckham tower block. With a couple of cameras rolling, the doors of the unit will be thrown open to reveal a stash of props and artefacts and bits of furniture, as used on the actual sets of *Only Fools*. And with any luck, I will have a reaction to said props and artefacts – though at this stage nobody involved in the production, and least of all me, has any idea exactly how strong that reaction will be.

Incidentally, the bits and pieces of memorabilia that I will be perusing form part of the collection of Perry Aghajanoff, who is a founder of the *Only Fools and Horses* Appreciation Society. Perry runs the annual *Only Fools* fans' convention. I've not been myself, because it's not my kind of thing, but apparently people tip up in costume and spend a few hours reminiscing about the show, and if you thought that only *Star Trek* generated this kind of event, and this degree of fanaticism, then you're wrong. Perry once got me to sign the bonnet of a yellow three-wheeled Reliant Regal, like the one that Trotters Independent Trading used. Just the bonnet, note. I don't know what had become of the rest of it or who had made off with its three wheels. Anyway, this remains, I can confidently say, the largest individual item that I have ever put an autograph on, and also the most absurd. Perry continues to find stuff related to the show from who knows where, and what he doesn't know about *Only Fools* isn't worth knowing; and, as I find out in that lock-up on that spring afternoon, what Perry can't somehow lay his hands on from the original programmes isn't worth laying your hands on, either.

It's Perry who escorts me to the lock-up, and it's Perry who opens the doors to disclose his hoard – and what can I tell you? It's overpowering. So many associations, all at once. A hundred feelings crowd in on me at the same time and I practically freeze to the spot. There are so many instantly familiar items here in this little walk-in space, from so many different places and times in the show, and wedged together in such tight proximity, that my senses can only reel.

Look at that! Here, against the wall, is the tacky green cabinet that stood in the Trotters' kitchen and held the plates and dishes. So straight away I'm spun back onto the set and into that crowded old council flat, with all its glorious and not so glorious junk. And here's the lion biscuit jar or – as recommissioned by Del – the cigar holder, with its daft lift-off lid, which I lift off again now, for old times' sake. No cigars inside, alas. Empty. But that dopey-eyed lion was in every episode. If its agent was any good, it would be seeing repeat fees. I replace the lid and instead pick up the flat's old pistol-shaped cigar lighter – that fancy 'antique' novelty ornament where you clicked the trigger to ignite the flame at the end of the barrel. All in the best possible taste.

But wait: put that pistol down because here's a chunky knock-off mobile phone with its aerial sticking out –

comically old-fashioned and brick-like now, but a swish, cutting-edge yuppie device back at the start of the 1980s, and something that Del was practically swooning with delight to get his hands on, albeit that when you pressed its buttons it changed the channels on the pub telly. So now, picking this phone off the table and remembering that scene, I'm whisked out of the flat and back down to the Nag's Head – a short walk across the studio, if we're going to be literal about it – and trading lines with Mike the landlord and Trigger and Boycie.

Hang on again, though, because down on the floor here, right by my feet, is the leopard-print suitcase that accompanied Del to Florida for the 'Miami Twice' Christmas special episode that went out in 1991 – my favourite of all the *Only Fools and Horses* episodes, if push comes to shove. It was deemed that Del would have tasteless luggage in mock leopard-skin – just as in another episode, he would disport himself in Spain in leopard-print budgie smugglers, in the wonderfully deluded belief that the women would be cutting themselves in half to get to him in that ludicrous swimwear. (Lord, my delight when I opened the script for that Spanish-based episode. 'Top work,' I thought. 'Some sun and some heat will go down nicely.' But, of course, BBC budgets, which were somehow never as automatically generous for comedy as they were for drama, were in operation. We filmed those Spanish scenes around Bournemouth. 'Don't worry,' they said. 'We'll light it so it looks like Spain.' Never mind what it looks like, one was tempted to reply, what about our suntans?)

The budgie smugglers were acquired from a shop, to the best of my recollection, but the BBC props department had to have the suitcase for Miami made to order. A quality piece of craftsmanship it is, too. Bless him, you could just make Del so naff, which was one of the wonderful things about him and a huge part of what made him such fun to play. He had this beautifully bold and uncomplicated view of what worked for him, fashion-wise, and you couldn't help but love him for it. And now, just seeing that leopard-print suitcase, I'm right back at Heathrow airport touting that bag proudly in the direction of the Virgin Atlantic check-in desk and then getting cross when some presumptuous bloke has the nerve to push in on the queue. ('Anybody would think he owns the plane,' I had to say at that moment, and when the bloke turned round, we got to see that it was Richard Branson. Whatever became of him? And whatever became of my free trip to Necker Island? Not a sausage.)

Wait a minute though, because here, directly behind the suitcase is, surreally, a bright orange lifebelt, rimmed with white rope and with a name painted on it in black capital letters: 'INGE', the boat that Del, Rodney and Uncle Arthur hired to travel to Holland on the trail of a batch of diamonds in 'To Hull and Back', the Christmas special from 1985. But wait another minute: are you kidding? What's this big white thing the lifebelt is leaning against, all weathered and with its paint peeling? It's only one of the *Inge's* funnels. How the hell did Perry manage to lay his hands on that? (Perry merely stands to one side and smiles enigmatically.) So now I'm no longer at Heathrow, bound for Miami, I'm in the freezing cold North Sea, pitching and tossing in a battered, old, pockmarked tub of a boat, and shouting up to a bloke on an oil rig, 'Excuse me, pal, which way is Holland?' – second for second, in terms of what it cost to shoot, probably the most expensive gag in the history of BBC comedy. (Fair play: the corporation got the chequebook out for us occasionally. But blimey, you had to pester them.)

Then, almost straight away, I'm off the boat, because here by the lifebelt is our old friend, the collie. So that sends my memory streaming back to the flat again, and suddenly, running my fingers across my canine chum's cold head, I'm wondering what became of the collie's mate – a strange-looking, white creature, much the same size and just as gawpy, which strayed onto the set one week and stayed there a while. It was part Dalmatian, as I recall, but perhaps with a bit of pottery greyhound in its ceramic ancestry. That was the dog which enjoyed a cameo role in the 'Three Men, a Woman and a Baby' episode, in series seven. It's the episode more commonly known for the big scene at the end in which Del's Raquel gives birth to their son Damien and Del carries the baby to the hospital window for his first view of the world, again stretching the limits of where comedies were supposed to go. It's also, while I think of it, the episode in which Del has accompanied Raquel to a maternity class where some of the other future fathers have been rendered a little queasy by the instructional video, but not, as it happens, our man Del. 'I was all right because I used to run a jellied eel stall.' Oh, the joy of delivering zingers like that.

And it's also the episode in which Del has bought a box of wigs off Mustapha, the Bangladeshi butcher. During the camera rehearsal, it occurred to me that Del might want to comb the wigs out a bit, and smarten them up – 'dress' them, as they say in the make-up department. And what better model or 'wig block' than the head of the spotless Dalmatian? Well, he wasn't doing anything else at the time. So there's a scene which opens with Del, in the lounge, sitting, straddle-legged, behind a china dog, combing a wig on its head, as if it's the most natural thing in the world for a man to be doing at home of a weekday evening. These were the moments in the shooting of the show that I really loved, when you added something daft that wasn't in the script, found an additional bit of business to get up to and conjured an extra laugh out of nowhere.

Hold up again, though: this place is like Aladdin's cave. Over here on the floor are some unopened bottles of Peckham Spring Mineral Water, from the 1992 Christmas special, 'Mother Nature's Son', where Del enterprisingly uses the product of the kitchen tap to enter the burgeoning refreshment business. It's good to see them, although, as it happens, these items are not so startling to me, because I've got a couple of bottles of Peckham Spring at home, which I have 'laid down', as I believe the wine experts like to say. They're the centre piece of my own comparatively meagre *Only Fools* memorabilia collection, which otherwise only really includes the following: a small, framed 'Trotter Air Gets You There' poster which was on the set during Rodney's futuristic dream sequence at the beginning of 'Heroes and Villains', wherein Rodney fantasises that the Trotters have successfully expanded, Branson-style, into the airline business; a couple of Del's jumpers, which may be a little snug in the fit these days, but sentiment precludes me from junking them; and Del's very first sheepskin coat, which I don't have much occasion to wear around the house, it's true, but to which I am sentimentally attached, and for which, by the way, I paid the BBC wardrobe department a fee. This was midway through the show's life, when Del was deemed to have moved on a bit and become slightly more yuppie in his aspirations. The original, market-trader look wasn't relevant any more, and the sheepskin – a magnificent item, made using patches of many different sheep, it would appear – was cluttering up the wardrobe. Did I want it? I was asked. Well, yes I did – how much?

'I don't know,' said the wardrobe person. 'Twenty quid?'

'But surely it must be worth more than that,' I replied, not wishing to rip off the BBC which is, after all, publicly funded by the licence payer (and also feeling slightly offended on behalf of Del, whose precious coat it was, after all).

'It's only going to be chucked out,' said the wardrobe person.

'Even so,' I said. 'What about sixty quid?'

'Thirty,' said the wardrobe person.

'Fifty,' I replied, in best Del Boy dealing mode.

'Forty.'

'Forty-five.'

'Done.'

There you go – no flies on me. We shook hands, with me having forced the deal up to £25 above the original asking price. I've had the goods ever since. In my innocence, I thought it would make a really good winter coat – heavy, yes, but extremely warm, if not stylish. Of course, the minute I put it on, I became recognisable as Del Boy everywhere from Land's End to John O'Groats. So it went in the cupboard and has largely lived there since.

Anyway, back in the lock-up, I turn slightly, away from the Peckham Spring bottles, and see the urn from the 'Ashes to Ashes' episode in series two – the colourfully painted china pot which held the precious mortal remains of Trigger's grandfather, Arthur. Or, at least, it held them until Rodney mistakenly rested the urn on the pavement and its contents got inadvertently sucked up by a road-cleaning lorry. Me and Rodney had to tell the bloke in the cab: 'Stop! You've just sucked up our urn.' And the bloke in the cab says: 'Oh my God. What was he, a little kitten?' We had a huge problem with that scene because the cameraman was in the cab, shooting down at us, and every time the driver said that line, he would laugh and shake the camera, and then me and Nick would go, too. We must have tried it about six times. Eventually we had to get the cameraman out and put somebody else in.

But I can't think about that for too long, either, because next to the urn is some jewellery – a couple of Del's gold sovereign rings and the matching dog-tag bracelets that he and Rodney wore in a show of their brotherliness. Rodney's, of course, said 'Rooney', rather than Rodney, but Del convinced him otherwise. Hold up yet again, though, because next to these exquisite bits of bling is, God love us, the showpiece item, I guess – the crown jewel at the heart of this memorabilia collection: the actual 'silver', eighteenth-century fob watch that Del unearthed in his lock-up, in the 1996 Christmas special, and casually tossed aside, but which later sold at Sotheby's for £6.2 million, meaning that finally – finally – the Trotters were millionaires. Quite a few people saw that episode: 24.3 million, to be precise, a British record for an entertainment show and one that isn't likely to be broken any time soon. I weigh the fob watch very fondly in the palm of my hand and ask Perry how much he paid for it, but he won't tell me. Quite a lot less than £6.2 million, I'm fairly sure. Not that it isn't, in its own way, a very rare and precious item, of course. Mind you, there was more than one made for the show, as I recall. We had to have one that could be chucked about with impunity because when Del first turns up this precious item, he flings it onto an old gas cooker to convey its worthlessness. Going by the weight and the detail, the one I'm holding here is the smart version, as seen at Sotheby's. Whisper it, but neither version was silver. They both had cases made of nickel.

Yet, strange as it may seem, amid this array of objects – the watch, the urn, the rings, the lifebelt, the china lion cigar holder – with all their specific attachments to particular stories and with all the individual memories that flow from them, it's the cardboard boxes that hit me hardest. It sounds stupid, I know, but it's true. They're piled up at the side of the lock-up – just a stack of empty containers, printed up to look like they hold dodgy Russian video cameras. Yet their impact on me is bewildering. The flat was always stacked with boxes – Del's latest acquisitions, ready for the market – and now, confronted with them again, they're the trapdoor that plunges me right back into the heart of those times. Nothing around me sums up the Trotters' home in all its glorious impermanence like the cardboard boxes, and nothing so immediately kick-starts the feeling that I used to get when I walked on the set in those years. The boxes were what the flat was, really. They bring back to me the sense of constant change, the continual toing and froing of the characters against that ever-shifting backdrop of dodgy boxed goods.

I say 'dodgy', but the stuff was never stolen, it's important to insist. The goods were cheap and tacky and very often broken, yes, and they may have owed their availability, somewhere back down the line, to a little underhand activity here and there, perhaps involving lorries and the cover of darkness. But they were always legitimately acquired, at least by Del, because Trotters Independent Trading was, at heart, a straight organisation, which people sometimes forget in the retelling. Del was a geezer who sold dodgy things, no question: but he was not at heart a dodgy geezer and I'm not sure the country would have come to love him so wholly and unreservedly if he had been.

The goods certainly came and went, though. As, indeed, did the furniture. I remember saying one day, 'Shouldn't we have the furniture changing as well?' It had occurred to me: wouldn't the Trotters' furnishings be up for sale, if a deal could be done, as much as anything else in the flat? I was remembering somebody I knew who did a bit of antique dealing. When you went round his house, you would suddenly notice that the chair you were sitting on had a price tag on it. And then you would notice that the lamps, too, were price-tagged, and all of the ornaments and the coffee table ... The stuff was in and out: nothing was permanent and everything had its price.

So, one week we changed the Trotters' sofa. No explanation was offered: we just shipped it out and had another one brought in. At which point I suggested keeping the plastic wrapping on it, to imply that this sofa, too, might not be hanging around too long. So the family had to sit on a plastic-covered sofa for a while; and then that one, too, changed and in came another, and so on it went.

But these cardboard boxes . . . Oh my. Of all the unlikely time machines. In the movie *Back to the Future*, Michael J. Fox had a specially tricked-out DeLorean car to blast him back into yesteryear. For me, it wasn't even a Reliant Regal, or any individual part thereof: it was a pile of bogus packaging, rigged to look like it might have contained a batch of hooky electronics. Which says it all, really, about *Only Fools*.

Just before we finish filming in the Milton Keynes lock-up – and before I get back in the car and head for home, greatly tenderised by the experience – a plastic crate is brought in and set down on the floor. Inside it is a batch of John Sullivan's original typewritten scripts. I reach into the crate and lift a few out, and it's genuinely stirring to find my hands on those sheets of paper again. Right away I'm remembering the excitement and eagerness I used to feel, pulling them out of the envelope when they were sent to me at home. 'What's he come up with *this* time?' you'd be thinking. I'd be like a boy with the latest edition of a comic. I thumb through a few pages now, observing the difference in weight between the early, half-hour ones and then the fatter ones from the sixth series onwards, when we persuaded the BBC to take the show from the seemingly statutory sitcom thirty-minute length, up to a more drama-like fifty minutes per episode. Because that's what *Only Fools* was, really: a drama. A drama with thick streaks of comedy in it.

It all sprang from here – these bits of paper. I set John Sullivan's old scripts back in their plastic crate and wonder aloud how many laughs there must be in that one box.

# CHAPTER THREE

## *Derek Trotter, a brief history*

So, who was Derek Trotter? Who was this bloke who came to occupy so much of my life and to reach so deeply into so many other people's lives? To get to the heart and root of him, you probably have to understand where John Sullivan, the writer, was coming from – a place, coincidentally, not so far, culturally and geographically speaking, from where I came from.

I grew up in a small terraced house in Lodge Lane in Finchley, London, with no bathroom, a tin bath on the kitchen door, an outside privy and a little concrete backyard. John grew up (starting six years later) in a small terraced house in Zennor Road in Balham, London, with no bathroom, a tin bath on the kitchen door, an outside privy and a little concrete backyard. My mum worked as a charlady. John's mum worked as a charlady. My dad was a fishmonger. John's dad was – guess what. You've got it – a plumber. OK, so that was a difference. Both of us left school at fifteen, without sitting any exams, and, whereas I went into the employment centre and pulled out the card for a job as a mechanic's help at Popes Garage, John started work as a messenger boy, first at Reuters news agency and then in an advertising company. At one point he apprenticed as a plumber with his dad, but he didn't take to that really, much as my apprenticeship at Popes Garage fizzled out and I went off and trained as an electrician. Instead of plumbing, John cleaned cars and then had an unsuccessful stab at selling them, and he eventually wound up working in a Watney's brewery, packing beer crates.

All the time, though, he was writing – just as all the time I was doing amateur dramatics. John was determined to break into television comedy. This probably seemed as remote a likelihood to him as making it as a professional actor seemed to me. But he had noticed how Johnny Speight, in the sixties, had gone from a humble background in Canning Town in London to a career as a celebrated script-writer by creating the legendary character of Alf Garnett and coming up with *Till Death Us Do Part*. He saw how Ray Galton and Alan Simpson had done much the same with *Steptoe and Son*. Inspired by those successes, John was constantly devising his own comedy shows and sending proposals and pilot scripts to the BBC – refusing to be set back by the standard rejection letters which inevitably flopped onto the doormat a few weeks later, but, instead, sitting down again and writing another proposal, another script.

He used to say that it was a hobby – and one that had the advantage of saving him a fortune in beer money because he would stay at home in the evenings and write rather than head off up the pub. But even if it was just a hobby at first, this was clearly a man who had entirely convinced himself that it would eventually amount to more than that. Someone once said to me, in the early stages of my career, 'If you want to be a comic, you're going to need an idiotic determination to succeed.' I think they were trying to be encouraging. But whatever they were trying to be, they weren't wrong. The phrase has stuck with me: an idiotic determination to succeed is what it takes. And the same goes, clearly, for comedy writers. John believed that if he just kept working and knocking hard enough, he would eventually break through.

He was right, too, of course – but it took a cunning move on his part to bring the desired ending about. John applied for a job in the props department at BBC Television Centre – humping the furniture around for *The Morecambe & Wise Show* and *I, Claudius* and all sorts – and thereby tunnelled himself into the beating heart of the organisation where he could become his own advocate and start to lean on people a bit more heavily. A very shrewd ploy, that. If the corridors of power won't come to your house, go and live in the corridors of power. This was in the mid-seventies, and at one point, John found himself in a position to saunter up to Dennis Main Wilson, the vitally significant

BBC comedy producer who worked with the Goons, Tony Hancock, Eric Sykes, Marty Feldman – in fact, pretty much every one of the great names of British television and radio comedy alive at that point. And Main Wilson was clearly persuaded enough by John's confidence to sit down with him and hear him out and give him some advice, the most significant piece of which was that if John wanted to make it as a scriptwriter, his best way in was to start out smaller and write some sketches – short, one-off numbers for variety shows.

John duly went away and did so. It just so happened that, around this time, his day job found him humping the furniture on and off the set for *Porridge*, the great Ronnie Barker prison-based sitcom – in which, the gilded annals of broadcasting history will show, I took the part of Blanco Webb, an ancient inmate, imprisoned for murdering his wife, though continually and convincingly professing his innocence, even while preferring to stay in prison rather than accept the pardon that has been granted to him by the prison governor. I loved playing Blanco – and, of course, I got that great story-clincher of a moment in an episode in series three, called, 'Pardon Me', where Ronnie Barker as Fletcher, after much painstaking and concerted effort, finally persuades Blanco to accept the official pardon and leave jail. As Blanco readies himself to walk out into the world, Fletcher begs him to promise that he's not to go getting himself into trouble by avenging the man who genuinely did murder his wife. Whereupon Blanco says, 'No, I know him what did it. It were the wife's lover. But don't worry – he died years ago, that I do know. It were me that killed him.'

It was a lovely and completely unforeseeable twist, wonderfully enhanced by the freeze frame on Blanco as he turns to leave, which just gives you a beat to absorb the gag before the end of the show swallows it – a comic effect of the highest order, worked to perfection by the director, Syd Lotterby. There was a neat and satisfying roundedness to the construction of that twist, too, because justice had been served, albeit it in a circuitous way: Blanco had been wrongly imprisoned for a crime he didn't commit, but he had also served his time for the one that he actually did commit. Dick Clement and Ian La Frenais, the writers of *Porridge*, knew what they were about.

Incidentally, in the final scene of that episode, just prior to his release, Blanco was to be seen for the first time out of his prison clothes and back in the suit that, imaginably, he was wearing when he was put away, and there was a notion that the suit shouldn't really fit him any more, after all this time. I had the additional idea, though, that it would be even funnier if it looked as though the jacket and trousers had been folded up and left in a drawer for twenty-five years. So I spoke to the wardrobe people about it and got them to iron some strong creases into the clothing so that it had these really stiff lines across it in the wrong places and hung really badly on Blanco's body, as well it might if it had been folded away for a quarter of a century. The suit and its condition were never alluded to in the script. It was one of those gags that was just left there: you might notice it and get the joke, or you might not, but it was in there anyway, ready to provide a bit of added value for any takers.

Did John Sullivan's and my paths cross during that happy time on *Porridge*? Not so that either of us ever did recall. But John certainly crossed paths with Ronnie Barker and was bold enough to put some of his freshly written sketches into Ronnie's hands with a plea that he should consider them. Ronnie didn't just consider them; he used them in *The Two Ronnies*. They were the Sid and George sketches – little bits and pieces in which two cockney geezers sit in a pub and chew the fat, mostly at cross purposes with one another. More than that, Ronnie organised for John to get put on contract at the BBC as a writer, a fantastic break for him, meaning he was now getting paid to come up with material for, not just the Ronnies, but shows with Dave Allen and Les Dawson which were right at the centre of the BBC's Light Entertainment roster in those days.

Yet another parallel, then, between us. It was Ronnie Barker who took me, too, under his wing – using me, at the recommendation of the producer Humphrey Barclay, for sketches in *Hark at Barker* and then eventually getting me to play Granville opposite his Arkwright in *Open All*

*Hours* and becoming in the process my biggest influence and closest friend in the industry. John, then, like me, had the door into mainstream television held open for him by Ronnie B, without whom who knows how differently things might have panned out for both of us.

Anyway, as encouraged by Dennis Main Wilson, John graduated from sketch-writing to full-length scripts, coming up, almost straight off the bat, with the enormously successful sitcom *Citizen Smith*, starring Robert Lindsay as Wolfie Smith, the faux-Marxist leader of the Tooting Popular Front, who campaigned assiduously, albeit largely unsuccessfully, for 'freedom for Tooting' and 'power to the people'. *Citizen Smith* ran for four series between 1977 and 1980 before John came to the conclusion that he had taken those characters about as far as they would go and decided to move on. John was football-mad – something I never shared with him, but each to his own – and the next project he came up with was a show entitled *Over the Moon*, about a failed and failing football manager endlessly attempting to bring his team back from the dead. He had his lead actor in place – Brian Wilde, who played Mr Barraclough, the gullible prison warden in *Porridge*, and Foggy in the practically never-ending *Last of the Summer Wine* – he seemed to have the enthusiasm of the BBC behind him, and he had a formidable director, Ray Butt, about whom these pages will have much more to say. Ray had directed a number of episodes of *Citizen Smith*, not to mention *The Liver Birds*, *It*

47

*Ain't Half Hot Mum* and *Are You Being Served?* – all of them
series that would come to have some staying power. A pilot
of *Over the Moon* was made and, after the BBC had had a
look at that, John was given the nod to go away and start
writing six episodes for a first series.

All was clearly set fair, then, for another ratings-grabbing
success, à la *Citizen Smith* and lashings of ginger beer for all
concerned – or not, as it happened, because the BBC
promptly turned round a few weeks later and cancelled the
project. Apparently the Light Entertainment department
had decided in the meantime to make a sitcom about boxing (*Seconds Out*, starring – that man again – Robert
Lindsay) and the BBC felt that that was probably enough
comedies on a sporting theme for now. Thus does the mys-
terious corporation move, its wonders to perform. *Seconds
Out*, incidentally, lasted two series and mustered very little
in the way of repeat action (just one rerun, for the second
series). We'll never know now, of course, whether the BBC
backed the wrong horse, but I know what my suspicions are
telling me.

Anyway, from the point of view of this tale, it's a good job
*Over the Moon* did get cancelled, given what then happened. John was understandably miffed, but, as we've
already established, he was not the sort of person to take a
setback personally or brood for very long. He only had a
couple of months left on his annual writing contract at this
point, so he immediately got together with Ray to try and

come up with something as fast as possible to replace the football comedy. In the course of those discussions – and quite possibly out of expedience as much as anything else – John returned to an idea he had hatched a while back for a show that featured a street-market trader and all-round wheeler-dealer. The downside was that John had already run a version of this idea past the BBC once, a year or so earlier, in the form of a page-long treatment, and had seen it cast aside without ceremony by the then Head of Light Entertainment, Jimmy Gilbert. A programme centred on a working-class market trader and fly-pitcher, with a roll of notes in his back pocket and a casual approach to the principle of taxation was not, at this juncture, the BBC's idea of a good time, apparently.

Ray Butt, though, hadn't heard the fly-pitcher idea before, and he loved it. It didn't only seem potentially strong as a comedy; it seemed timely. We're talking about that period at the beginning of the 1980s when Margaret Thatcher's Conservative government was setting off on a long period in power and preaching free enterprise and deregulation, thereby (inadvertently or otherwise) creating a mini boom time for dodgy entrepreneurship and the black market. Wheeling and dealing, get-rich-quick schemes, flogging the family silver – these things were the fabric of the daily news at that time. John's fly-pitcher could sit very comfortably in the context of all that.

That said, the actual models for Derek Trotter (in so

much as you can ever pin these things down) seem to have preceded the Thatcher years and included, so far as I'm aware, various would-be shysters and likely geezers that John had come across during his time in the second-hand car trade. There was also, in particular, a bloke that John had known in south London with the excellent name of Chicky Stocker. Chicky, in John's descriptions of him, was a special kind of cockney archetype: a working man, but imposing and always immaculately turned out, with hair just so and rings on well-scrubbed fingers, intent on cutting an impressive figure in the pub, peeling notes off a wad of readies. 'Readies', in fact, was the title that John gave to this new show in its earliest incarnation. I believe he also toyed for a while with the idea of calling it 'Big Brother', which was the title of episode one. But apparently another sitcom writer – a certain George Orwell – had beaten John to that phrase and it wouldn't have been clever to imply that there was any link between this new sitcom set in Peckham and a dark vision of a fascist future. Very soon after that, though, he came up with the notion of slightly abbreviating the old saying 'only fools and horses work' (a saying coined by nineteenth-century American vaudeville performers, apparently). John preferred the obliqueness of that title, the way it pulled you up a bit short and therefore potentially snagged itself on the edges of your mind – though it was a touch too oblique for the BBC initially, it seems, who wanted him to find a name for the series that hit the nail more squarely on the head. John prevailed, though, as he tended to do – largely, in this case, I think, by pretending that he simply couldn't think of anything else. The old 'play dumb' tactic: always worth a try.

Anyway, Ray Butt knew exactly what John was getting at with this project. After the war, Ray's father had converted an ex-army wagon into an ice-cream van and had driven around London, flogging ice lollies. He had also worked the local markets on a stall selling ladies' stockings one week, shampoo the next, sweets the one after – whatever was to hand. This was a comedy that was quite literally up Ray's – or his dad's, at least – street.

I, too, related closely to all of this. When I eventually read John's first script, the person that Del instantly brought to mind was a kind of Chicky Stocker figure from my own past – a bloke named Derek Hockley whom I had stumbled across while working for the electrical business that I set up in my twenties with my mate Bob Bevil. For the full and unadulterated history of B. W. Installations of Lodge Lane, Finchley ('no job too big or too small, estimates gladly supplied on application'), you will need to refer back to my first autobiographical volume which is still (did I mention this?) widely available from outlets of distinction. But, to recap briefly: casting about for business, Bob and I had gone door-to-door in selected areas of London, offering our bespoke services, and had lucked out when we knocked at the premises of a building contractor in the East End, who just happened to have the contract for doing up London's still war-battered Ind Coope pubs and was therefore in a position to offer a whole pile of work to a couple of willing sparkies. The man in charge of this East End operation was the aforementioned Derek Hockley, a proper, working-class cockney geezer and yet a guy who dressed like a king, with a fastidious attention to detail; the pricey-looking shirt, the beautifully knotted tie, the spotless camel-hair coat, frequently worn on the shoulders as a kind of Napoleonic cloak. He also had a superbly curated hairstyle, moulded with grease and set to perfection. This was a man who profoundly understood the power of appearances and how a little care in the area of what you wore could massively boost your social standing.

Quite coincidentally and rather conveniently, I also had a fascination of some long-standing with fly-pitching. I mean, I'm not saying it was a hobby of mine on the weekends, or a burning ambition, but it was definitely an object of curiosity for me. Through the 1970s, I was living in a rented flat in Newman Street, north of Oxford Street, slap bang in the centre of London. One of the things that made me happy about this location was that, when I was in a play in London, I could simply walk to work in the afternoon, head down across Soho to Shaftesbury Avenue and 'theatreland', strolling with my hands in my pockets, absorbing the buzz and very much fancying myself the young and swinging actor about town. Crossing Oxford Street on that journey, where the crowds of shoppers were normally thick, I would often stumble across hawkers, who had thrown down a blanket on the pavement and set up a pitch, maybe flogging perfume or watches or transistor radios, sourced from who knows where. I'd stop off and watch them because I loved the way they worked: the patter, the bluff, the banter, the teamwork, the way they would position a plant in the crowd, one of the lads who would eventually step forward and buy something, which would then encourage other people to take the plunge. There might also be the lookout guy, checking up and down the pavement for strolling coppers on the beat, at which point the alarm would be raised and the blanket would be snatched up with the gear folded away inside it, and the operation would vanish down a side alley as quickly as it had arrived. I was enthralled by all this. It was like street theatre to me – and really, without wishing to cast aspersions upon my noble craft and the law-abiding gentlefolk who nobly practise it, there's quite a lot in common, all in all, between an actor with a role to play and a spiv with a bundle of hooky radios to flog. Both are playing a part, both are trying to hold people's attention, both are trying to hook an audience with some lines they've learned, both are doing their best to persuade. Frankly, they're as good as in the same business. Sir Laurence Olivier and Darren from Herne Hill with a knocked-off box of Latvian Chanel No. 5: one struggle.

Anyway, I mention these biographical details – John's,

Ray's, mine - simply by way of illustrating how, at the core of *Only Fools and Horses* and responsible for developing the character of Del, you had these three people with a natural proximity to working-class London. This was where we had come from, what we were, and, to the extent that the show and Del Boy managed to be convincing, I'm sure it was in no small measure as a consequence of that.

Not that I was the first choice to play him, I should swiftly add. It's no secret by now that a couple of other actors were ahead of me in the queue for Del Boy and what turned out to be the part of my lifetime could very easily have turned out to be the part of somebody else's lifetime. But that, of course, is very much the nature of the casting business – a game of swings, roundabouts and lottery tickets. And I speak as the man who, following a successful audition at the BBC in the 1960s, held the highly covetable role of Corporal Jones in *Dad's Army* . . . for precisely two and a half hours. The corporation had badly wanted to cast Clive Dunn in the role, but were told they couldn't have him. So they got me in, heard me read, and gave me the job – only to discover, within an hour of me leaving the building, that they could have Clive Dunn after all. I was at home, very smugly fixing myself a sandwich and meditating on the stardom and glory that lay ahead of me, when the phone call came from my agent. 'Er, David . . . about that *Dad's Army* part . . .' So, what could have been the part of my lifetime turned out to be merely the part of my lunchtime. I've had some lousy sandwiches in my time, but the one I made that day ranked among the most dead that I have ever tasted.

But what can you do? You adjust, you dig deep, you find your inner steel, you move on. Of course, the fact that, over the ensuing decades, *Dad's Army* proved to be such a massive flop that nobody ever talked about it certainly acted as a helpful and convenient balm. [*Author lowers head and sinks teeth into leg of desk. After a short while, he unclenches jaw, extracts teeth from desk leg, sits upright again and continues.*]

Anyway, as I said: swings and roundabouts and lottery tickets. Once John had gone away and worked those early ideas up into a script, Ray and John initially pitched the leading part to Enn Reitel, the Scottish actor and voice-over expert, who later went on to be a big contributor to *Spitting Image*, the landmark 1980s satirical puppet show. But I think Enn had already signed up for something else. So then they approached Jim Broadbent – but Jim had a theatrical project on the go in the West End, and he, too, turned the job down. Jim, in fact, would later show up in series three of *Only Fools*, playing the wheedling detective Roy Slater. Jim and I were on set together a lot during the filming of those episodes, and we got along famously, but we didn't talk about the fact that he had turned down the part of Del Boy, because I think both of us were a little bit too embarrassed to go there, and anyway, it's not really the done thing. Old theatre adage: what happens in the audition room stays in the audition room. Unless it makes for a really funny anecdote, in which case out it comes. However, Jim once generously described his decision to walk away from Del and open the door to me as his 'greatest contribution to British culture'. That's a wonderfully kind thing to say. Certainly if he knew any ruefulness about that decision, Jim recovered from it in time to become one of the most respected British actors of his generation; and he wasn't so crippled with disappointment that he didn't manage to land a Best Supporting Actor Oscar and a Golden Globe for his role in *Iris*, that terrific film about Iris Murdoch. All in all, I think we can fairly resoundingly conclude that not being Del Boy didn't exactly hold Jim Broadbent back.

You might remember that first episode Jim was in. It was called 'May the Force Be With You'. Roy Slater, a childhood enemy of Del's who has since become the meanest copper on the force, turns up at the Nag's Head on the trail of a stolen microwave oven and, more importantly, its thief. The microwave, in fact, is up in the Trotters' flat, Del having taken it off the thief's hands for a nice price. Indeed, when we first see this cutting-edge and potentially life-transforming culinary device, Grandad is bent over its controls, trying to tune it in time for *The Dukes of Hazzard*. Meanwhile, at the pub, Rodney, who is too young to know the dark history between Del and Roy, invites Slater back to the flat for what he imagines will be a happy and touching school reunion over a beer. Jim's Slater is a brilliant piece of work. It's hard to know what's more chilling: the constant threat in his tone or his gape-mouthed, entirely mirthless laugh. Slater observes the microwave, arrests Del, Rodney and Grandad for receiving stolen goods and then, down at the police station, leans on them to grass up the thief. This leads to an extended interrogation scene between me and Jim which is one of my favourite sequences from *Only Fools* and one of the bits of acting in the show of which I'm most proud. It's a parody, of course, of the typical detective drama procedural scene – the smoky, sweaty station room, the cheap desk and chairs, the anglepoise lamp – but there's quite a lot of straight dramatic heat in it as well, which is what I really love about it. It's also one of those quite rare examples of a comedy having the courage to sit tight in one place for an extended period of time. Jim and I properly go at it across the desk – an instance of that enormously energising tennis-like thing that sometimes happens when two actors go head-to-head in a scene and the lines start fizzing backwards and forwards and each of them makes the other up his game. It's a terrific thing to be involved in when it happens.

In the course of that scene, Del has to go through an entire wrestling match with his conscience, weighing the morally repugnant thought of turning informant against the dire personal consequences of not doing so (Del and Rodney will be sent to the nick, and Grandad will be left alone to fend for himself on the estate). Rodney and Grandad return to the interrogation room just in time to see Del signing off on the paperwork and about to become, unthinkably to them, a copper's nark, while Slater meanly enjoys the sight of 'the great Del Boy, the man who can talk his way out of a room with no doors, reduced to this: grassing'. (Permit me to explain, from my advantageous position on the edges of the criminal fraternity, some of the arcane terminology here. A 'grass', being one who 'grasses up' another, thereby functioning as a surrogate policeman, appears to be an abbreviation of the phrase 'snake in the grass', though there is also a theory that it derives from cockney rhyming slang: 'grasshopper', meaning 'copper'. The term 'nark', meanwhile, allegedly derives from a nineteenth-century Romany word for nose – hence 'copper's nark', or copper's nose, as in one who sniffs around on behalf of a policeman. Glad to be of enlightenment in this critical area.)

Anyway, at that point, accused of grassing, Del has to turn round from the desk and give Rodney and Grandad the agonised look of a trapped and defeated man. Quite a bit of thought went into that look, I can tell you. After which, paperwork double-signed and checked and immunity from prosecution guaranteed, Del gets to reveal to Slater the man who stole the microwave with the resounding programme closer: 'I did.' It was such a lovely, tidy set-up and a classic piece of Sullivan in the way that it danced you through a whole range of emotions on the way. That was writing that could only bring the best out of you – writing you could feel yourself expanding into.

But I'm getting ahead of myself. Back at the auditions, after Enn and Jim had failed to enlist for Del Boy, muggins here was choice number three. Or possibly choice number four, if the rumours about Robin Nedwell are true. (Robin was Duncan Waring in the *Doctor in the House* series and its assorted sequels. I know John thought about Robin for Del, but whether he actually got around to offering it to him, I'm not sure.) Or possibly I was choice number five, if they offered it to Billy Allen, who later worked prominently on *The Bill* and *EastEnders*, and which is another story that gets told. Again, it seems that Billy was in John's mind for a while, and then no longer in John's mind, and was perhaps none the wiser about it either way.

Whatever, eventually there was me. Fifth (maybe) on the list! Flattering, no? That's just how it works, though, and you've no option, really, but to develop as thick a skin as you can about it. I mean, I'm sure that, if they hadn't thought of those other four, I would have been the first person they called . . .

Actually, to tell the truth, if John, in particular, had been writing a list at the time, I'm not sure he would have had me on it at all. This was before I read for him, I should add. But when Ray casually threw my hat in the ring, saying 'What about David Jason for Del?', John's reaction was to kick my hat straight back out again.

The reason Ray brought me into this discussion at all was down to Syd Lotterby. A BBC man since the late fifties,

Syd was producing *Open All Hours* at this point, with me and Ronnie Barker. I loved working with Syd. He was a slim, gentle, enormously conscientious figure. He had this wonderful way, on the set, of keeping things moving by very politely calling out a question. 'Lighting, I'm waiting for you, aren't I?' he might say, or, 'Make-up, am I waiting for you?' And they would say, 'Yes, Syd – just need a couple of minutes here,' or, 'No, we're all done and ready, Syd.' He was nudging and cajoling the crew, in other words, but phrasing it as question, as if he needed to find out, which meant that nobody really felt nudged or cajoled.

Syd, Ronnie and I were in rehearsals for *Open All Hours* in Acton – and that's when, in the lift on the way up to the rehearsal room, Syd slipped me the brown envelope containing the script which would eventually form the first episode of *Only Fools*. (The surreptitious passing of brown envelopes from person to person is a routine feature of the television business. It's not necessarily as shady as it sounds.) Ray Butt and Syd knew each other well because Ray had been Syd's assistant on a number of projects, including on an earlier series of *Open All Hours*, and Ray had now sought Syd's advice on this casting dilemma of his. Syd took a look at the pilot script and definitely thought he could see a role for me in this show – and so did I, when I took the script home to the flat in Newman Street and read it in one sitting overnight.

The thing is, what Syd saw and what I saw didn't match.

I remember him asking me the next day if I'd liked that script he'd given me, and me saying that I thought it was brilliant and that I would love a shot at the Del character. Syd's face dropped slightly and he said, 'Oh. Not the grandad, then?' In his vision of *Only Fools*, Syd clearly saw me as the cranky patriarch in the armchair, the still centre around which so much of the show would come to revolve. Fair enough, I suppose: under Syd's guardianship, I'd done Blanco in *Porridge*, who looked to be on his deathbed most of the time; and I'd been Dithers, the raggedy hundred-year-old gardener who looked after Lord Rustless's estate on *Hark at Barker*. I suppose I was beginning to work up a bit of a reputation as a man who played decaying (indeed, already decayed) oldsters who were more than twice his age – your go-to man for a bit of gaga, if you like. Well, everybody needs a calling card, and if it's working for you ... But that wasn't the way I saw that script of *Only Fools*. It was Del for me, no question.

Syd reported back to Ray Butt and told him what I had said – and once more, apparently, as a bitterly cold wind blew eerily through the gaps around the windows, the sound of tumbleweed was heard in the room. Ray couldn't imagine me in the part of a cockney grifter at all – simply couldn't picture it; and the conversation would have ended right there if Syd hadn't pressed my case by dredging up a memory of a moment in our mutual past, a feat of recollection for which I will owe Syd for the rest of my life.

61

The memory dredged by Syd dated from 1974 and revolved around the setting of a hotel snooker room in the north of England. Syd, Ray and myself were all staying in this hotel while on a location shoot for a Roy Clarke-written show called *It's Only Me, Whoever I Am* – the story of one meek man from Rochdale's attempt to escape the clutches of his domineering mother. We had been commissioned to make a pilot and had high hopes of landing a series subsequently – or I certainly had high hopes of doing so, eager as I was for a big break into television at that point. (Reader, the show didn't quite work out. Let us quietly draw the kindly curtain of forgetfulness and move on. Let us also observe that, a number of years later, Ronnie Corbett had a considerable success with a show, *Sorry!*, based on a very similar premise to the one mentioned above, about the meek man and the domineering mother. But let us harbour no unduly regretful feelings.)

Disappointment at the hands of *It's Only Me, Whoever I Am* was a long way ahead of us at this point, though. One evening after another optimistic day of filming was concluded, me, Ray and Syd met downstairs in the hotel for light refreshment and a game of snooker. Now, right from the moment I had first set ear on it, I had been fascinated by Ray Butt's accent. I sound a bit London, too, but nowhere near as London as Ray did. Ray had the full-strength, no-filter cockney thing going on. This man's voice was all Bow Bells, all the time. In fact, after you'd met Ray, it was tempting to redefine the definition of cockney, from 'born within earshot of the bells of St Mary-le-Bow', to 'born within earshot of Ray Butt's voice'.

On the fate-shaping night in question, as we moved around the snooker table, I'd been doing impressions of Ray – rather accurate ones, if I may say so myself. Syd now reminded Ray of that night, producing this memory as proof that I was someone who could turn on the deep cockney if required. So strange how these things all hook together. I must be one of a very small number of actors who have auditioned for a part in a major television series by taking the piss out of its director during a game of snooker, without either of them realising and three or four years before the part had even been written.

Anyway, that memory, stirred up in Ray by Syd, was enough to get me summoned for a reading of the initial *Only Fools* script with Ray and John one afternoon in one of the BBC's famously featureless offices at Television Centre, over a cup of the BBC's famously disgusting coffee. At this point, frankly, I still had a lot to do to persuade both of them – but especially John. John's problem wasn't that he saw me as a natural grandfather, as Syd had, nor that he saw me as an unnatural cockney, as Ray initially had; it was that he saw me as a natural loser. Not in real life, you understand; in terms of the characters that I played. John had seen me in *Open All Hours* where Granville, the beleaguered shop assistant, is trapped in his job, a victim of circumstance, and more than a little bit sad at the edges. Life's vicissitudes haven't defeated Granville, but they have certainly softened him. In addition to that, I think John had seen me in *The Top Secret Life of Edgar Briggs*, the (ahem) not entirely successful comedy series I had made for ITV in 1974 – and Edgar Briggs, too, was an unassuming and inward type of character whose victories were achieved despite rather than because of himself. By contrast, John envisaged Del Boy as an out-and-out winner – not in the sense of being materially successful, because obviously Del was the opposite of that a lot of the time; but a winner in his attitude, in the way he took the knocks, rode the bumps and bounced back, a man of insuperable energy and considerable ingenuity, with optimism always renewed and a new scheme always ready to be hatched. Hence the definitive *Only Fools* proclamation and the programme's central take-away message: 'This time next year, we'll be millionaires.'

Could I be that kind of person? Could I convincingly play Del? It was down to me in the reading. That was my first proper meeting with John, and I always say that I had a difficulty at first equating the figure in front of me with the script I had read. When I got to know him better and we relaxed in each other's company, it was easier to see the connection. But while the writing was so lively and outward, John seemed so quiet and withdrawn. It's an obvious category error to make with writers, though. You assume that the person who can be this funny with words on paper must be alight in the way a comedian is alight. When they prove to be more muted than that, it catches you off guard. The same goes, by the way, for Roy Clarke, the writer of *Open All Hours*. The funniest person on the page isn't necessarily intent on being the funniest person in the room.

At the audition, I read some bits and pieces from that initial script – 'Big Brother', the one that became the opening episode of the series, where Del acquires a batch of combination-lock briefcases off Trigger for a bargain price (but the combinations for the locks are, somewhat typically, locked inside them) and where Rodney, in a strop, leaves for Hong Kong, but is soon back, having forgotten his passport. I thought I read OK and Ray and John seemed happy enough, but you never really know in those circum-stances. People aren't necessarily going to hit you with the truth of their feelings, there and then. You close the door and leave them to their thoughts and just hope that the phone rings in a couple of days' time.

Guess what? In a couple of days, the phone rang. It wasn't a job offer, though. It was a request to go back in to the BBC and read again, this time in the company of a couple of actors who John and Ray were considering for the parts of Rodney and Grandad. So that's how I found myself for the first time in a situation that would become enormously familiar to me over the next few years: sitting in a room with Nick Lyndhurst and Lennard Pearce, reading a script by John Sullivan and trying not to laugh while doing so.

Nick and Lennard and I were as good as total strangers at this point, professionally speaking. Nick and Lennard had never met before. I had acted with Lennard in a repertory production of *The Rivals* at Bromley Theatre – but that was twenty-five years earlier and neither of us remembered anything about it until it was brought to our attention much later. As for Nick, as a kid-reporter on an ITV children's show in 1976, he had interviewed me on air when I was starring as Shorty Mepstead in *Lucky Feller* (another TV sitcom to whose mast your author nailed his youthful hopes, only to see them torn down after one series-long voyage). As with Lennard, I had no recollection of that prior meeting.

The usual niceties exchanged, down we all sat and started to read. It sounds suspiciously blithe and easy to say the chemistry was there straight away, but I don't know what else to tell you, because it absolutely was. You could hear right from the get-go, in the blend of the voices, that this thing was going to fly. Far from being a whiskery old man in battered clothing, Lennard was actually a well-dressed and rather dashing gentleman of the theatre – someone who, I later discovered, after a respectable life on the boards, actually believed his career was winding down at this point and who absolutely wasn't expecting the boost into public prominence that this show would eventually and relatively quickly hand him, late in his sixties. But that wonderful, cracked, grumbly tone was entirely convincing as the voice of a Peckham tower-block dweller from the moment he opened his mouth to read.

The same went for Nick's deliberate, gawpy take on Rodney. For me, the line that in many ways summarises Rodney is this one: 'If there is such a thing as reincarnation, knowing my luck I'll come back as me.' Nick had the perfect tone and expression for that sense of put-upon hopelessness, and he had it from the start. Even though we were only reading, and not acting it out properly, it all seemed to line up physically, too. Nick and I couldn't have looked less like brothers, of course. Nick was blond and I was dark. Nick was north of six foot tall and I . . . wasn't. But the differences between us were what was perfect about it, allowing the possibility to linger forever more that Rodney and Del might not, in fact, share a father – a thought which seems to occur at some point to everyone in the cast, except, sweetly, to Rodney himself. (The mystery of Rodney's parentage was only revealed to him as the clinching development in the very last episode of the series – a moment, incredible to think, still twenty-two years off at the point of this first read-through.) The physical disparity between us also meant that when Del was shoving Rodney around and giving him verbal stick, it could happen in the absence of real intimidation, which would have soured the fun of it. The fact that there was a twenty-one-year age difference between Nick and myself was also next to irrelevant because the story insisted on a thirteen-year gap and my spiritual youthfulness, freshness of skin and natural ebullience – not to mention the masterful work of the make-up department – would no doubt eliminate the other eight years. Also, as Del explains in that first episode, their father walked out on them, two months after the death of their mother, when Rodney was six. True, in a later episode, 'Thicker Than Water', Del claims that Rodney was five when their dad left – but let's not get bogged down with numbers. The point is, we were to understand that Del had largely been mother and father to Rodney, making the bond between them parental as well as brotherly and giving Del an additional sentimental investment in his brother, which again could be usefully in play when the two of them were at each other's throats.

I don't think any of us had been given reason to believe at that point that we were the chosen ones. At the end of that reading, though, the cast was set. Ray turned to John and said, 'That'll do for me,' and John nodded, and Nick, Lennard and I put our coats back on and headed off downstairs to the BBC bar to toast the new show we were in.

# CHAPTER FOUR

## *Becoming Del*

Those early days, when you start building a new character – that's the most exciting part of the whole process
for me. You're working out who this person is, how they're
going to sound, how they're going to carry themselves, how
they would behave and react in different circumstances;
and then you're honing the character and trying to get to
the point where those reactions and bits of behaviour can
start to happen without you thinking about it, becoming
almost second nature. Again, it's that chance to leave yourself behind and become some other person for a while,
which seemed to me the best reason for applying for a job in
the acting business in the first place.

One of the first things we needed to establish about Del
Boy was what he was going to wear. So much about him
would flow from there, clearly. When I was working in repertory theatre, I nearly always used to start with the shoes.
The shoes would often give you the class of person you were

dealing with, maybe their walk and how they would stand, and you could work upwards from that base. I did the same thing on television with Dithers, the character Ronnie Barker gave me for the Lord Rustless sketches in the 1969 television series *Hark at Barker*. If Dithers had reached the grand old age of one hundred, it stood to reason, as far as I was concerned, that he would be suffering from corns; so we found him these soft, white, broken-down plimsolls and hacked at the ends of them so that his toes poked out. That immediately gave you so much to work with in the way he flopped about the place and generally carried himself. Dithers aside, though, building characters on the shoes-first principle stopped when I got into television. You don't feel your feet are going to be on display so much, the way they inevitably are when you're stomping about on a stage all evening, so you start out with the more obviously exposed items further up.

The costume designer appointed to the first series of *Only Fools* was a young woman named Phoebe De Gaye, who, in the course of her research, spent a lot of time walking around London markets, getting a sense of what the well-turned-out trader was wearing that season. In one of the earliest sketches of Del that Phoebe drew to begin to get a feel for him, he already had a tweed flat cap and a brown, sort of blouson-style leather jacket, both of which would become key elements of his look. He was also, however, in that drawing, a man with a fairly significant beer belly and

I felt obliged to point out I didn't have one of those to supply. Had I been a method actor, like Robert De Niro, I suppose I could have gone away for a month or two and grown one. But I wasn't too keen on the idea – and anyway, I felt Del could benefit from having a perfectly flat, magazine-shoot-ready, washboard stomach, such as my own. [*Author clears throat noisily.*] In any case, I wasn't sure that paunchy was quite the right build for Del. In my vision of him, he was quite spry and nippy, physically active around the place. That's the direction I ended up taking him, and the beer-belly idea withered on the vine, as it were.

Acquiring Del's first set of clothes necessitated a special trip to the shops. Go clothes shopping for myself? Not remotely my notion of fun. Indeed, in the general scheme of things, I would rather fall under a lawnmower or gargle drawing pins. Or even fall under a lawnmower *while* gargling drawing pins. Shop for clothes for a character that I'm going to play, on the other hand – well, what time do you want to meet? The prospect actually fires me up, and so it was with eager, even puppyish anticipation that I jumped into Phoebe's battered old Mini and set off for Oxford Street one spring afternoon in 1981.

Mind you, that Mini wasn't in the best of repair. Indeed, judging by the air quality in the interior, more exhaust fumes were percolating through the carpet on the floor than were going out through the exhaust pipe. Somehow, though, the pair of us got up to central London without either fainting or exploding, and, once our eyes had stopped watering, we spent a happy morning trawling the stores for cheap and nasty suits. I must have tried on about a dozen different types in various shades, until we found a grey one that we agreed was perfect in both the essential areas of cheapness and nastiness. We paired it with some Gabicci shirts – brightly coloured, slightly shiny in finish, just a little bit showy, but not too much. Gabicci, an Italian company with a warehouse in Edgware, were to end up being the predominant label in Del's wardrobe – more by accident than by design, I have to say. Theirs were just the clothes we kept finding ourselves drawn to on the racks. When the series eventually started broadcasting and grew in popularity, this did not go unremarked by the directors of Gabicci. You can see how they might have had mixed feelings about the publicity: many a fashion line might have baulked at being thought of as the official supplier of smart-casual leisure-wear to Derek Edward Trotter. But they took it in great spirit and even had me over to the warehouse for a show-round at one point. Nice people.

The cheap grey suit from the Oxford Street shopping trip, and the red Gabicci shirt with fetching black breast pocket – those are the clothes I'm wearing in the opening episode of *Only Fools*, walking into that lounge for the first time, and little imagining that I'll be walking into it, on and off, for the next decade and more. The flat cap and the leather blouson that came later were BBC wardrobe items, as far as I remember. Phoebe also dug out that patchwork sheepskin coat from somewhere or other – the one I mentioned earlier which, following clever Del-style bartering, now proudly resides in the globally esteemed Jason Collection of Trotter-related artworks, viz. my cupboard. What a piece that sheepskin is. One has seen far smarter sheep, definitely. But it suited Del. Or it certainly did so at first, before the 1980s wore on and he became more yuppie and a touch more city-wise and slick in his tastes. That's when he graduated to Austin Reed suits at a couple of hundred quid a pop. But whatever Del wore, it was always important, I felt, that it should fit him properly. Even when he wore jeans, I insisted that they should be tailored, just to be communicating that care and fastidiousness about his personal appearance at all times – the little touches that say, 'I'm a classy geezer, me.'

We turned our attention to accessories. John Sullivan wanted me to wear a fistful of jewellery. He saw Del with sovereign rings on every finger and with a chunky gold necklace – a bit of a 'medallion man', as we used to say. Though still highly visible in the 1980s, medallion men had their real prime in the 1970s, where it was considered a sign of immense virility to unbutton your shirt to the navel and dangle a piece of gold jewellery the size of a car's hubcap in a field of rippling chest hair. Never quite saw it myself, but there you go. It worked for Tom Jones, and in no uncertain terms, so who am I to quibble?

I am reminded, though, of my only personal encounter with the late, great Eric Morecambe, who was by no means a medallion man – a meeting which occurred in the immediate aftermath of some long-forgotten industry dinner or other.

On this occasion, the dining done, I had retired to the bar for a drink with Robin Nedwell, the aforementioned star of *Doctor in the House* who may or may not have been considered for the part of Del Boy, although that prospect lay several years ahead for both of us at this point in time. On the evening in question, the pair of us were propping up the bar and sipping our lemonades, with Robin clad for the night in the de rigueur international jet-setter uniform of the time, which is to say: velvet jacket with lapels you could land a plane on; a slashed shirt rent boldly asunder; and a massive medallion, possibly as much as half a stone in weight, proudly on display. Why? Because that was simply the look, wasn't it? Suddenly, Eric, accompanied by Ernie Wise, massive legends of the industry, breezed through, on their way to the exit. Whereupon both of them paused where we were standing, and Eric reached forward to take hold of Robin's medallion. He lifted it slightly away from Robin's chest, looked at it through his famous black-rimmed glasses as one might scrutinise a piece of small-print in a newspaper, and said, 'Ah, Robin: I see you've come second.' With that, Eric carefully returned the glittering showpiece to its place between Robin's pectorals and left. It was a devastating put-down, to which Robin did not take entirely kindly, and a memorable warning lesson about the dangers of wearing an outsized medallion in a built-up area containing Eric Morecambe.

Should Del Boy wear a medallion like Robin's? More than that, should he wear a medallion, a broad selection of rings and some bracelets? I disagreed with John about this. I thought there was a danger of tipping Del into parody, and certainly of giving people the wrong impression about him. When you see that amount of ostentation on a person in real life, it's often easier to read it (rightly or wrongly) as an indication of a character flaw, rather than as a sign of a strength in them. You perhaps instinctively wonder if they're compensating for something, or covering something over, or creating a glossy distraction for themselves – and, again, you could be completely wrong and they might just really like jewellery. But I didn't want people to entertain even for a moment those sorts of uncertainties about Del. There was a big streak of ostentation in him, yes – but not desperation. You wanted to bring out a flamboyance in the character but not to the point where it started to look like a need, which would possibly have taken people's response to him closer to pity or contempt. So I wanted to back off on the jewellery. We settled for a smaller number of rings – just a couple on each hand – and a necklace with, not a medallion, but a gold letter 'D', for Del, which I felt was naff to just the right degree. Phoebe sourced these precious accessories in Chapel Street Market in Islington, north

London. We got through three different variations on the 'D' necklace during the show's lifetime but the basic joke never lost its sparkle.

There was a similar debate between us all about Del's hairstyle. It was definitely important that Del should be regarded as someone who took care of his hair – indeed, as the kind of man who was careful with all of his personal grooming. But how *much* care, and how far would you push it? John, who would have been remembering Chicky Stocker, the south London geezer who was his key inspiration for Del, thought there should be a lot of grease involved – that Del would have one of those styles where the hair was set, just so, every strand carefully stuck in place with lacquer. (Derek Hockley, my early model for Del, was similarly exact in his hairstyle, which was essentially a sculpture chiselled from pure Brylcreem.) John also raised the possibility of giving Del thick and well-tended sideburns, in a passing tribute to Elvis Presley, whom geezers do generally adore. Phoebe, the costume designer, on the other hand, saw Del with permed hair – fresh out of the hairdresser with lots of lush ringlets in the 'bubble' style that was popular with certain late 1970s footballers and also (as her research in the field revealed to her) with London market traders. I would have needed a wig for that one. Again, though, my instinct was to rein back a bit and be calmer about it. We used my own hair, tidily backcombed into a very low and understated quiff, and held in place with some grease, but not too much of it – the hair of a man who has clearly spent some time in front of a mirror, and has obviously taken a moment or two to enjoy the reflection coming back at him, but without heading for parody territory. And no Elvis sideburns, as adorable as Elvis was.

Looking back now, I can see how lucky we got with the styles and the clothing we used – not just Del, but Rodney's dowdy jeans and battered jackets and Grandad's crumpled trousers and beaten-up hat – and with the look of things in the show in general. The years have gone by and what the characters are wearing is not substantially different from what you might plausibly see people wearing today. *Only Fools* is not immediately locked into a period, visually speaking. Consequently, younger viewers, coming to it for the first time, don't see something which straight away looks like a historic artefact. I wonder whether a bubble-permed Del would have survived as long. The chances are that he wouldn't, or that he would be generating a different kind of laughter. You take these tiny decisions at the time and have no idea what they could amount to in the long term.

With the clothes and the accessories and the hair in place, I could start to work properly on the physical gestures, building up Del's body language. My feeling was that he should be physically quite busy – that he would go in for flexing his neck, twitching his elbows away from his body, rolling his shoulders a bit, shooting his cuffs. I'd seen it in

London lads – the peacocking, the showing out, a form of strutting even when you're standing still. You will recall, I hope, Lord Foppington, from the beginning of this book – the character from Restoration comedy that I played early on in my career in the theatre. Lord Foppington was a far more extreme version of the type, clearly, but there's a basic connection with Del, I think. It was explained to me when I played Foppington that, in the eighteenth century, in polite society, the display of an elegantly turned male calf was a sign of distinction – even a bit of a turn-on, it seems. Well, let's not forget, they were making their own entertainment in those days. But once you had that concept in mind, you were gifted an entire manner of standing – one leg out wide, with the foot twisted to bring the calf into view. And from there, you could go on to evolve an entire, calf-centric walk, which worked upwards from the legs, through the hips and into the spine, ultimately forcing your shoulders out wide, too, and lifting your chin. Now, it was less broad, obviously, in the case of Del Trotter, and the clothes were less noisy and the posing was less pronounced. Nevertheless, that slightly showy, arms-akimbo thing, and what that in turn does to your shoulders and your neck, and then your chin, and to the way you set yourself in relation to other people generally, is basically a version of the same thing. To some extent, as remote as it may seem, I saw Del as Lord Foppington on a council estate, Lord Foppington on a working man's budget.

Then there was the question of what Del should sound like. Voices have always been a huge interest for me – a hobby, really. I was a freelance impressionist from early days in the school playground, specialising in unflattering parodies of teachers, and I was mad about accents ever afterwards. Even now I sometimes find it hard to talk for more than a couple of minutes without lapsing into some kind of voice not quite my own. This obsession really came alive in the 1970s, when I worked on *Week Ending*, the Radio 4 topical satire show. I loved that programme – especially the on-the-fly nature of it. I would go along to the Paris Studios in Lower Regent Street bright and breezy on a Friday morning and we'd have a half-hour show knocked together by lunchtime. The producer would edit it together in the afternoon and it would go out that night at 11 p.m., and then get repeated on Saturday afternoon. Bill Wallis and David Tate were in the cast and we used to compete for the right to do the necessary impressions: everybody would have a crack at it, and the most convincing voice would win. I used to do Tony Benn, the fabled Labour MP who was in the Cabinet at that time, and Jim Callaghan. Bill Wallis would do Harold Wilson.

I was also doing a lot of voice-over work for television and radio commercials at the time, running in and out of little recording studios in Soho, as busy as a little bee. There was a lot of snobbery surrounding that kind of work, it probably goes without saying. A lot of proper actors wouldn't sully themselves. I always remember bumping into Michael Hordern (who was a proper actor, and no question) in a voice-over studio one afternoon.

'Michael! What are *you* doing here?'

'The same as you, dear boy,' Hordern replied, without hesitation. 'Being a vocal whore.' (To experience the full, Shakespearean richness of this response, you need to pronounce 'whore' as Michael did, with two syllables: 'whuuu-eerrr.')

Well, a version of light prostitution it might have been, but I jumped at it. In those days, before I had really broken through as a television actor, I was just happy to be working – and, in any case, I loved the challenge that doing those different voices provided. In fact, it was while recording an advert that I was given a technical acting tip that has stayed with me for all of my professional life, on into *Only Fools* and beyond. I was in a studio with Bill Mitchell, who was one of the true legends of the voice-over business – a deep, gravel-voiced Canadian, known as The Bear, on the grounds that if an enormous grizzly had come out of the woods to do ads for Carlsberg, this is what he would have sounded like. Bill, who was greatly in demand, habitually wore black from head to toe, with a pair of dark glasses completing the look, and he spent a lot of time lubricating his unique and extremely valuable vocal cords in the John Snow pub on Broadwick Street in Soho. I've long forgotten what the ad was that we worked on together, but it involved some dialogue for the pair of us and, after a couple of run-throughs, Bill pointed out that the conversation would happen a lot faster between us if I took my breath while he was speaking, rather than waiting until he had finished, which was my natural instinct. If I drew breath while he spoke, I would be ready to come right in at the end of his line, and we would end up with this seamless exchange with no surplus air in it at all, which was dead useful in the tight time constraints of a commercial, and also extremely natural-sounding. It was such a simple, tiny note that Bill gave me, but I have always remembered it when doing dialogue, and it has served me well.

My old appointments diaries from those times are inked all over with details of studio sessions for commercials – sometimes as many as four in a day. It got to the point where I had a pager – a piece of bleeding-edge communications technology at the time, though now, in the age of the smart-phone, it seems like the equivalent of a tin can and piece of string. The grey plastic unit, clipped proudly to my belt, would bleep and I would get a message to call Linda at the agency, who would want to dispatch me to Angel Sound or the Tape Gallery or Molinaire, or wherever, to do a voice for Esso, or Castella cigars, or McEwan's beer or Fisherman's Friend throat pastilles. I was on call, like a doctor. 'The voice-over artist will see you now.'

I watched that area of the advertising industry explode. In the beginning, the studios were spartan places, cramped and underequipped, frequently in damp basements from which you would emerge into the daylight after a two-hour session with your own personal layer of mildew. By the eighties, as the money flowed in and competition flourished, studios were suddenly popping up with black leather furniture in the foyer, glass bowls of sweets on the reception desk. Minions would be dispatched to bring back salt-beef sandwiches for lunch – unheard-of luxuries.

Even then, you had to roll with the punches a bit, it's true. Your idea of the perfect voice for a throat pastille (for example) and the producer's idea of the perfect voice for that throat pastille wouldn't always tally. You would do your bit and leave the studio with the cries of 'Thanks! That was great!' ringing in your ears. Then the ad would come out, and you weren't on it – dropped, without ceremony. It was good training, though, and it made me pretty confident with accents that weren't my own – confident that I could summon them up fairly quickly and get them locked down.

Indeed, the only time I can remember tripping up in that area was in something called *The Bullion Boys*. This was a feature-length drama that the BBC made in 1992, with Tim Pigott-Smith also among the cast. It was the story of how Britain's gold reserves were smuggled out of London in a top-secret mission at the start of the Second World War in order to protect them from the thieving mitts of the Germans in the event of the anticipated Nazi invasion. *The Bullion Boys* is a little-mentioned piece these days when conversations turn to the greatest war movies of all time, though I hope you won't mind me pointing out that it won an International Emmy for Outstanding Drama that year, so somebody must have enjoyed it. I hear a full-scale movie remake of it is in the works, too. Have they asked me to reprise my role? Funnily enough, no. Anyway, my character was a Geordie docker, and Geordie is a tough accent to nail – unless you're actually a Geordie, of course, although I wouldn't be surprised to hear that even Geordies have trouble doing a Geordie accent, because that's how tricky an accent it is. There were a number of occasions where the director would shout 'Action!' and I would set off strongly and get into my stride, only to feel my tongue starting to slip and to hear the vowels drifting away from me, and then it would be 'Cut!' and retake time.

There would be no such problems with Del's voice. As a working-class Londoner myself, I had a head start. I needed to vamp it up a bit though, increasing the cockney content, tightening the top lip, forcing it out through the nose more than I naturally would and using the back of the throat. I wanted him to operate at volume, too – not just when out in the market, but in the flat and the pub as well. He needed to be bright and noisy, crisp and loud, ebullient. The basic, irrepressible, optimistic energy that was the key to his character had to emerge in the voice. So, although I had the native foundations to build on, there were still aspects to add and fold into the mix. Even now, people expect me to sound like Del, and are sometimes slightly disappointed when I don't. In 2014, I was in a bookshop at a signing event for my autobiography, when a pair of women came to the table and we had a little chat while I was scribbling in their books. Then they said thank you and turned away, and just before they got out of earshot I heard one of them say to the other, 'Blimey, he don't half talk posh, don't he?' I was sorry to have let them down, of course. I had clearly failed to be Del enough for their liking – and not for the first time in my public life, I should say, nor the last, I'm sure. That said, I think 'posh' might have been stretching it a bit. Even post-knighthood, there's more Peckham than Mayfair in my speaking voice – or, to be accurate, more Lodge Lane, Finchley. I do, however, have a number of highly convincing posh voices in my repertoire if I'm ever called upon to produce one. Maybe I should adopt one of those permanently and remove the matter from doubt.

So, Del's clothes and jewels were sorted, and his hair and the mannerisms and, most important of all, the voice: I was all set to go. It fell together very swiftly and very naturally, which was a good omen. Indeed, I quickly got to the point with Del where it was as though I had a switch and I could flick him on and off. I'd watched Ronnie Barker do that countless times and had always been impressed by it. I'd seen him snap into Fletcher in *Porridge* and into Arkwright in *Open All Hours* almost like clicking his fingers. And then – snap! – he'd be out again when the scene ended. He barely needed a moment's pause and the voice and the facial expressions would be right there. Of course, you can only do it when you're absolutely sure you know who that person is, when they're coming from a place inside you. With Del, I knew.

# CHAPTER FIVE

## *Eating disorders and other bits of business*

We rehearsed *Only Fools* in the BBC's Television Rehearsal Rooms, or TRR, to give it the favoured acronym. Perfectly placed to enjoy the dust and traffic of North Acton's lovely Victoria Road, and known to one and all as the Acton Hilton, TRR was a seven-storey, blank-faced, brown-and-grey concrete chunk, embodying all the warmth, charm and approachability for which late-sixties, low-budget, British municipal architecture was celebrated the world over. I absolutely loved the place.

Why wouldn't I? It was the venue for some of the best days of my working life. The BBC had opened up in there in 1970 and from then on practically every drama, comedy and light entertainment show that the corporation had given a green light to had passed through this grimly functional building on its way to production. It was where I went with Ronnie Barker and Syd Lotterby to rehearse *Open All Hours*, and it was where I went with the *Only*

*Fools* team, mapping out moves, shaping scenes, gradually transforming those tales from the script to the screen. I would arrive on the dot at ten in the morning, striding purposefully across the forecourt and through the doors and getting myself checked in at reception, for all the world as if I were someone with a proper job to go to. Then I would head up in the unglamorously strip-lit lift, walk along the blank corridor and push through the functional numbered door into a large, barely furnished, slightly echoey room with yellow walls. There would then follow a three-hour session of preliminary comedy-making, after which, to fortify yourself ahead of the afternoon session, you would head downstairs to the TRR canteen and queue up for lunch, shuffling your tray along the silver rail, past the tureens of slop under the hot lights, the sausages, the chips, the eggs sliding around on their silver hotplate – eggs which were fried but were now also, courtesy of the hotplate and the lights, baked, and therefore roughly the texture and consistency of a rubber insole. Delicious. My plate would be stacked high. As Ronnie Barker always said, 'You can't be funny on an empty stomach.' Jam roly-poly and custard seemed to be the eternal dessert option, though I never went there. Nothing is *that* funny.

It wasn't just at lunchtime, though: quite a lot of food got consumed in the actual show. Quite recently, while I was working on *Still Open All Hours*, a director said to me, 'I watch *Only Fools* sometimes, and I'm always amazed that you can eat a whole meal in a scene.' But that's what people do, isn't it? They talk and they eat at the same time. You need to tuck in properly, too: none of this slicing off the tiniest piece of meat so that you can keep your mouth clear for your lines, which you will always see actors doing. None of this sipping politely at obviously empty cups, either. Del would never be so dainty; he would happily stuff his mouth. And then you would reap the benefits in terms of additional unscripted comic business. A pickled onion, for instance, could give you loads of work for your facial muscles, coping with the strength and the bitterness of it. Or you could chase it around your plate with a knife and fork for a while, struggling to pin it down and cut it.

You might, in the rehearsal room, decide to shift a piece of dialogue from the lounge to the kitchen, just to intro-duce some movement. (The parts of the lounge and the kitchen, by the way, would at this point be being played by a couple of stackable chairs and a table.) And then you'd say, 'I know: while we're talking, you make a bacon sand-wich, for yourself; and then, when you've finished it, and set it down on a plate and are ready to tuck into it, I'll take it.' So you've got this additional thing going on under the script, that doesn't need any extra words, but which adds colour and reinforces character. There were a couple of times where we had Rodney or Grandad arrive in the lounge with a meal of some sort on a tray and Del would merrily tuck into it as if it was his own – again, without remark. In rehearsals, one of us would say, 'What time of day is this all supposed to be happening?' We would work out that it was plausibly lunchtime. So Uncle Albert could load up a plate and carry it through, only for Del to snaffle it.

These were the kinds of things that would be knocked backwards and forwards at those happy rehearsal sessions in the Acton Hilton, and, looking back now, I can see how much of my input into that process rose directly out of my years in the theatre. Every show I've been in, I've considered it my duty to find things that I can add or invent to get a bigger laugh, and the presence of food in the vicinity has rarely let me down. I remember being in a production of *Charley's Aunt*, somewhere in the 1970s, where I was required to dress up as a dowager old lady and where a scene at the tea table was the perfect opportunity to insert some additional business. I asked for a bowl of unchopped lettuce leaves to be on the table every night, so I could use a fork to steer these huge pieces of floppy greenery into my mouth, making sure to cover most of my face at some point, as if the lettuce was a flannel, and then folding the flaps very carefully into my mouth. Meanwhile the other cast members were trying to concentrate on their lines, which isn't altogether easy when sitting opposite you is a man in a dress who is complicatedly chewing his way through sheets of vegetation.

Or there was the time I was playing Norman in *The Norman Conquests*, the Alan Ayckbourn trilogy from 1973,

How can you not respect the amazing work of the Counter IED Task Force? It was an honour to meet them at Camp Bastion (later Camp Shorabak) in Afghanistan in October 2010.

Receiving some TLC when I was out of my comfort zone.

Swapping the Reliant Robin for a Harrier jet and BBMF Spitfire. Do you think Del Boy would approve?

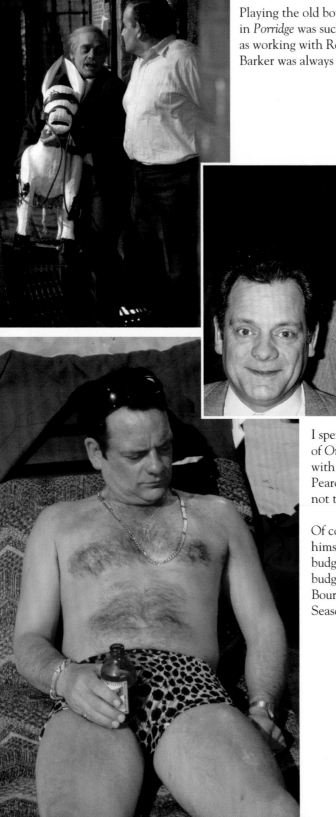

Playing the old boy Blanco
in *Porridge* was such a joy
as working with Ronnie
Barker was always a laugh.

I spent many of those early years
of *Only Fools* sitting in a room
with Nick Lyndhurst and Lennard
Pearce, reading a script and trying
not to laugh.

Of course, Del would disport
himself in Spain in leopard-print
budgie smugglers – except BBC
budgets meant 'Spain' was actually
Bournemouth – 'It Never Rains…',
Season 2, 1982.

'Which way to Holland?' – 'To Hull and Back', Christmas special, 1985.

It wasn't Christmas without an *Only Fools* special, with over 20 million viewers tuning in by the end.

Hitting the streets to film became increasingly difficult as public affection for *Only Fools* grew and we tried to keep the punchlines under wraps from the paparazzi – 'The Jolly Boys Outing', Christmas special, 1989.

Filming with Nick in Miami, seemingly recovered from meeting Al the Gater – 'Miami Twice', Christmas special, 1991.

where Norman makes an appearance at breakfast the morning after he has disgraced himself while drunk, meaning that nobody else at the table is talking to him and he ends up conducting a conversation with himself. All that the stage direction required me to do, against the backdrop of this awkward silence, was go over to the sideboard, pick up a box of corn flakes and pour some of the contents into a bowl, but even as we were rehearsing it, it came into my mind that I could work this moment for something extra. The noise that the flakes made in the box sounded a bit like marching soldiers to me, especially if you tipped the contents rhythmically from end to end. Bizarre as it may sound, I spent a considerable amount of time with the props maker, trying different things in order to get the corn flakes box to render its best and most amusing impression of marching feet. If you want to try this at home, the key is to remove the flakes from the inner bag, so that they're properly rattling around loose inside the box. Tip two: add some Shreddies to the corn flakes for extra bulk and heft, and therefore greater sonic depth. Other cereals are available – but they don't work as well. If you think I'm making this up, I'm not. It's what we did. 'Atten-shun!' Norman would shout by the sideboard. 'Left, right! Left, right!' And I would work the cunningly adapted corn flakes box: 'Shkronch, shkronch. Shkronch, shkronch.' You may be of the opinion that this was no sensible way for a grown man to spend his limited portion of time on this earth and, more importantly,

his limited portion of mental energy. You would possibly
have a point. But I will tell you something: it didn't just get
a laugh, it got a round of applause, every night.

*Charley's Aunt* and *The Norman Conquests* were at least
strong pieces. But the truth is, in the early days, when I was
slogging around on the touring circuit and doing seaside
summer seasons at pier theatres and picking up anything
that would come my way just in order to remain employed,
I wasn't always working with, shall we say, top-drawer
material. In a couple of cases (no names, no pack drill), if
you had left it to the play on its own to get you your laughs,
you would have been waiting a long time. So, even more
urgently in those instances, there grew inside me this urge
to go looking for extra stuff to bulk up the comedy. If, for
example, the production had been thoughtful enough to
furnish the stage with a tiger-skin rug, well, why would you
not, at some point during the play, come to accidentally-
on-purpose find your foot trapped in the mouth of that
tiger-skin rug? And if that seemed to go over well with the
audience, then why would your later interactions with that
tiger-skin rug not become even more elaborate, until you
were involved in a full-scale wrestling match with the
aforementioned tiger behind the sofa? That was the way
my brain became accustomed to work in those days. The
resulting freelance efforts on behalf of the production's
entertainment value may not always have endeared me to
some of my fellow cast members – particularly the ones

waiting to come on while I fought with the carpeting, or worked the simple ringing of a dinner bell for a few moments of extra farcical value and, with a bit of luck, a round of applause. But my interests were the overall comedy of the production, first and foremost, and instinctive self-preservation second.

It got to where I was quite neurotic about it. 'What's my input here?' That was the question I would always be asking myself. 'I've got to justify my involvement, haven't I? Else what am I doing in this play?' It was a form of under-confidence, of self-doubt, which was the thing that had nagged me all my life as an actor: the thought that I had come from nowhere, untrained, and that therefore I wasn't the proper deal, that I constantly had it all to prove. Working on *Only Fools* in that Acton rehearsal room, though, I realised that I was beginning to feel and behave differently. Because the script was so good, it gave me confidence to express myself using it. I was working with genuine quality and I didn't have to be constantly pushing outside the lines in the way that I had done many times before. The foundations were solid, the bricks and the mortar were properly laid, and because John had designed the structure so firmly, you didn't need or want to be working outside it. That's not to say that I stopped looking for things that I could add, for any extra bits that I could bring to the party – for a china dog that might work as a wig block, for instance, or for a bacon sandwich that might be rustled up and nicked. But I did so in the context of a script that was going to support me whatever, so I could relax a bit about it. That, as inadvertently as it might have been, was the show's great present to me as an actor and I was extremely grateful for it.

Don't bother looking for the Television Rehearsal Rooms now, by the way. The BBC flogged the building to Carphone Warehouse in 2009, cunningly timing the deal to coincide with the bottom of a recession for property prices. Carphone Warehouse in turn flogged the place to the London University of the Arts, and the London University of the Arts bulldozed it and put up a far prettier student accommodation block in its place. So the Acton Hilton is now, I guess, a seat of learning. Then again, from my point of view, it always was.

# CHAPTER SIX

## *Houston, we don't have lift-off*

Amid no great fanfare, the first episode of *Only Fools and Horses* went out on BBC1 on Tuesday 8 September 1981 at eight thirty in the evening, wedged between *The Rockford Files* (James Garner's American detective series, famous for messages recorded on self-destructing tapes) and the *Nine O'Clock News* (a British and international co-produced reality show, starring Jan Leeming and frequently featuring far worse problems than tapes that self-destruct). By all accounts, the nation's television viewers were more excited that week about the launch of *The Day of the Triffids*, a six-part sci-fi drama adapted from the John Wyndham novel, which attracted a lot more publicity than our show, and perhaps understandably so. Carnivorous plants on the rampage across Britain, terrifying a population struck blind by meteorites? Or a slightly dodgy geezer from Peckham in a naff shirt, trying to flog a batch of plastic combination-lock briefcases whose combinations have ended up locked inside them? You took your choice.

Still, whatever *The Day of the Triffids* had going for it (and I must confess, I didn't tune in), I would hazard that it didn't have an exchange as slick as this one, from that opening *Only Fools* episode, 'Big Brother', when Del, down at the Nag's Head, watched by Rodney, negotiates to take those briefcases off Trigger's hands.

TRIGGER: To you, Del Boy, seventeen pounds each.
DEL: You know what happened to the real Trigger, don't you? Roy Rogers had him stuffed.
TRIGGER: All right then – fourteen.
DEL: Fourteen? Leave it out! Five.
TRIGGER: Twelve.
DEL: Six.
TRIGGER: Ten.
DEL: Nine.
TRIGGER: Eight.
DEL: Done!
TRIGGER (to Rodney): That's the way to do business, Dave.

That classic piece of dopey wheeler-dealing was to set the show's tone in so many ways. It also instantly established the character of Trigger – profoundly slow-witted and yet, by his own reckoning, a sage. (You will recall, perhaps, the

ONLY FOOLS AND STORIES

Peckham road-sweeper's considered verdict on Mahatma Gandhi: 'He made one great film and then you never saw him again.') In place right from the beginning, note, was Trigger's habit of persistently, and despite all protests and demonstrations to the contrary, calling Rodney 'Dave'. Forgive me for removing my trumpet from its case at this point and giving it a quick toot, but that little quirk of Trigger's was my suggestion to John. I said, 'He should call him Dave, all the time, regardless.' John ran with it utterly brilliantly, seeding a running joke that would build and build and wouldn't reach its absolute peak until a whole decade later, in series seven, the final full season, when Trigger is charged with discovering the intended name for Del and his wife Raquel's imminent baby. 'If it's a girl, they're gonna name it Sigourney, after an actress. And if it's a boy, they're going to name him Rodney. After Dave.' Ten years in the making, that line. Sometimes, with gags, you have to be prepared to play the long game.

Judged on the number of lines he got, or on the relative amount of screen time, it would be conventional to describe Trigger as a secondary character. But that doesn't wash in my reckoning – and not only because so many of his lines were just so plain great. (Sample: 'What's the name of that bloke who invented the Dyson vacuum cleaner?') Trigger wasn't a secondary character for the simple explanation that John Sullivan didn't do secondary characters – not in *Only Fools*. Trigger, Boycie, Denzil, Mickey Pearce, Mike the landlord – there was nothing remotely secondary about these characters, they were just characters, full stop, and proof of the imaginative commitment with which John was prepared to people his fictional world. It wasn't only Del, Rodney and Grandad (and then, later, Uncle Albert); everybody in that extended *Only Fools* family seemed to resonate in no small measure with the audience and would continue to resonate long after the show had gone.

Certainly it takes more than a 'secondary character' to slip loose from a comedy programme and make it into the pages of the philosophy books. In 'Heroes and Villains' in 1996, Trigger gets a medal from the council for managing to keep the same broom for twenty years. It subsequently emerges that the broom has had seventeen new heads and fourteen new handles over that period, but never mind. This, apparently, is an example of Theseus's Paradox – which I used to think was some kind of extra-powerful bathroom cleaner with the capacity to fight limescale, but which I subsequently learned is a Greek conundrum from ancient times. The conundrum is this: if you take an object (a ship in the original Greek case, though there are later versions featuring an axe, too) and individually change its component parts, in what sense is it the same object thereafter? In other words, can you still technically call it Trigger's broom once it's had a new handle and a new head? There are potentially hours of fun here for your brain cells. The main point is, since Trigger won his council medal for broom conservation, some philosophers now happily shove Theseus aside and refer to 'Trigger's broom' as the textbook illustration of this mental quandary. Whatever you end up concluding about the newness or otherwise of his road-sweeping equipment, the fact that Trigger, of all characters, has come to sit at the heart of an academic philosophical enquiry seems deeply satisfying to me – surely one of John Sullivan's rarer and finer achievements.

Trigger was played, of course, by Roger Lloyd Pack, an immensely capable, RADA-trained actor, and as down-to-earth a bloke as you could hope to meet. He was far from dopey, too: he had A levels and everything. Ray Butt spotted Roger when, during the development phase for *Only Fools*, he went to the West End to see a Bernard Slade comedy called *Moving*, on the pretext, I believe, of having a look at Billy Murray as a potential Del. I'll let that slide. But it was Roger's big-featured face that stayed in Ray's mind on that particular night. He could see him unmistakably as Trigger and, in due course, millions of people would come to agree. Like all of us in the show, Roger had no idea when he signed up how much appearing in *Only Fools* would convert him into public property, and how much he would be required to wrestle with that. Off the set, Roger took to wearing a battered trilby in the hope of avoiding recognition, but it rarely worked. Once, with his hat firmly on his head, he travelled to Iceland with his friend, the actor Kenneth Cranham, in the hope of seeing the Northern

Lights. Instead, they somehow got lost in a blizzard on the outskirts of Reykjavik. However, as they wandered the frozen tundra in their confusion, they were relieved to see a figure emerging from the ice and darkness ahead of them who could perhaps offer them some guidance out of this remote region. So they approached him. The figure took one look at Roger, shivering in his hat, and said, 'All right, Dave?'

Roger was to die too soon, of pancreatic cancer, in 2014. He was sixty-nine. We were all at the funeral – Nick Lyndhurst, John Challis, Tessa Peake-Jones, Sue Holderness, Paul Barber, Patrick Murray – and we were all hollowed out, although Roger had done his best in advance to lighten the burden of the day for us. At his insistence, the coffin, his battered trilby atop it, arrived in a bright pink hearse. Stylish to the last.

But I'm getting ahead of myself. After Del bought Trigger's briefcases in that classic piece of series-opening bartering, it would be nice to relate that nothing afterwards was ever in doubt: that *Only Fools* surfed smoothly onwards, amid rapidly gathering acclaim, and rose untrammelled to its inevitable place in the comedy firmament. Alas, nothing in television is ever simple – apart, possibly, from Trigger. *Only Fools*, certainly in its early years, rode a sometimes bumpy road dotted with obstacles, ranging from blessedly temporary inconveniences, at one end of the scale, to one occurrence in particular that could have terminated the show altogether.

*Only Fools* was born in chaos. Indeed, it almost stopped before it started. It's amusing to reflect on that from a secure position, sat here on the sunny uplands of my posterity, as it were. But I can remember not finding it especially funny at the time. We were only three days into shooting the first episode when Ray Butt, who had been instrumental all the way down the line in putting the show together and who was slated to produce and direct all six of the episodes that would comprise the first series, woke up and wondered why he could barely move. Somewhere in his sleep, with scant respect for the job at hand, he had contrived to slip a disc, and the only thing he could do was go to hospital and get himself fixed. There he was to remain for three weeks, removing him as director from the entire first series which he had developed, nurtured, cast, planned ... Credit to him, though: he phoned John Sullivan to tell him about the back situation before he even phoned for an ambulance. Proper priorities there, of which today's emerging programme makers would do well to take note: the production first, medical emergencies requiring surgery second.

Gareth Gwenlan, who would later become the BBC's Head of Comedy, stepped in to cover for Ray as producer and – because we couldn't lose our shooting days without jeopardising the schedule for the entire series – to hold the director's baton for a day or so until another director could be found. This was Martin Shardlow, who had done some episodes of *Last of the Summer Wine* and *Terry and June*, but who was requisitioned without ceremony or notice from a BBC drama production and had the shortest time in which to get his bearings. Credit to him: he found those bearings faster than anyone could have reasonably expected him to and went on to do a classy job with the rest of the series. Nevertheless, there we were, a matter of days into production, and we'd already had three different directors. Which doesn't do much for your sense of stability, I probably don't need to say. That first week was a glorious old mess – amateur hour, really. I remember standing on the set and being comprehensively deflated. I'd had such a good feeling about this show, going in, and had a really firm sense that I was on the verge of making something strong and funny. Now I was thinking, 'Oh, here we go again. Another bomb. More hopes dashed.'

In due course, though, the ship steadied and by the time we had finished filming those initial six episodes my anticipation for the success of the show had recovered to its previous levels. It was really solid work, I thought. John Challis, who is such an easy guy to get along with, had superbly nailed the character of Boycie, the second-hand car dealer, in an episode that allowed Nick and me the pleasure of tooling around in a Jaguar E-Type, which was not to be sniffed at. There was the 'A Slow Bus to Chingford' episode, with the Trotters running a wonderfully crappy open-topped bus tour of south London, taking in the glories of the Lea Valley viaduct and Croydon by night. There was

'The Russians Are Coming', where Del and Rodney con-struct a DIY fallout shelter against the possibility of a nuclear attack. It was, surely, a veritable cornucopia of comic delights. Certainly it all seemed to have played really well with the studio audiences at the Sunday-night record-ing sessions, and that's always a good litmus test. The only thing left to do was to sit back and wait for the nation to swoon in ecstasy and wonder.

Plumpf! Another deflation. The first series of *Only Fools* generated a reaction which these days we would probably describe using the word 'meh'. The critics felt largely able to ignore us. Certainly nobody was inspired to write a review that said, 'I have seen the future of television comedy, and it is *Only Fools and Horses*.' Nor, indeed, did anybody have the prescience to come out and say, 'Heed my words: one day, 24 million-plus people will be swarming all over this.' We had barely any presence in the media at all, in fact. I would have been happy to go out and publicise the show, and John battered away at the BBC press and publicity department to organise features on me and Nick for the magazines, to act as trailers for the programme and get it under people's noses. But nothing happened. Whether the publicity department tried to drum up some interest and were knocked back by an entirely indifferent British press, or whether they saved themselves the inconvenience and embarrassment by not getting their drums out in the first place, I could not tell you. All I know is, my boundary-breaking *Vogue* cover story was not forthcoming. I wasn't even in *Good Housekeeping*.

Alas, the press were not alone in largely ignoring us. That first series generated audiences of between seven and nine million, the kinds of numbers for which channels would bite off your hands as far as the elbows these days. But this was back in the terrestrial-only period, when people had far fewer claims on their attention. Indeed, British television wouldn't even know the bewildering plenty of a fourth channel until the following year, 1982. So seven to nine million didn't really qualify as setting the world on fire – nor even, really, setting *Radio Times* on fire. During and immediately after the series, there was, accordingly, a general feeling of flatness – a sense that the spark hadn't caught. Given the hopes I'd been harbouring, it was fantastically dispiriting. Moreover, still more troublingly, with the future of the show by no means guaranteed, indifference seemed to be coming off the relevant BBC executives in misty waves.

But then, I suppose, to a certain extent, all of us involved in *Only Fools* were already used to a touch of corporate coldness. At some point during the screening of that first series, the BBC had decided to decorate the foyer and main corridors of Television Centre, the mothership of their broadcasting operation in Shepherd's Bush, with giant colour pictures celebrating the corporation's current comedy output. I remember passing through there one day and thinking, 'Ah, well, that's nice of them.' Penelope Keith and Peter Bowles were on the wall, beaming out from the set of *To the Manor Born*. Kenny Everett was up there – Dave Allen, also. Ronnie Corbett was depicted in *Sorry!* and there was a tribute in image-form to *The Hitchhiker's Guide to the Galaxy*, too. 'How great,' I thought, experiencing an anticipatory tingle of flattery. 'Any moment now I'm going to see *Only Fools and Horses* saluted among this illustrious company.'

Wrong. We were nowhere in sight. The galaxy of BBC comedy talent deemed worthy of hanging in the foyer (in a manner of speaking) did not include our humble unit. Rumour had it that there was a snap of us somewhere in the vicinity of the lift shaft, up on the sixth floor, though I never set eyes on it. It was all rather disheartening and hard not to take personally. John, in particular, felt slighted by this omission and complained bitterly about it. I don't know whether it was the BBC's reaction to our working-classness, or our working-class reaction to the BBC – and the chances are it was a bit of both. But in those early days, before the show found its rhythm and its audience, we never quite shook the impression that the BBC was slightly embarrassed by us. It only added to the feeling that we, and our show, were a bit of an outsider as far as the powers that be were concerned – urchins with grubby mugs at the gates of the big house – and that we had it all to prove before we would find love and acceptance there.

Indeed, maybe it was just the way the BBC operated,

something to do with the culture of the place, but a certain amount of reserve characterised its relationship with the show even once it was successful. None of the actors in the series, me and Nick included, was ever put on a retainer, which would have locked you in place and given you a bit of job security – and which, just as importantly, would have given you the sense that they were thinking about the series in the long term. Instead, whenever a series finished, you were left in limbo, wondering whether another one would ever be commissioned. Getting a straight answer to the question 'are you going to let us come back?' was extremely difficult. 'Possibly' was about as precise a response as you would be given. I would be ringing up John Sullivan and saying, 'Have you heard anything?' and John would say, 'No. I'll ring Ray Butt and see if anyone's said anything to him.' Weirdly, people didn't seem to be involved in the process. Each time, it was as if the machine had to finish churning though the figures before finally clanking out an answer. At some point in the mid-1980s, after four or so series, when the show had established itself but was again in its annual limbo period, I found myself seated at a dinner next to Bill Cotton, who was then the BBC's Managing Director of Television. A big cheese, in other words. Nick Lyndhurst was also at the table and he was nudging me all evening to ask Bill outright if we were going to get another series. I felt a bit awkward about doing so, not wanting to seem gauche or desperate. But I bided my time as the meal went on and at what I considered the optimum moment, adopting a tone of casual diffidence, I finally went for it.

'So, er, Bill. Do you reckon *Only Fools* will get another shot sometime?'

He laughed loudly. 'Oh, don't ask me, old chap,' he said. 'Nothing to do with me.'

I had aimed too high, clearly. Those kinds of decisions were for people elsewhere in the machine. But the machine was so big that you could work inside it for years and still not feel you had a proper grasp on the mechanics of it. And I say this as someone who is quite good with machinery, too, and who has been known to restore motorbikes and classic fairground slot machines in his workshop at home.

Whatever, the heat certainly wasn't under us at the end of series one. In fact, John was getting some pretty strong hints from above that maybe he'd like to try something different now – kind of 'so, that was fun – what else have you got?' But he was still backing the show, and so was I. I knew it was funny and I still thought it had the potential to strike a really huge chord with people. If it had a problem grabbing attention, it was partly the fact that nobody in the cast was a star. Me and Nick had some prior television experience, but not in leading roles, and neither of us was the kind of actor whose name alone would guarantee an audience from the off. The only way to get around that was to give it time.

There was also the matter of the title, an ongoing bug-bear for the BBC, as I mentioned earlier, which didn't directly explain what the show was about and which was always going to take a bit of getting used to. Changing it after one series was completely out of the question – and in any case, John Sullivan had already dug in hard on the title's behalf and would brook no challenge to his authority in that area. So one thought was to make the theme music work a bit harder on the title's behalf. For the first series, the theme was an instrumental, written by Ronnie Hazlehurst, who was no slouch when it came to the composition of signature music for television. Indeed, at one stage in the seventies and eighties, it seemed to be the law that before a BBC programme could be passed as fit for public broadcast, Ronnie Hazlehurst had to do the theme tune. No Ronnie, no show. In addition to his piece for the first series of *Only Fools*, younger readers may care to check out his work at the front and back end of such programmes as *The Generation Game*, *Yes, Minister*, *To the Manor Born* and *Some Mothers Do 'Ave 'Em*, and especially his famously cash-till-driven opener for *Are You Being Served?*. It's well happening, as we say in the music industry.

For series two, at the risk of offending against any number of existing broadcasting statutes, the decision was taken (and this was way above my pay grade, let me hastily add) to set Ronnie Hazlehurst's work aside and, assuming lightning didn't strike us all dead for our blasphemy there and then, use something different, with helpfully illustrative lyrics. It wasn't automatically assumed that scriptwriters would come up with opening numbers for their shows, but John, helpfully, had some previous in this area: he had written the theme tune for *Citizen Smith*. So he duly composed a theme song for *Only Fools*, the lyrics of which included the whole of the original expression ('why do only fools and horses work') and went at least a little way towards explaining it. It also went on to become quite an item in its own right – a catchy number that came to embody the show and that people found themselves singing and humming even at times when they weren't in front of the television. You can't underestimate the importance of that. Behind every great sitcom, there's an iconic theme tune. Or rather, in front of it, obviously.

John even sang the song himself, due to the unavailability of Chas & Dave, the 'rockney' double act, who had agreed in principle to record the new theme for us, but then inconveniently had to go and have a huge smash hit record ('Ain't No Pleasing You') which set them on the path to national stardom and left them too busy to meet their engagement with us. I wonder how Chas & Dave feel now about that little dink in their career path. It's one of those oh-so-poignant, 'road not taken' moments. They could have sung the theme tune for *Only Fools* but instead they had to settle for massive chart success. How different things might have been for them, one ruefully ponders, if they hadn't had that smash hit.

Anyway, the second series got made and it contained all sorts of good stuff, including the aforementioned 'Ashes to Ashes' episode, with the urn containing the mortal remains of Trigger's grandad, and the now famous 'chandelier drop' from 'A Touch of Glass', with Del and Rodney up the ladders, carefully holding the blanket under one of Lord Ridgemere's priceless crystal chandeliers while Grandad, upstairs, loosens the other one. That's another *Only Fools* sequence that people have warmly admitted to their annals, if I may put it that way. It's worth making the point, in relation to the second series, that this was the first time John Sullivan had been able to write with all of our faces specifically in his head. The six episodes of series one were finished before the show was cast. The scripts were adapted slightly, to fit our voices and natural timings and so on, and to insert various set-ups and jokes as they arose, such as the running 'Dave' gag. But that was clearly very different from sitting down at the start of the writing and being able to summon Del's and Rodney's voices and expressions. If the scripts tightened in series two, then it was on account of that.

So how did it go over this time? Well, in response to these new and exceptional offerings, the audiences duly . . . stayed pretty much the same. Apart from the 10.2 million that tuned in for the chandelier caper, the figures held steadily around the eight million mark – and even though Channel 4 had now officially joined the national broadcasting party, this was still a few million short of what the BBC would have been hoping for from one of its primetime sitcoms.

Accordingly, when it was time to take a decision on making a third series, things really were trembling in the balance. John Howard Davies, who was the Director of Comedy at the BBC at the time, summoned me, Nick and Ray Butt to a meeting in his office somewhere along the daunting forty-mile-long corridors of Television Centre. Now, something I can tell you about John Howard Davies is that when Ray Butt originally sent him John Sullivan's draft script for 'Big Brother', the first episode of *Only Fools*, Davies sent Ray a memo saying that, although he had enjoyed it, he didn't think it was strong enough to work as an opening episode and kick off a whole series. And Ray was so piqued that he kept that memo stuck to the wall of his office at the BBC until the day he left, by which time *Only Fools* was well under way, its opening episode having been, of course, 'Big Brother.'

Anyhow, John Howard Davies sat behind his desk with, on one side of him, a stack of scripts and, on the other, a sheaf of paperwork. He said to us gravely, 'Over here I have some scripts for a third series of *Only Fools and Horses*. And over here I have some viewing figures for the last series of *Only Fools and Horses*. The scripts on the right are telling me we should definitely make another series. But the figures on the left are telling me we should definitely pull it.'

There was a silence here, while Nick and Ray and myself shifted uneasily. And then Davies said, 'Well, balls to the figures on my left – we'll go with the scripts on my right!'

Cue much relief and rejoicing. God bless John Howard Davies and his balls. Of course, the third series got made, and from there the show really started to bound forward and the audiences snowballed. By the time of the fourth series, the first series' figure of seven million per episode had doubled. Series five and series six would see audiences of between 16 million and 18 million as a matter of course, and the Christmas specials would end up peaking even higher than that, all the way up to those record-breaking, 20 million-plus levels by the end. Yet if Davies had been a different kind of broadcasting executive, the sort who only scrutinised the bottom line, the show would have been chopped in its infancy. *Only Fools* survived and grew because somebody had the courage to ignore the maths and nurse it and give it the time to develop. It wouldn't happen like that nowadays. Now everybody seems to want success straight off the bat, and the BBC feels obliged to join battle with the commercial operations and the whole world seems to be chasing numbers rather than excellence. It's a salutary reminder, really, of the part that luck played in the success of *Only Fools*. Yes, it was a fantastic creation, but we happened to come along at the right time, to the right place, with the right people in control.

Of course, luck isn't inexhaustible. The show had arguably just hit its stride when it was knocked flat on its back by a major upset, the worst it would know in its lifetime.

The last I ever saw of Lennard Pearce was outside the magistrates' court in Kingston in December 1984. We were filming, I hasten to add, rather than responding to a summons. We were doing some scenes for a daft series-four story in which Grandad takes a tumble into a pub's beer cellar and Del and Rodney then join him in pursuing a hefty compensation claim against the brewery, only to discover, when their case is heard, that this is not the first time that Grandad has tried this ruse. That was a Sunday morning and, as he wasn't needed on set, Lennard was due to join up with us again seven days later. But on the Wednesday, Lennard's landlady found him lying at the foot of the stairs to his flat after a heart attack.

He was taken into intensive care at the Whittington Hospital in Highgate. John Sullivan visited him there and took in a replica of Trotter, the china pig that used to be placed in the control room at the *Only Fools* studio sessions and which it was Lennard's habit to touch for luck before every show. Sadly, the pottery pig couldn't work any magic in these circumstances. Lennard suffered a second heart attack in the hospital. On the Sunday morning, Nick and I were getting made up, when Ray Butt came and stood in the doorway. He didn't say anything. He just shook his head and walked away. We had spent the week fearing the worst, and here it was. We knew, before this, that Lennard's health hadn't been the best. He was sixty-nine and had had some troubles the previous year with his balance and he had been taking pills for hypertension. But the actuality of it – the finality of it – was overwhelming. Neither Nick nor I knew what to say or do with ourselves. I remember just sitting silently in a chair for a long time, trying to absorb it and failing. The day's work, obviously, was abandoned. As we left in silence to go home, as if in some kind of maudlin film, there was a sudden flurry of snow.

At that point, I thought the show was probably over. I couldn't see any way around it. Obviously, a meeting was rapidly called, led by Gareth Gwenlan, who had by now graduated to that Head of Comedy role. John and I were part of that meeting, and Ray Butt and a couple of other BBC people, and when I walked into that room it was on the pretty firm assumption that we were going to talk about calling it a day and about what the exit strategy would be. But that wasn't the case. Broadcasting can be a fairly ruthless and logistical business, and I never completely worked out, in the discussions that followed, how much the BBC's position was driven by the fact that transmission dates were now locked into the schedules, and how much it was about their will to keep the show alive for its own sake. No matter. What I do know for sure is that John and I very quickly crushed the idea that some bright spark had of getting in a lookalike to play Grandad. Just blithely sailing on like that, as if nothing had happened, would have been an insult to Lennard that neither John nor I, or anyone else in the cast, would have been able to live with, and we made our feelings on that issue very clear.

It was John who suggested that if *Only Fools* was going to survive, then he should write Grandad's death into the show, give him a proper funeral scene and fittingly mark the exit of his character. Then, somehow, the life of the show could gather itself and resume, just like our lives outside the show. I don't know about the rest of the people around the table, but, as firm as John sounded about this, I had my doubts that he could make it work. This was not an area you had seen television comedies venture into, for fairly obvious reasons. How could you actually record and explore the death of one of your central characters, without doing something utterly disruptive to the comic tone? That stuff was too big for comedy, surely.

Of course, I should have had more faith in John's talents. What he came up with was, in terms of its drama and reach and the unflinching way in which it went about its grim but necessary work – and also, we should add, in its continued comedy – probably his greatest piece of writing for the show. This wasn't just a matter of the funeral scene, although that's the centrepiece of it, with Del's stern and bottomlessly touching admonition to the gravediggers as they spade the soil onto the coffin ('Gently!'), and with the beautiful clinching gag wherein he and Rodney drop what

115

they take to be Grandad's trilby into the grave as a final mark of honour and walk away, only to hear the vicar wondering if anyone has seen his hat. All that stuff is truly brilliant but, for me, there is another significant moment, after the funeral, in the aftermath of the gathering back at the flat. Del has, as ever, brightly played the part of mine host at that occasion, welcoming the guests and serving drinks, inspiring a bewildered and angry Rodney to accuse him of getting over Grandad's death too quickly. The speech that Del then has is, I think, among the most poignant that John wrote for him.

Get over it? What a plonker you really are, Rodney. Get over it? Ain't even started yet. I ain't even started, bruv. And do you know why? Because I don't know how to, that's why. I've survived all my life with a smile and a prayer. I'm Del Boy, ain't I. Good old Del Boy. He's got more bounce than Zebedee. ''Ere, pal, what you drinking?' 'Go on, darlin', you 'ave one for luck.' That's me, that's Del Boy, isn't it? Nothing ever upsets Del Boy. I've always played the tough guy. I didn't want to, but I had to, and I've played it for so long now that I don't know how to be anything else. I don't even know how to . . . oh, it don't matter. Bloody families – I'm finished with them. What do they do to you, eh? They hold you back, drag you down and then they break your bloody heart.

After which Rodney, who has been utterly silenced by this torrent, whispers, 'I'm sorry.'

It's a great outburst, that. Del's heart comes off his sleeve and it all comes pouring out. It was such a clever way to get at Del's true feelings without in any way dissolving the character of Del. You're reminded of how much Del gave up in order to raise Rodney and look after Grandad. But the key to it, I think, is the self-knowledge that Del is allowed. 'That's me, that's Del Boy, isn't it?' What was crucial about the people John Sullivan created in *Only Fools* – and this is perhaps the reason they continue to inhabit viewers' minds and lives all this time later – is the way he gave them the scope to know themselves, and to see themselves as other people do. At that point Del isn't just some sitcom cypher that everybody laughs at. He's a rounded character – a person. The funny stuff in *Only Fools* speaks for itself. But the reason the show has become part of the national psyche is because, ultimately, as at that moment after the funeral, it was about real people behaving in real ways.

I'm very proud of what we did in that episode, 'Strained Relations'. It suggested that there were broader, more complex aspects of life that the show could now go on and meet – which it duly did, in the form of Del's relationship with Raquel, played by Tessa Peake-Jones, and Rodney's relationship with Cassandra, played by Gwyneth Strong, and in the form of love and marriage and birth and all of the big stuff. Above all, it enabled us to feel that the programme had done right by Lennard. We missed him terribly, and I still do. But it's some slight consolation to think that part of his legacy to *Only Fools* was that greater depth and breadth and confidence that it had thereafter.

At Lennard's actual funeral, which took place a couple of weeks before filming resumed, we were asked to stand and sing a hymn at one point, and I opened my hymn book, took a breath . . . only to discover that the relevant page in it was missing. Some of us had a quiet giggle about that there and then, and I know Lennard would have utterly approved. It seemed a suitably Trotter-like occurrence to see him out on.

John's other stroke of brilliantly redemptive invention was to create the character of Uncle Albert, Grandad's long-lost brother, who turns up, naturally enough, for his brother's funeral and then never leaves. Buster Merryfield's path to sitcom fame must be among the most unlikely in history. His photo seemed to emerge almost at random from a pile of long-ago submitted actors' CVs in Ray Butt's office, just at the point where Ray was looking for somebody to play a white-whiskered former navy man old enough to have seen action (or thereabouts) in the Second World War. Happening on Buster's face, Ray had no choice but to put in a call. Until that point, Buster was a bit-part theatre player who had only turned to acting in retirement after a career as the manager of a NatWest bank in Thames

Ditton. He was living with his wife in a bungalow on the south coast and he claimed never to have seen the show. He would spend the first month of his time in the cast of *Only Fools* flashing up and down to London in a BBC car, honouring the remainder of his contractual commitment to a pantomime in Bournemouth.

Buster had some early problems with the recording sessions in front of the audience, which was work he had never done before and which takes a bit of getting used to. You're poised somewhere between theatre acting and location filming and there's cameras and crew and microphones between you and the audience and it can be distracting and odd. Buster was fluffing his lines and drying and I found him backstage in a right old state because he felt like he was in over his head. So I did what I thought might help: at the next take, I deliberately screwed up a line myself and turned it into a joke with the audience. It happens to us all, was the only point I was trying to make – and, above all, it doesn't really matter. In fact, the audience love it if you screw up, because you're in on the moment together. When he knew he could relax, Buster was fine, and he was a fully blended-in team player from that point on.

Buster's trademark and calling card was, it goes without saying, his beard. He was extremely attached to it, in more senses than one. Nick and I spent a long time nagging him to bring in a photo of himself without the beard, but he absolutely refused. We began to think that maybe there was no such thing, and that Buster had emerged, fully white-bearded, from the womb. Eventually we convinced him that John was writing an episode of the show in which Uncle Albert would appear in flashback as a young man, for which scenes, it stood to reason, Buster/Albert would not have had his beloved beard. The prospect upset him enormously, almost as if he believed his very strength, in some vaguely Samson-like way, would drain away with the scissoring of that vital hair.

'It'll be OK,' I reassured him. 'You'll be able to wear a false one after.'

'But it will take ages to grow back,' replied Buster.

'Well, you could wear the false one for ages, then,' I suggested helpfully.

He wasn't happy.

Eventually we got John in on the wind-up and brought him in to confirm to Buster that the beardless flashback episode was go. John could never keep a straight face for long, though, so the jig was soon up – although not before Buster had plaintively asked John if he couldn't just cut the beard back a bit and then cover it with make-up, which would have looked marvellous on camera, no doubt.

# CHAPTER SEVEN

## *A fight with Nick Lyndhurst, and the party that wasn't*

Only *Fools* threw me and Nick Lyndhurst together in a working partnership. That was all that was expected of us. We didn't have to become a pair of physically unlikely brothers in real life, just because the script for a television comedy show told us that's what we were. Yet, during that intense decade of filming in the 1980s, over the course of those seven series, a pair of unlikely brothers is what we did become. Nick was twenty when it all started. I was twenty-one years older than him, but the gap somehow didn't seem to matter. Indeed, it seemed to close when we were around one another. There was an easy rapport there – and, quite coincidentally, a bunch of interests in common outside of acting, too. Both of us, for example, thought there was nothing better in the world than going diving – except, possibly, flying gliders, planes and helicopters, which were hobbies we both eagerly explored during this period. And both of us got an enormous and perhaps disproportionate amount of pleasure out of winding people up by means of elaborate practical jokes.

There was one morning when we became ragingly keen on the idea of going into the wardrobe store, bright and early, and turning every item of Lennard Pearce's costume inside out. Hours of fun. Well, a few minutes of fun, anyway – though not for dear old Lennard, God rest his soul, who took this assault on his clothing very personally and had a significant meltdown about it, during which it became clear that he believed this pointless and intrusive disturbance to his working day to be the work of juvenile hooligans. He may have had a point. Nick and I certainly promised Lennard that we would do all that was in our power to identify those juvenile hooligans as quickly as we could and ensure that some measure of punishment befitting their delinquency was meted out to them.

The thing is, as I'm sure you will be aware, filming television programmes is an occupation in which bursts of furious activity are broken by long, long periods in which nothing happens at all, and sometimes even less than nothing. It's a bit like war in that sense, I suppose – except that you get your own trailer. Or, at least, you get a trailer to share with Nick Lyndhurst. Actually 'trailer' might be rather a fancy word for the temporary shelter that was our refuge during *Only Fools* location shoots. 'Grubby caravan' might better convey the lower-than-Hollywood standard of the accommodation provided for us during those long days. Almost terminally aged by having been dragged around the country on film shoots for a couple of decades, and with its internal walls and ceiling joyfully yellowed by many years of heroically sustained cigarette smoking by idling actors, this highly undesirable wagon boasted a dirt-coloured carpet, a couch ruined by we dreaded to think what, and space which prohibited the swinging of cats. Not that we ever tried to swing a cat in there, although, during a rain delay, had we been bored enough and had a suitable cat been available, I wouldn't have put it past us. Left to loll about in this wagon for extended periods while lights were rearranged, or cameras positioned, or sets adjusted, or during the thousand other delays to which filming is prey, Nick and I would very quickly find ourselves in the kind of mood in which messing about with Lennard Pearce's costumes just to get a rise out of him could seem like the only appropriate course of action.

Boredom would also explain the time in 1986 that Nick and I got into the most almighty row, a truly monumental shouting match – the one and only time, I can honestly report, that this happened in the entire course of *Only Fools*. It started in the caravan, where, for important reasons which I will duly disclose, words were exchanged between us at great volume and where, I'm afraid to say, one or two loose items that happened to be to hand were flung angrily at the walls, thumping against it and inevitably startling members of the cast and the crew walking around outside.

The row continued with Nick throwing open the caravan door and exiting in a hurry, visibly upset and shouting, 'That's it. I've had it. I'm not working with him any more.' Whereupon he stormed away to the canteen, with me standing in the caravan's doorway, shouting after him, 'Yeah, that's right. Run off and cry to the crew, why don't you?'

The argument was as surprising for its violence as for the way it blew up out of nowhere, and these must have been genuinely shocking scenes for those obliged to witness them. Certainly a hush now descended on the set, with people exchanging anxious and embarrassed looks. The most anxious and embarrassed of them all was probably Mandie Fletcher, who had just graduated from being the show's assistant director to being its director, and whose first day in the bigger job this was. Hard to reckon with how panicked and generally sick this bust-up must have made her. She had only been in charge a couple of minutes and two of the stars of the show had already fallen out with each other, seemingly terminally – every director's nightmare. For the next hour, Nick and I sat separately in our fury, refusing to talk to each other and refusing to discuss the matter with anyone else, including Mandie, to whom I merely communicated that I was no longer prepared to share a trailer with Nick and that our working relationship was over as far as I was concerned.

The day carried on, as best it could. The bits of filming on the schedule – none of which, conveniently, involved Nick and myself – were getting done, but there was no sign of any break in the silent impasse between the two of us and the general atmosphere continued to fester. Eventually, around teatime, not sure what else she could really do, Mandie phoned John Sullivan at home and said, 'John, we've got a real problem here. David and Nick aren't talking to each other, and they're not talking to anyone else, either. It looks bad.' Recognising that this presented a potential disaster for the future of his show, John immediately agreed to get in his car and drive out to the location to play the role of Henry Kissinger, and see what he could do to bring about a workable peace between our two warring factions.

Fortunately for John, a second call reached him just before he left. Nick and I had just cracked. The whole thing had been a wind-up – a staged spat, meticulously planned by the pair of us during a quiet moment in the caravan at the beginning of the day. The best bit, as we happily explained, through eyes damp with laughter and merriment at how clever we were, was being able to see everybody's frozen reactions out of the caravan window while we were in there bellowing at each other and chucking the ashtray against the wall. Oh, how Nick and I chortled and clutched at our aching ribs. For some reason, the rest of the crew, however, including Mandie, seemed not to find the big reveal at the end of this gag quite as funny as Nick and I did. Obviously they were in some measure relieved and glad to see the tension dispersed. But at the

same time, their reaction appeared to be not so much amused
as . . . well, unamused, I suppose, is the word that I'm looking
for here. Possibly even angry. I guess it's true that you can
allow these things to go on too long, and in this case Nick and
I may have misjudged it by – oooh, maybe an hour or two. Or
possibly three. Ah, well. It had passed some time, which was
the main thing.

On an earlier occasion, Nick himself was the victim of
the wind-up – though this time the duration of the prank
was just right, I would suggest, and the eventual denoue-
ment didn't lead to widespread anger and irritation, but to
general joy and happiness, which is perhaps how it's meant
to be. We were on location in April 1982, a couple of days
into filming scenes for an episode in series two called 'It
Never Rains . . .' That's the one I mentioned earlier, that I
had got all excited about, upon reading the script, because
it featured extensive holiday scenes in Spain, and who
wouldn't fancy a few days working in the sunshine and sam-
pling the local paella if the BBC was paying? Except, of
course, the BBC, as usual, weren't paying and we were sent
to Studland Bay in Dorset instead. No disrespect to Studland Bay, obviously, which is a very nice place. And I'm
sure you can get a perfectly respectable paella there, too, if
you try hard enough. But if your work requires you to lie on
a beach in April in no more than a pair of leopard-print
budgie smugglers, Spain is likely to be the more accommo-
dating location. Let me tell you, pretending that you're hot

and relaxed when in fact there's a typical English coastal wind pounding away at your most intimate recesses calls on the very deepest reserves an actor can muster. They were beating down my goosebumps with a mallet that week. Thank heavens this was in the days before high-definition TV, or I would have looked like a roll of bubble wrap.

Anyway, the mock-Spanish film shoot in Studland Bay coincided with Nick's birthday – his twenty-first no less, on the occasion of which, obviously, he would be expecting a bit of fuss and ceremony. So, realising that this was a very special day in the life of my acting partner and dear friend, I decided that we should all completely ignore it. No cards, no presents – no mention of it . Everybody in the cast and crew was in on it and secretly briefed: don't say anything to Nick about his birthday. If he mentioned it himself – which he did – the instruction was to move the conversation along briskly to some other matter entirely.

Now, given that he had done his best to put the word out, you can imagine the tingling anticipation Nick must have been experiencing as he came down for breakfast in the hotel that morning. He would have been expecting a card or two, at the very least; maybe presents – certainly a friendly 'Happy birthday!' from his friends and colleagues on the production. Not a dicky bird. Same thing at lunchtime, when we broke from filming. Nick was probably thinking, 'This is where they'll bring in a cake or something, surely.' He must have been bracing himself for a burst of the birthday song and the arrival of some flickering candles. He may even have been quaveringly awaiting the moment where we suddenly ambushed him and gave him the bumps. Silence, though. Utter silence. Nothing whatsoever to that effect.

By the time we got back to the hotel at the end of the day, Nick's disappointment had clearly consumed him to the point where it was now openly visible in the hang of his shoulders and the downcast nature of his face and he was obviously – and justifiably – feeling thoroughly sorry for himself. Twenty-one – and nobody cared. As we separated to go to our rooms, I asked him if he wanted to join me in the hotel bar for a drink a little bit later. 'Just a quick one, mind,' I told him. 'Want to be fresh in the morning. Show to make, and all that.' Having no alternative, Nick agreed to see me there.

That evening, at the appointed time of 8 p.m., we descended from our rooms into the lobby of what appeared to be an almost entirely abandoned hotel. 'Where is everyone?' Nick asked. 'I think they've all gone off to Bournemouth,' I said. 'Bit of a night out.' With perfect timing, a couple of members of the crew crossed the lobby at this point. Nick, with faint but detectable desperation, asked them if they fancied joining us. 'Sorry, mate,' came the reply. 'We're going out. We'll see you later, maybe.' I don't know about crestfallen: Nick's crest had completely disappeared. Indeed, it was as if he had never grown a crest in the first place. Bad enough to be away from home on his twenty-first birthday, removed from family and loved ones. But on top of that, his big day had been completely overlooked and he was going to be spending the last hours of it with one other bloke from work in a Dorset hotel that, far from being Party Central, was rapidly coming to resemble the *Marie Celeste*.

We went into the bar, thereby becoming the only two people in it, apart from the barman. We sat on our stools for a while and toyed with our drinks – for which I had, of course, let Nick pay. As we drank, I mostly maintained a remote silence, the only noise in the room being the gentle wash of muzak from the bar's speakers. After about fifteen properly inconsequential minutes, I drained my glass and said, 'Well, I think I'm going to go up now.' Nick's face fell another five feet. 'But before I do,' I added, 'I've got an idea. Let's go down to the wardrobe store and nail Lennard Pearce's shoes to the floor.'

It speaks volumes about what passed for regular, quotidian behaviour on an *Only Fools* shoot that Nick would entertain this as a perfectly plausible proposal, not even worth blinking at, let alone questioning. To him, it would have seemed like a natural follow-up to the 'turning Lennard's costumes inside out' prank. Also, in the context of what was now officially the worst birthday of his life, the idea of devoting a few moments to spoiling Lennard Pearce's composure in the morning might even have had something of a redemptive glimmer about it. Maybe, Nick most likely thought, the night was not yet completely lost.

He was right: it wasn't. The wardrobe store was actually a large, windowless room in the basement of the hotel, normally used as a gym but which had been requisitioned by the production team for the duration of our stay. I led the way, and down we went. At the door, I cast a surreptitious look behind me to check the scene was clear, then quietly opened it, nudged Nick inside, and switched on the light.

Ta-da! With the costume racks pushed out to the walls and the floor cleared, the whole cast and crew were there, touting drinks, presents, cards, balloons and a whacking great birthday cake. Nick was delighted, of course, although he did greet the moment of revelation with the utterance traditionally heard on such occasions: 'You bastards!'

Did we take it too far? Was this a step too bastardly? I hope you don't think so. From a more mature perspective, and as the father of a teenage daughter rapidly approaching those landmark birthday ages, I can see how this agonisingly protracted set-up might come over as a bit harsh – a touch cruel, even. But you have to place it within the fiercely competitive context of Nick's and my practical jokes, and our determination to top each other royally in this important department. Had we been on location on the occasion of my fortieth, say, I'm sure Nick would have come up with something equally fiendish, if not more so. Anyhow, let's not overlook the redemptive nature of the end-moment. A grand party duly ensued, and when the evening had worn on and numbers had thinned slightly owing to varying degrees of exhaustion and over-refreshment, the revels adjourned upstairs and continued in Nick's room. The specially commissioned birthday cake hadn't been touched at that juncture, so, with a view to performing a ceremonial cake-cutting in due course, it was carried upstairs with us. Whereupon, in necessarily crowded and slightly unsteady circumstances, John Sullivan accidentally sat on it.

We fooled around a lot, then, me and Nick, but we also clung to each other for support when we needed it, and not least on those Sunday nights when we were filming the studio portions of the show, in front of the audience. Those were seriously tense times – a completely different level of anxiety from shooting on location, generating an altogether different surge of adrenaline. I had spent years playing to theatre crowds and knew how jittery that could make you in the moments before the curtain went up. But the combination of cameras and a roomful of expectant people was something else. You were always worried about whether you had your lines down, how it was going to play with the crowd. It used to really get to me and Nick. Nobody else in the cast seemed to catch it quite so badly. One of the mental images I hold most vividly from that whole period is of being backstage at those sessions, getting ready to go out and perform, both of us stricken every time, without fail, by nerves, pacing up and down and looking at each other and saying, 'Why? Why do we do this?' – but sharing it, and making it easier in the process, which is how things worked between us.

Not long after Nick's uneventful twenty-first, I was the victim of a cruel prank myself – though, for once, neither Nick nor any of the crew was behind it. We were filming on location and I came down from my hotel room for breakfast to find some kind of trade fair going on in the lobby. There was a bunch of stalls set up and people were selling their wares off trestle tables – mostly electrical items, it seemed. So I had a little browse and the one thing that caught my eye was an electric carving knife. The guy at the stall had a whole batch of them stacked up in cardboard boxes and he was good enough to give me a little demonstration of the machine in action, carving perfect slices off a lump of ham, quietly and effortlessly. The price for this clearly brilliant and enormously labour-saving device, though not cheap, didn't seem exorbitant, so I bought one.

Back home a few days later, with anticipation around the dining table at feverish levels, and bearing the proud demeanour of a man who is confident that he is about to bring carving the Sunday joint screaming into the late twentieth century, I got ready to wield my magical appliance for the first time. With the meat sitting ready, and the machine plugged in, I unsheathed the blade and depressed the ON/OFF switch, whereupon, all of a sudden . . . nothing happened. Nothing continued to happen for the next few minutes, while I repeatedly clicked the ON/OFF switch, checked the plug, examined the machine from both ends, shook it, rapped it on the table, consulted the instruction manual to ensure that the ON/OFF button genuinely was that button with ON and OFF written on it, as I had inferred, and so forth. Absolutely nothing. The standard, non-electric carving knife was humiliatingly retrieved from the kitchen.

I was furious. What kind of chancer sells dodgy imported electrical goods off a stall to innocent and unassuming passers-by?

What kind of chancer, indeed. Suckered. Done up like a kipper. Del Boy had been properly Del Boyed.

# CHAPTER EIGHT

## *Trains and boats and press photographers*

I was on board a ninety-foot boat on the North Sea, moored off the Yorkshire coast near Spurn Point, and it wasn't looking pretty. I lay on a bed in the aft cabin, clutching my stomach and groaning quietly. Ray Butt stood over me in consternation. 'I've never had seasickness like this before, Ray,' I muttered, between deep breaths. 'You're going to have to leave me behind.'

This was not news Ray needed to hear. As if the stakes weren't already high enough. Ray had had to go on his knees to the BBC to get the budget for this shoot. Shooting on the high seas doesn't come cheap. There was the cost of our vessel, a safety boat, a helicopter on stand-by to fly a skeleton crew onto a British Gas rig, tight timings to meet – and here, at the very start of the day, with the sun barely up, his leading man was already groaning on a bunk bed and wanting to get off.

I couldn't keep it up for long, though. After half a minute

or so of glimpsing, between groans, the colour drain from Ray's face, I jumped up and clapped him on the shoulder. 'Gotcha.' I had rarely felt better, actually. Having suffered seasickness in my time and knowing full well how unfunny it is, your author had smartly dosed himself in advance with Kwells anti-nausea tablets, to which I wholeheartedly recommend you the next time you're filming a Christmas special edition of a sitcom on the North Sea. Excellent work that day by the make-up department in the greening of my gills, by the way. It's the little touches, the attention to detail, that make all the difference in the delivery of a convincing wind-up.

This was the early autumn of 1985 and we were in the middle of making 'To Hull and Back' – the first of the proper *Only Fools* Christmas specials, which followed series four. I mean 'proper' in the sense that was a full-blown ninety-minute story rather than a standard-length extra episode of the show packaged for the season, which had been the case of the earlier series. John Sullivan had come up with a corking feature-length tale in which Del agrees to act as a mule for a shipment of diamonds procured in Amsterdam by Boycie and his business partner Abdul Khan, played by Tony Anholt, who was familiar to viewers around this time from his role in the drama series *Howards' Way*. To avoid the scrutiny of DC Slater (our old friend Jim Broadbent, back again), who is on to Boycie's smuggling ruse and is having the airports watched, Del decides to travel to Amsterdam by water in a privately hired boat. He also decides to call on Uncle Albert's nautical experience and appoint him as ship's captain. Of course, the truth is Albert spent his navy career in a storeroom in Portsmouth and he can barely captain his own way out of a lavatory block, so the trip is doomed. On the morning I'm talking about we were off at the crack of dawn to film the now famous sequence where Del, by this point thoroughly lost at sea, calls up to a worker on a gas rig for directions.

The *Inge*, our commissioned vessel, wasn't exactly a gin palace, or in any way the kind of item on which you might go swanking into the harbour at Monte Carlo. In fact, it looked as if it had been recently dredged up off the ocean floor. A blistered and creaking old tub in a fetchingly municipal shade of pale blue, it wasn't built for comfort, and once in open water it was soon rocking about like something at a fairground. Me (suitably medicated), Nick (also medicated) and Buster (somehow oblivious) seemed OK. But the production crew were all over the place. As the six-hour voyage out to the gas rig wore on, and the *Inge*'s pitching and tossing showed no signs of abating, illness among the cameramen, sound operatives, make-up girls, etc., was rife and the packed lunches so thoughtfully provided for our voyage by the hotel in Hull – ham and egg sandwiches in cling film, cheese-and-onion crisps – began to look less and less like a good idea.

Particularly grievously affected was one of the dressers, a lovely but rather delicate man who also happened to wear a hairpiece. Now, as I probably don't need to point out, it takes a well-attached hairpiece to withstand an attack of seasickness in gusting winds on the North Sea. Thus our journey found the poor bloke slumped over the side of the boat, emptying the contents of his stomach into the sea while simultaneously, with one carefully applied hand, holding his supplementary head-coverage in place. This vision of distress provoked a profound reaction from one of the electricians, a cockney, who, far from being moved to sympathise with a struggling fellow crew member, became loudly convinced that this was the funniest thing he had ever seen. The electrician stood on the deck, pointing at the heaving dresser and crying out to me through his tears of mirth, 'Dave – he's losing his Irish!' (Cockney rhyming slang: Irish jig, wig. 'Dave, he's losing his syrup' would also have qualified: syrup of figs, wig(s).)

For a while it looked bad for our chances of having enough able bodies to form a workable crew, but fortunately, by the time we reached the rig, we were just about fit enough to go. We were down below on the sea, with a camera shooting up; and Ray Butt was on the rig with the actor playing the rigger, and a cameraman, shooting back down at us in the boat. The moves were all coordinated via walkie-talkies. With both cameras rolling, I duly shouted my line ('Which way to Holland?'), and the man on the rig duly delivered his shouted reply ('Holland? [Points] It's over there!'), and that was it. I think we had it down first take, but we did a few more, just because it had been a long way to go and it would have felt wrong not to, given the money that had been spent getting us out there in the first place.

Everyone assumed that Ray had secured himself a cushy number by electing to be part of the skeleton crew on the gas rig. This was a man who generally knew how to look after his best interests, after all. Ray's standard, and very smart, approach to the rigours of on-location night-shooting was to stuff the pockets of his big, furry-hooded director's parka with a healthy serving of miniatures from the hotel minibar, to the point where you would sometimes find him clanking around the set like a milk float. On this occasion, rather than travel with us on the six-hour trawl from Spurn Point, having seen us all on board, he had gone back ashore, hopped on a British Gas helicopter that was doing a routine crew run, and flown direct to the rig. This would ensure, very conveniently, that he missed the six-hour return trip, too. However, he got his comeuppance. After the shoot, Ray had to sit around on a gas rig with the cameraman, twiddling his thumbs and bored out of his box, waiting for the British Gas helicopter to turn up, and the *Inge* actually beat him home. Also the production crew, who were never slow to spot a potential party opportunity in the schedule, had thoughtfully loaded the *Inge* with booze for the return journey. By the time the boat berthed back in Hull, those who couldn't stand up on account of seasickness had been joined by those who couldn't stand up on account of alcohol consumption.

'To Hull and Back' was filmed entirely outside London – another first. We had already started using Bristol for exterior shots, because it was cheaper and simpler to film there than in the capital. But we had always done the interior studio stuff back in London. Here, though, the sets for the flat and for the Nag's Head were driven up from Television Centre and replicated in a Hull warehouse and there were no studio sequences with an audience anywhere in the show, which made it feel more like a feature film than a television production. I think we were all rather thrilled about that. Also thrilling, but at the same time disconcerting, were the first signs we saw of the extent to which the show was now becoming a public item – and us with it. I'm not saying it was Beatlemania for us, up there in Hull. People weren't screaming and flinging themselves on top of us and trying to collect hanks of our hair and strips of our clothing whenever they saw us. More's the pity, perhaps. Yet it seemed that the temperature around the production had suddenly risen. We were creating a gathering wherever we went, and there were people outside the hotel and in the lobby, apparently just standing around and waiting to catch a glimpse of us. The press were more visibly present, too. They weren't going after us personally, but they were certainly going after the show. Photographers were trying to get pictures of the action on location and you realised that what the *Only Fools* team was getting up to was somehow now a viable news story – a potential exclusive. For those of us who had travelled through life more or less incognito up to this point, it felt very strange.

By the time we made 'The Jolly Boys Outing', the one about the fateful seaside day out and the exploding coach, which was shot on the seafront and the streets of Margate in 1989, the public attention we were getting had reached such a level that the production was routinely hiring security guys to keep an eye on the crowds and prevent people getting in the way of the filming. It was becoming increasingly difficult to go anywhere without being noticed and attracting a knot of fans – which was nice, of course, but also a bit intimidating sometimes, and occasionally, when you were trying to get on with something, it could be a bit of a hindrance. The security guys were a useful buffer.

One day, during a break in shooting, John Challis realised he needed some cigarettes and asked one of the guys standing on the edge of the cordon if he would mind accompanying him to the shop, just in case he got swamped by bystanders. Off they went up the road. John slipped into the newsagent's, bought his cigarettes and then, as the pair of them headed back to the shoot, he engaged his minder in conversation, asking him how long he'd been doing this kind of work.

'What do you mean?' said John's minder.

'You know – doing security for people,' said John.

'Oh, no,' the bloke said. 'I manage a supermarket. I was just on my lunch break. Can I have your autograph, Boycie?'

The presence of the paparazzi was a problem that the programme needed to take particular precautions against. A snap of your big set-piece moment, or your long-planned visual gag, printed in a newspaper before the show was broadcast, could be a horrible spoiler, ruining the surprise for the viewers and thereby nuking the joke. When Tony Dow was directing (he took over from Ray Butt in 1988 after Ray was given his own department to run at ITV), he would get particularly agitated about it. There was more than one occasion on location when photographers were spotted lurking furtively nearby, and Tony had to be physically restrained from going over and lumping them. In the case of the Batman and Robin sequence from 'Heroes and Villains', in 1996, the secrecy surrounding the set reached virtually FBI levels of density. Those pages of the script were circulated only to people who genuinely needed to know about them, on a 'for your eyes only' basis. If we had had the whereabouts to transpose them into an uncrackable code, I'm sure we would have done. The filming was conducted on a closed street in Bristol with security posted at both ends, and was done very late at night to minimise the likelihood of prying eyes, and more particularly prying lenses.

As it happened, our biggest problem that night wasn't unwanted press intrusion; it was an outbreak of disgraceful corpsing on the part of the leading players, who ought to have known better. Nick and I, dressed for the publican Harry Malcolm's party as Batman and Robin (though, of course, that party turns out to be a wake, Harry Malcolm having died in the week, unbeknown to Del and Rodney), were doing the conversation sequence in the broken-down van – a set-up, by the way, inspired by a passing comment of a friend of John's who was going to a vicars and tarts party with his wife, having decided that his wife should go as the vicar and he should go as the tart, and was worrying about breaking down in Stockwell on the way there. By this point in the shoot, it was about two in the morning and everybody in the crew was more than ready to finish up and go to bed. Unfortunately, every time we went for a take, Nick would start talking in that ridiculous costume and he would look so stupid that I would start to go. That, in turn, would set Nick off and the pair of us would be reduced to a giggling mess, within the space of about half a line. Tony Dow was not best pleased. But that's crime fighting.

It all finished happily, of course. The Batman and Robin segment is one of the *Only Fools* sequences that people still constantly hark back to – the particular genius of it being, in my opinion, the mist that Tony Dow decided to spread across the street for the pair of us to emerge through, as we abandon the van and run to the party, inadvertently interrupting the mugging of Councillor Murray, whose attackers turn and flee in fear and confusion at the sight of the caped crusaders. It was one of those moments where it all comes together: the set-up, the location, the costumes, the characters and the tiny extra details, all gelling in one very funny moment. It was Nick, by the way, who remembered how Batman and Robin used to bunch a fist and punch the palms of their hands before going into action, a gesture which we were rather childishly pleased to be able to incorporate into our impression. One leaked photo, though, could have ruined it.

# CHAPTER NINE

## Only Fools *and sex toys*

Did we go too far with the blow-up dolls? Clearly there were a few people who thought so. It was the sole time *Only Fools* found itself accused of overstepping the mark for a family show. In Del's defence, he didn't know what kind of dolls they were when he agreed to take them off Denzil's hands. He just thought they were dolls. He didn't know they were . . . you know . . . *dolls*.

Still, there's no getting away from it: the 'Danger UXD' episode in series six stirred a public controversy regarding taste and morality which was unique in the history of the show. (That title, by the way, possibly hasn't aged well. You need to know that there was a seventies television drama called *Danger UXB* about the work of the force sent to deal with the unexploded bombs, or UXBs, that were left lying around in London after the Blitz. Hence, in our case, UXB became UXD, for unexploded doll. Thank you for your attention.) John Sullivan had apparently been to a party where somebody, for a lark, had filled the room with inflated dolls and this amusing approach to interior decor had planted in his head the idea for a plotline. Partly these dolls looked funny en masse; but also, how was the host of this party going to get rid of these dolls discreetly? So he cooked up a story involving a batch of self-inflating dolls – but with faulty valves, making them prone to going up at the wrong moment and in unfortunate places, such as in the back of the Trotters' Reliant Regal and behind the bar of the Nag's Head. Just to add to the chaos, it also becomes apparent that these dolls are filling up with highly flammable propane, meaning that they are essentially bombs waiting to go off. Slapstick opportunities galore here. Albeit slightly adult slapstick.

*Only Fools* had always been a clean show, ever mindful that there were children in the room. Certainly nobody swears. In 'Miami Twice', Boycie had a line, when he caught a whiff of Del after the latter emerged from an unfortunate dunking in a swamp (of which more later): 'Blimey, Del, you smell like a vegetarian's fart.' That was probably about as close to the wire as *Only Fools* ever got – and that was in 1991, in a period when the rules around acceptable language on television were rapidly relaxing, and in the slightly looser circumstances of a Christmas special. I'm not sure the show would have risked even that line in a regular series in the 1980s.

Now, I'm not prudish about swearing, by any means.

ONLY FOOLS AND STORIES

Indeed, I have been known to crack open *Roget's Profanity Thesaurus* myself and turn straight to the pages under 'F' when the situation has arisen. For instance, the time I ran over my own foot with a Flymo, I believe I automatically unleashed a torrent of the kind of language that would have bothered the late Mary Whitehouse enormously had she been tuned in, which fortunately she wasn't. But, with due respect to the memory of Mrs Whitehouse, who I'm sure meant well, there's no point being overly censorious about these things. Those words are part of the language too, as far as I'm concerned, and as long as it's between consenting adults, you might as well use them to express yourself when you need to. And as I lay on the grass beside my Flymo that afternoon with one of my shoes in shreds, I definitely felt I needed to – and took, I think, some small measure of comfort from so doing.

Incidentally, during my convalescence in East Grinsted hospital after that horticultural mishap, Ronnie Barker, typically, sent me – or, at any rate, Dithers the gardener – a letter of commiseration, written on headed notepaper in orange ink and purporting to be from Lord Rustless of Chrome Hall. 'My Dear Dithers,' it began, 'what's all this I hear about you cutting off your toes, you damn fool? I never did like that lawnmower, and neither did Bates, ever since the time you came up behind her a bit sharpish when she had her head down that rabbit-hole, and you hit her amidships up the back rockery. Do take more care, old fruit.' For the record, I should point out, contrary to Lord Rustless's inference, that no toes were actually severed during the mowing of my lawn, but the big one on my left foot, which bore the brunt of this mechanical assault, was never the same afterwards.

So, it's a firm 'yes' to swearing from me, in the right circumstances. It's just that I don't think a comedy show on television is the right circumstances. Again, this is not prudishness on my part. In my view, swearing in comedy conforms to the law of diminishing returns: and I speak as someone who recently sat in his living room watching an Amy Poehler movie with his teenage daughter. Swearing has its initial impact, that big buzz of transgression for both the audience and the performer, but then you've got nowhere to go with it, I reckon, except down. Also, as far as mainstream television comedies are concerned, you have to remember that there is still, even now, a significant portion of the audience that are going to be offended by swearing – and not just mildly disapproving of it, but actually upset by it. They're entitled to feel that way and I've never worked out how you could decide that those people, and their offence, wasn't worth anything to you. That strikes me as a bit arrogant. One thing I do know is that I never received a single letter from anyone complaining that they didn't enjoy an episode of *Only Fools*, or *Frost*, or *The Darling Buds of May*, or whatever, because it didn't have any swearing in it.

With *Only Fools*, a commitment to cleanliness in the

language department worked to the show's advantage. The restriction on swearing forced John Sullivan into feats of linguistic ingenuity for which the programme is now loved and remembered. Words like 'twonk', 'plonker', 'nerk' and 'dipstick' were the show's hallmark, its incidental catchphrases and calling cards. Then there was Del's catalogue of misappropriated French exclamations: 'mange tout', 'menage à trois', 'boeuf à la mode', 'bonnet de douche'. Again, you had to wonder: if John had been able to access the full panoply of the English language in all its historic saltiness, would he have gone there? If he had felt free to flick through the profanity thesaurus, would we ever have seen Del respond to an explosive situation by shouting, 'Châteauneuf du Pape'?

John also had cockney rhyming slang, of course, to colour things up and also to act as a screen against vulgarity – although there was one time when the screen was so thick that even I, a fellow Londoner, couldn't see through it. We were sitting around a table, the cast and John, having a first read-through of an episode called 'The Losing Streak', from the second series, in 1982. We had reached a rather moving sequence where Del tells Rodney about the night their father walked out on them, taking everything with him, including the money from Rodney's piggy bank and Del's birthday cake – sobering details which Rodney was too young to know at the time. At that point, I got to the following line:

'From that day, I swore that I would never run away from anything in my life. I mean, you know, if a wild lion were to come in here now, my old April would be pouting like a good 'un, but I'd stand me ground.'

This rather pulled me up. 'John,' I said. 'April? My old April? I don't understand. What's April got to do with it?'

John said, 'That's modern rhyming slang. It means "arse". In other words, "my old arse would be pouting like a good 'un". You know – in fear.'

I said, 'Come again? How the hell do you get from "April" to "arse"?'

John said, 'April in Paris – arris. Aristotle – bottle. Bottle and glass – arse.'

There was a considerable silence while the brains around the table all engaged with the complex parts of this equation. Not since I badly failed maths at school had I known a knotty sum quite like it. Eventually I said, 'John, that isn't going to work. Nobody's going to understand that.'

John said, 'It'll fly – trust me.'

So we get to the live show, in front of the studio audience, and I've still got my doubts, but I'm trusting in Sullivan, a policy which, let's face it, hasn't tended to let me down thus far. We duly reach the moment:

'If a wild lion were to come in here now, my old April would be pouting like a good 'un, but I'd stand me ground.'

I then pause to allow space for the laughter. Silence. Absolute silence. The line goes for nothing. All Nick and I can do is gather ourselves and move swiftly on, and hope that the post-production people can patch up the mess.

Afterwards, I said to John, 'My old April actually *was* pouting like a good 'un out there. Your so-called April got sweet nothing.'

That was a rare lapse on John's part, though – and perhaps the inflatable dolls were another one. What possessed him? I think John just saw it as one more part of the rich tapestry of human life – the rich latex tapestry of life, in this case. Let me be clear, the decision to involve the show in a drama about sex toys was not taken lightly. The pros and cons were batted back and forth during a series of painstaking discussions, which, as so often in comedy production, would probably need to be filed under 'Is this any way for serious grown people to be spending their time?' The question was, if we were resolved upon the use of inflatable dolls in the show, should we make our own, more innocent ones, whose purpose was more obscure, without real hair or gripping hands, to say nothing of the gripping other bits? This approach seemed to have due caution on its side. On the other hand, if the dolls came across as innocent, how would you sustain the comedy of embarrassment around disposing of them? It was clear that we needed to have, if not the real thing, then the nearest thing to the real thing. So the eventual plan was to acquire some actual inflatable dolls and then, in the privacy of a BBC props workshop, slightly amend them with the sensitivities of the wider audience in mind.

Now, this was 1989, before the days of accessible and

discreet online shopping – a development which has revo-
lutionised the purchase of all manner of goods, from sex
toys to copies of my first volume of autobiography, which,
in case I haven't already done so, the publishers have asked
me to mention is still available, both on- and offline.
Accordingly, having little alternative, representatives of
the props department were duly dispatched to Soho to
source, compare and then bulk-buy appropriate dolls for our
purposes. Oh, to have been a fly on the sex-shop wall during that particular shopping mission. Back they came with
their mucky plunderings and work began on the necessary
alterations. The dolls' vital areas were glued over with flesh-
coloured patches, not so much in order to spare their
modesty as to create some modesty where there wasn't any
in the first place. The thoughtfully created open mouths
proved a little more difficult to work with. We had to live
with that ultimately unalterable trait and hope that innocent viewers would merely interpret it as an expression of
permanently delighted surprise.

As for the faulty valves which John's script called for,
well, I hope you will believe me when I say that I am well
outside my areas of expertise here, but apparently there is
no such thing as a self-inflating sex doll. Or, at least, there
wasn't when the props department looked into it, at the
end of the eighties. That could have changed, of course;
technology does evolve at a startling speed. After all, we
didn't even have the Internet or decent coffee at that point,

and now look at us. What I can say for sure is that, in 1989, the props people had no choice but to take a dozen or so of the standard, manually inflated dolls and doctor them so that they could be attached to a gas cylinder, concealed from the camera's gaze, and go up like a bouncy castle when required to do so.

A couple of the dolls were brought into the rehearsal room, precipitating much mirth of a schoolboy nature among us. The banter that went on around these temporary additions to the cast was, I'm afraid, unprintable in a book of this kind. Let us simply say that it did its protagonists very little in the way of credit, and quietly draw a veil across it.

Next stop for the doctored dolls was Bristol, where the episode's external scenes were to be filmed, including the impromptu inflation in the back of the Reliant Regal and the climactic explosion scene (not necessarily what you think; watch the episode back if you're in any doubt here). At one point, the crew were using the hotel lift to transfer a number of these dolls from the room in which they had been inflating them to the space that had been commandeered as a stockroom. Of course, an elderly couple had to call the lift during that journey, only for the doors to part and reveal a man, a woman and an assortment of fully enlarged sex dolls. Somehow one imagines the explanation they were offered – 'It's OK – we're just doing some filming' – didn't automatically set their minds at rest.

Anyway, the show went out and there were complaints. I don't know exactly how many complaints, but it doesn't take a lot of people to phone the BBC switchboard to kick off a controversy and soon the papers were onto it. There was no doubt the story was being whooped up a bit, but it seemed prudent to go into damage-limitation mode. Nick and I went on daytime television – sort of to apologise and sort of to defend the show at the same time. A woman came at us with a question about how we thought she should explain the dolls to her children, which I don't think either of us could convincingly answer. Apart from stressing the lengths to which we had gone to make the dolls less sexually obvious, there wasn't really any satisfactory argument you could mount – if that's the verb I'm looking for. That daytime telly appearance was one of the most awkward experiences of my life.

In due course, the storm, such as it was, died down and the controversy went away. Or did it, in fact? In 2013, an *Only Fools* fan in Sussex, named Richard Foster, got into trouble with the police for driving his yellow Reliant Regal van with a sex doll in the back, visible through the windscreen. It was, he claimed, an innocent enough tribute to the 'Danger UXD' episode, but the police weren't so sure. Mr Foster was threatened with a penalty charge unless he removed the offending item from sight. A police spokesman was quoted saying, 'The officer felt [the doll's] obvious attributes were not appropriate for family viewing.' Nearly a quarter of a century later, the debate was still rumbling on, clearly.

While we're on the subject of scandals stirred up by *Only Fools*, this would be a good moment to recall the time the Trotters were accused of being a pernicious immoral force. Not by anyone who actually watched the show, of course. People who watched the show understood the Trotters to be no such thing. Politicians in search of a headline, on the other hand ... Well, sometimes when you stand up and talk loudly about something you don't really know much about, you're quite likely to end up embarrassing yourself, and that's what happened in 1997 when Chris Woodhead, then the government's Chief Inspector of Schools, decided to take a pop at the Trotters for being a corrupting influence on the nation's youth, no less. 'If Del Boy and Rodney are the only role models available to the young then we have a problem,' Mr Woodhead said sternly, during a lecture in London, arguing that the programme encouraged the idea that education was irrelevant to success in life.

Hmm. 'But what about Rodney's GCEs in maths and art?' one was tempted to ask. You could hardly accuse the show of failing to promote the value of those particular two qualifications. Indeed, Del never failed to fall back on them while reminding Rodney that he was 'the brains of the operation'. But, in all seriousness, Woodhead seemed to have formed the impression that the Trotters were reprobates and criminals through and through, which was, of course, far from being the truth. Del might turn a blind eye to the source of a bit of 'hooky gear' every now and again; and he might flog Trigger a wig he didn't need, 'just in case'. But he was no thief. He wasn't wittingly on the wrong side of the law and, as I've mentioned before, he wouldn't have been such a strongly sympathetic character if he had been. Then you have to think of the things that the show was so obviously in favour of: love, support, self-improvement, a solid family life and, above all, the enduring truth that the most important things are the things that happen at home. Yes, there were things that Del and Rodney were poor at, but that didn't necessarily make them a poor example – neither for impressionable children nor for anybody else. Anyway, who said they were meant to be role models in the first place, rather than characters to be laughed at in a television show?

It was rather like the time at the 1992 Republican Party Convention when George Bush Sr laid into the cartoon Simpson family, saying that he wished American families were closer to the Waltons than to the Simpsons. The implication was that, where the Walton family was wholesome and admirable, the Simpson family was merely corrupt and corrupting – though as aggrieved fans of the show, and its writers, were quick to point out, the Simpsons embody and promote family values extremely avidly, much like the Trotters. They just happen to do their embodying and promoting in a show that is funny and ridiculous – much like the Trotters.

Ah well. Politicians and comedy never were an especially happy mix.

Incidentally, when we had finished shooting the inflatable dolls episode, the props department faced (just as Del and Rodney had done) the task of disposing of a small army of supplementary rubber cast members. As we were leaving at the end of the day, Nick and I were asked if either of us wanted to take one home as a memento. The question was put to us perfectly matter-of-factly, as if this stock of unwanted sex toys were just a plate of uneaten sandwiches – kind of 'you might as well take them, because they'll only go to waste otherwise'.

Nick and I exchanged a look. We would have had to rack our brains to recall even a single other occasion on a BBC shoot where we had been offered something for free. No question, either, that it would have been an item to remember the episode by. However, none of this outweighed the fact that the gift in question was, at the end of the day, a sex doll, and the idea of walking into the kitchen at home with one of those and saying 'Look what I've brought back' was hard to feel entirely comfortable about. Both of us politely declined the kind offer and left.

With regard to the rumour that, somewhere along the way, two or three of these dolls had gone missing, I will not be drawn to make a comment. I did not count them all out, and therefore I was not in a position to count them all back. Nothing would surprise me, though. People have their needs, after all. And as long as those dolls found a stable and loving home, that's the main thing.

*   *   *

I WONDER WHAT Anthony Hopkins would have made of all this. He was nearly in *Only Fools*, you know. And no, before you ask, he wasn't on the seemingly ever-expanding list of people who were considered for the part of Del before I was. But he did nearly make an appearance.

What happened was this. Part way through the 1980s I met Anthony Hopkins and his wife in a restaurant. He hadn't yet played Hannibal Lecter in *Silence of the Lambs*, but he had played everything you care to mention in British theatre, and he had starred in *The Elephant Man* and had played opposite Mel Gibson in *The Bounty* and was unquestionably a mega-star: a powerful actor and a huge name. It should have been *me* who was fawning all over *him*, yet, as so often with *Only Fools*, embarrassingly, the tables were immediately switched and, while I was still drawing breath, he promptly came out to me as a Trotters fan. 'I love that show,' he said. 'I've always wanted to be in it.'

'Really?' I said.

'Always,' he said.

Well, this was a bit of a scoop.

Casting a surreptitious look over each shoulder, I leaned in a little closer and spoke quietly into the legendary actor's highly respected lughole. 'Listen,' I said, 'I have influence. Strings I can pull. Levers I can activate. Not for any old geezer, it goes without saying. But in your case, Ant? Leave it with, my son. Leave it with.'

Actually, I don't think I did say that. I was too busy swallowing my surprise. But I duly told John Sullivan about what had happened and he was practically melting with excitement. 'Anthony Hopkins? Are you kidding?' Just to have him in the show would have been at once monumental and hilarious. John immediately sped off and started work on writing him a part. I think John pretty quickly realised that he couldn't simply make him a character – couldn't have him pitch up as a gangland boss or somebody's long-lost relative, or something. You can't just parachute a Hollywood star into the middle of a television sitcom, unexplained. His stardom would have eclipsed the show and the whole thing would have become unbalanced and fallen over. But if he could come on as himself, that might work; if something could bring Anthony Hopkins, the film star, into the world of the Trotters, or take the Trotters into the world of Anthony Hopkins, it could absolutely fly. So John began to play around with ideas for which the Trotters and Anthony Hopkins could end up brushing past each other and meanwhile excited members of the *Only Fools* production team started to talk to Anthony Hopkins's people about availability. Alas for us – though probably not for him – something came up for him in Hollywood and

159

removed him from our grasp. After that hot flush of enthusiasm, the idea dwindled away. You catch these things at the flood, it seems, or you don't catch them at all. Ah well. Maybe it would have lost the show some credibility if it had been seen to be bending itself out of shape in order to incorporate a Hollywood big gun. We never found out.

We did get Joan Sims, though – and British comedy film stars surely don't come much bigger. The queen of all those *Carry On* movies played Reenie Turpin, Trigger's aunt, in 'The Frog's Legacy' episode, which was the 1987 Christmas special. The idea was that Reenie had been a great friend of Del and Rodney's mother, enabling her to raise some questions regarding Rodney's paternity, which, in one of those massive, long-term narrative arcs that John Sullivan was so good at, the show would later resolve. Joan was great. She was infinitely more experienced than anybody else on the set, but she brought no air of superiority with her and had no desire to get her part enlarged to suit her standing. She knew exactly where the centre was, did what the script asked and was real. She also related to us that the *Carry On* team were paid reasonably well, but nowhere near as well as you might have imagined and certainly not to a degree that was commensurate with the vast and still ongoing success of the series. Joan wasn't bitter about it, by any means – and all credit to her for that. But she did think it was a touch unfair. Their deals gave them no part of any of the TV airings, apparently – and presumably the repeats of *Carry On* films must by now have generated enough to purchase and finance a medium-sized country. Fairness surely suggests the cast should have had some of that treasure.

That's not the way we rolled on *Only Fools*. Had the queen of *Carry On* joined us in 'Danger UXD' she would at least have been offered the compensation of an inflatable doll to take home. You were in the wrong episode, Joan. Or maybe not.

# CHAPTER TEN

## *Oi, Bazza!*

One simple way to measure the increase in the show's leverage at the BBC: in 1982, during the second series, we were obliged to pretend that the Dorset coast was Malaga in order to save money. In 1991, by contrast, at the end of series seven, we were all off to Miami to film the second part of a double-episode Christmas special in and around the Everglades. Wind back nine years, and the part of the Everglades would probably have been played by Thetford Forest while the Miami skyline would have been represented by some carefully framed shots of office blocks in Croydon. Now, though, it was Florida here we come. We considered ourselves blessed indeed.

When I say we were all off to Miami, I should immediately qualify that and say that some of us were. The plot took Del and Rodney to the States, Del having bought Rodney and Cassandra a holiday to help heal one of their frequent lovers' tiffs. However, when it turned out that

Cassandra was too busy at work, Del had taken up the ticket himself. (The holiday, you may remember, was bought with Rodney's pension money. It would also emerge that Del was fully cognisant of Cassandra's work diary at the point at which he made the booking. Fairly standard Del behaviour, then, all things considered.) The plot also involved a trip for John Challis and Sue Holderness, because Boycie and Marlene were meant to be on holiday in Florida, quite coincidentally, at the same time as Del and Rodney – and, of course, would be only too delighted to have gone three thousand miles west only to run into their friends from Peckham. Gareth Gwenlan and Tony Dow were naturally in the travelling party, as producer and director respectively, and many of our usual crew members. To the rest of the cast – to Buster, to Tessa Peake-Jones and Gwyneth Strong, to Ken MacDonald and Roger Lloyd Pack – we could only wish a fond farewell and issue a promise to bring them back a novelty fridge magnet, or something, if we remembered, which, on reflection, I don't think we did.

Mind you, exciting though it was to fly abroad, this didn't look like it was going to be much of a holiday. Scanning the itinerary eagerly for the bits where it said 'Time at Leisure', I noticed that filming was only scheduled to last for three days, at the end of which, with our body clocks barely adjusted to US time, we'd be flying straight back home again. There was no 'Time at Leisure' built into the itinerary at all.

Imagine our disappointment, then, when, upon arrival, the production immediately ran into difficulties with the local union laws, difficulties which took a number of days to resolve, thereby expanding the trip so that it ended up lasting a week and a half, much of it necessarily downtime. Nick and I were so upset we had to go to the hotel pool and lie in the sun for hours just to recover. And when that didn't quite work, we had to adjourn to a Miami bar and drink margaritas while watching the sun go down. Those were tough times. But, again, our close professional relationship kicked in, we clung to one another for support and some-how made it through.

Those union difficulties related to the fact that we had turned up with an all-BBC crew and the tight US regula-tions insisted that we employ a certain percentage of American unionised labour. Gareth was in negotiation for hours on end and the situation was only resolved when he agreed to take on some additional, American drivers, who then mostly spent the time on location standing around and not doing anything, apart from being additional and American. But thus are the wheels of international industry greased and at least we could now get on with making our television programme.

I think I can say without fear of contradiction that this was the first time that I had ever acted alongside an alliga-tor. They say you should never work with children or animals, and they may be right. But you should certainly never work with animals that have sharp teeth and snapping jaws – and the same undoubtedly goes for children.

The alligator chosen for the part in 'Miami Twice' – after bitterly competitive auditions, I'm sure – went by the rather unimaginative stage name of Al the Gator. Al was roughly the length of Ipswich and, in common with many alligators in my experience, had a demeanour that said 'Don't mess with me' – which I suppose could also be said about Ipswich. His role was to take a run at me and Nick, who were perched on a log, ready to sprint off in terror. No tricks, mirrors, screens or smoke were used in the assembling of this shot: when you see Nick and me sitting on our log, with Al just behind us, looking mean and moody and, above all, unmessable with, that's actually how it was. What you don't see is the ranger with a loaded rifle, who was standing by at all times – which was faintly reassuring, although you had to hope, in the absence of any rendered proof, that he was a good shot. You also don't see the bucket of alligator-friendly titbits that were there to act as bait for Al and to get him moving in the right direction.

With each take, Sean, Al's impressively muscled handler, would release him, Al would scuttle straight for the food, being filmed all the while, and then, when he was occupied eating, Sean would jump on him and render him captive again. Sometimes this would work like a dream. At other times, Al, who I think had some issues with concentration, wouldn't budge and Sean would be required to give him a prompt with his stick. On one occasion, Al set off quickly, as planned, but not in the direction of the food. Instead he decided to run straight at the camera crew who, naturally, scattered to all corners of Florida, screaming. Sue Holderness happened to be videoing the action at this point, and would have had some possibly award-winning footage of panicked film crew fleeing an attack by a ten-foot reptile if she hadn't panicked herself and ended up making a short movie of her own feet running across the grass. No future for Sue alongside David Attenborough in the BBC's Natural History department, one sensed.

As well as the tangle with Al, the script also called for me to plunge into a swamp. How I wasn't on an absolute fistful of danger money for this episode completely baffles me. Of course, John, writing away off the top of his head back in England, had probably assumed that this scene would be mocked up in the Thames somewhere around Henley, where the threat of actual alligators is generally low. But no. Del's plunge into the alligator-infested waters of an Everglades swamp took place in the actual alligator-infested waters of an actual Everglades swamp.

It was actually me who did the plunging, too. I've always done my own stunts whenever I could – partly because I had among my role models, from the very beginning, the great men of physical comedy, such as Buster Keaton and Laurel & Hardy, practitioners of a brand of comic acting which is rarely seen these days but which will never cease to be funny as far as I'm concerned. Any chance to emulate those people, in the slightest of ways, I jumped at – often literally.

But the other reason I would do my own stunts was simply because I thought it looked so much better. When a stunt-man steps in and takes over, you can generally see the join and that spoils it for me. The problem is, there's a strong imperative felt by directors to keep the leading actors out of trouble – and not necessarily for purely sentimental reasons, either. The director knows that if his lead gets crocked then the whole programme goes up the spout. I learned this early, during a series I did for ITV in 1974 called *The Top Secret Life of Edgar Briggs*, about a humble pen-pusher at the British Secret Intelligence Service who, despite his general inadequacy in the face of life, somehow becomes the hero of the hour, time and again. There was a sequence which required me, as Briggs, to roll out of the way of a moving car. When we were setting it up, I was urging the director to let the car get closer to me before I rolled. Buster Keaton, for heaven's sake, bust his neck falling off a moving train; surely I could be permitted this one slightly risky tumble in the vicinity of some passing hubcaps? The director, with one eye very firmly on his shooting schedule, insisted that the car was coming quite close enough, thank you, and he'd make it look good in the edit. So, I survived to film another day. But when I eventually saw that sequence back, I was bitterly disappointed because the moment didn't look anywhere near as dangerous as I wanted it to look. It was another victory for health and safety and another blow to the memory of Buster Keaton.

On the same show, eerily prefiguring my time in Miami, I had to take a plunge into Regent's Canal in London. The set-up was that I would go to leap aboard a barge from the canal path, miss and land up in the water. The feeling among the production team was that this was definitely work for a stuntman, but, again, I insisted on doing it myself – not for macho reasons (or not purely for macho reasons), but in the interests of the purity of the shot. Again, after much tutting and fretting, the director reluctantly agreed. The first concessionary requirement was that I get myself inoculated against the various diseases rumoured to be lurking in that suspiciously brown canal water, a body of liquid, it was made clear to me, into which barge owners were not averse to emptying the contents of their septic tanks. Accordingly, I was dispatched to the doctor's to have myself chemically proofed by injection against diphtheria, cholera, tuberculosis, spots on the tongue and all stations to Edgware. I had never seen so many needles in one doctor's plastic tray, and I returned to the set feeling like someone who had rolled on a hedgehog.

There was meant to be a coming together between two barges at the point at which I landed in the water. The two craft were meant to bump each other, end to end, well clear of my body in the water. When we did a dry run, though, the barges didn't just meet, as intended; one of them rode up on top of the other and, in a horrible grinding of metal, they both twisted. Had I actually jumped into the water at that point, rather than stood assessing the scene from the bank, I would most likely have been flattened to the thickness of a newspaper between two vessels, and this book would quite simply never have got written. Thank heavens we did that dry run, then, rather than adopt the usual corner-cutting, time-saving approach of 'shoot the rehearsal' which was very much the policy on that show, and many others like it in my early years.

So, what this meant was that I approached the swamp-plunge moment in 'Miami Twice' as a man who was more than acquainted with the business of dropping into risky waters in search of a laugh. No injections were needed on this occasion because, of course, you can't inoculate against the Everglades' biggest threat, which is Al the Gator and his relatives. In I plunged, into those troublingly populated waters, for one take and one take only. I tried not to think too hard about the extent to which my thrashing about in the water could have been interpreted, by alligator families in the vicinity, as a dinner gong. My bravery and apparent sangfroid were much praised by the rest of the cast, but I can't deny that, when I pulled myself back up the bank afterwards, it was with some relief that I observed myself to be in continuing possession of a full complement of limbs.

Considerably less risky was the scene with Barry Gibb

from the Bee Gees. I have no idea who set the wheels in motion to make this appearance happen. I only know that John Sullivan was extremely excited about having a bona fide, multimillion-selling singing legend on the show, while big, bluff Tony Dow would rather have been eaten alive by Al the Gator than given anybody the impression that he was in any way star-struck. Or maybe he was just concentrating hard, because it was quite a complex shoot. Barry was on the shore, in his garden, which backs onto Miami bay, and Nick and I were aboard the tourist boat from which we had to spot him (and from which I had to unleash the very Del line, 'Oi, Bazza!'), and the whole thing had to be coordinated with walkie-talkies. Shades of Spurn Point and the gas rig, during the filming of 'To Hull and Back', although of course the water in Miami was calmer and bluer, and the weather was warmer and the boat was more comfortable and there was a member of the Bee Gees on the shoreline . . . So, actually, not many shades of Spurn Point and the gas rig after all.

Budgetary concerns were still in evidence, though. The tourist boat that Nick and I were on wasn't chartered by the production, which would have cost a lot of money, but was an actual Miami tourist boat, doing its routine rounds of the bay. Had we messed up, we would have had to wait until the boat had completed its tour and commenced its next one before we could try again. Barry, meanwhile, would have had to hang on in his garden, and maybe his patience would have run out because how long, ultimately, can you keep a Bee Gee waiting for someone to shout 'Oi, Bazza!' at him? Thankfully we nailed it first time, so I never found out.

When the filming was done, Barry had me and Nick round to his house for tea and biscuits. He was a lovely chap, and a massive fan of *Only Fools*, who, in the days before the Internet, used to have tapes of the latest episodes sent to him in the States so that he could keep up with it. I have a picture that I cherish, taken that afternoon, of me, Nick and Bazza Gibb, standing at the end of Bazza's jetty, Bazza in a police patrol T-shirt and shredded jeans and me in a flowery shirt and a Dolphins baseball cap. Ah, Miami.

So, yes, 'Miami Twice' is my favourite of all the *Only Fools* episodes – and that's not just the still vivid memory of the margaritas speaking. It's also because I got to play two roles – Del, and Don Vincenzo Occhetti, the Mafia boss who happens to be a Del lookalike, creating the confusions around which the episode revolves. The latter part gave me scope to wear a terrific white suit and offer the world my best Al Pacino impression. Tremendous fun. And in the Florida sunshine, too. It's staggering to reflect that we called this 'work'.

# CHAPTER ELEVEN

## *A nation trembles*

'Time on Our Hands', the third part of the 1996 *Only Fools* Christmas trilogy, is the most watched programme in British television history. It's one of four episodes of *Only Fools* in the all-time top 12, in fact, meaning that the show occupies a third of that list. The 2001 Christmas Special, 'If They Could See Us Now', gets to number 10 with an audience of 21.35 million. It's the only programme from the twenty-first century that figures in the chart, which tells its own story about the way television audiences have dispersed in the years since then. The first two parts of the 1996 trilogy, 'Heroes and Villains' and 'Modern Men', had audiences of 21.31 million and 21.33 million respectively. But it's the final episode that earns top place. When it went out on 29 December, it was viewed by 24.35 million people, all drawn to their screens by the prospect of seeing the Trotters flog an antique watch at auction – Del actually passing out with excitement and disbelief at this outcome – and thereby finally fulfil Del's constant and undimmed prophecy, that one day they would be millionaires.

You didn't find out the audience figures straight away. There was no such thing in those days as 'overnights' – practically immediate assessments of viewer numbers from digital data. I'm not even sure how audience figures were arrived at in 1996, to be perfectly honest with you. Maybe the old analogue system was still in operation, whereby a selected group of people carefully logged their viewing habits in a printed notebook, and then handed it back in to be examined and extrapolated from. Maybe they had upgraded to set-top boxes by then, which is the current system. Or maybe the BBC was sending out an army of people with clipboards and biros to peer through the nation's curtains. It doesn't really matter. All I know is that we had to wait about a week before the results were in. And the results said: 24.35 million people.

It was perfectly amazing to me. You couldn't get your head around the number. You simply couldn't imagine that quantity of people in any way that made sense or rendered it graspable. You couldn't put them into a theatre in your mind and imagine playing to them. Your brain ended up reeling. There was, however, one aspect of the whole thing that brought it into focus for me. Before the show was broadcast, we were solemnly informed that the national electricity grid was braced for action. They were anticipating some serious interest in the show and, by extension, in their product. Accordingly, in addition to all those television sets being switched on, it was understood that when the programme ended, the number of people going into the kitchen to put on their kettles and make a cup of tea would cause a surge in demand for electricity that the grid would be required to take measures to insulate itself against.

This notion really got to me – perhaps inevitably, as a former electrician myself. It was exciting and ridiculous at the same time. Glorious sci-fi visions danced in my head: of troubled street lamps flickering across the nation as the credits rolled; of giant pylons spitting and crackling and swinging in the wind with their wires glowing hot; of blokes in lab coats in remote facilities, straining over levers, shouting, 'I cannae hold her any longer, Captain!' as 10 million households simultaneously reached for the PG Tips. And all because Del, Rodney and Uncle Albert had been mucking about in a flat. But sci-fi visions aside, this was the detail that hit home, that crystallised the magnitude of what we were involved in and how big this daft sitcom of ours had got. We had gone from fooling around in an obscure rehearsal room in North Acton to the point where we were officially a threat to the nation's infrastructure.

Success of this magnitude wasn't in my personal game plan – assuming there had actually been a personal game plan, which there hadn't, not really. Did my head swim with it? Yes, a little bit, from time to time, and sometimes the feeling of swimming was enjoyable and sometimes it was less so – a little more like drowning. It was, for instance, fascinating and amusing at times to notice my growing media presence as the *Only Fools* effect kicked in. OK, there was still no interest from *Vogue*, but I did find myself on the cover of *Radio Times* – and that, in those days, seemed to be a signal of some kind of arrival. As for being on the cover of the *Radio Times* Christmas edition – well, that was agreed to be the Holy Grail, the sign beyond all others that you had been summoned to a place among the small-screen immortals. That happened for the first time in 1985, and very satisfying it was, too. (These days *Radio Times* tends to put a drawing on the cover at Christmas – largely because there's too many people who get upset about being left off at that special time of year, and a drawing is the simplest way to avoid the offices getting stormed by miffed TV stars with agents in tow and vengeance in their hearts. Smart move.) Setting those specific glories aside, though, there was one piece of press in particular which seemed to me to be indicative of a change in the air. It was a feature about me which appeared in a broadsheet newspaper – a long piece with a big photograph of me, not in costume but as myself. It was surprising enough, at that stage, to be deemed newsworthy by a broadsheet. But the thing that really struck me was the headline above the article: 'IT'S A DEL OF A WAY TO MAKE A LIVING'. Something clicked when I looked at that. For the first time I was aware that I was being identified with the character, the boundary blurring in the public eye between me and Del.

That blurring continued when I was out and about. The success of the show meant I was now being recognised and approached in a way that was new to me. 'There's Del!' people would say. 'It is you, isn't it? It's Del!' This was attention that I didn't quite know how to react to or what to do with. Yes, it *was* Del, but at the same time, it . . . you know . . . wasn't. Should I be me for these people, which might disappoint them, or were they expecting me to drop into character and be Del? Mostly it left me in a state of confusion and embarrassment. I took to wearing baseball caps and scarves in an effort to prevent the dilemma arising. I would have lunch out with friends and then, when I stood up to leave, before reaching the street, I would start binding myself in the scarf and pulling the cap down over my head. This baffled them at first. 'What, has it turned cold or something?' I had to learn to accept that, wherever I went, people would want a piece of me, which they had a perfect right to, but it took some getting used to. I started thinking a bit harder before I went out: 'Do I actually need to go there?' It was like it had snowed outside – but permanently, so that I was always asking myself, 'Is your journey necessary?'

Still, I had plenty of grounding. I was in my forties when *Only Fools* took off. Jack Nicholson said that nobody should be famous before they're forty. He didn't say that to me personally, I hasten to add. He said it to someone else, in an interview somewhere. He was absolutely right, though – and I would have happily said as much: 'Jack, mate, you've

slapped it smack on the nose there.' Clearly fame can mess
you up if it comes at you too fast or too young. But neither
of those things applied in my case and, accordingly, my feet
were fairly firmly on the ground when attention eventually
did come barging through the door. I had been through my
jobbing actor phase, plugged away on tour, done summer
seasons – been Mr Nobody in every provincial theatre
going. I had grabbed at any part that was offered to me and
tried to make it work. I had gone out in mediocre productions of mediocre farces, taking the roles that Derek Royle
had made hay with in the West End and flogging them
around the country. (Royle was the king of the West End
farce, in my view. Brian Rix used to get all the credit, and
grew, indeed, to be the outstanding legend of the genre. But
I always found him a bit too heavy-handed. Royle was the
one I looked up to and borrowed from.) I wouldn't go so far
as to say I bore the scars of those touring experiences, but I
certainly bore the memories: of the six-day weeks, with
Sunday for travelling; of the gloomy bed and breakfasts
with the starchy landladies and their bri-nylon sheets,
which were permanently on the brink of setting fire to your
leg-hairs. Not to mention their nit-picky rules. You had to
be out by 10 a.m., but you weren't due at the theatre until
late in the afternoon, so there was nothing for it but to go
walkabout, wandering around Bradford or Hull or Aberdeen
or Stirling or some other town you didn't know, in the tipping rain, trying not to spend money because you didn't

really have any, homesickness and loneliness creeping up behind you and sometimes catching up with you, to the point where you thought, 'Just what the hell am I doing with my life, frankly? What can ever come of *this*?' I'd had a long time to work out who I was, what I was doing and why I was doing it, and I had paid a few dues along the way. Consequently, success wasn't in a position to ambush me. Indeed, I would have been more inclined to say, 'What kept you?'

I also had behind me the sobering experience of *Two D's and a Dog*. My first adventures in television had been littered with misfires, and this was surely the one which fired widest. It was the series that came my way in 1970, after *Do Not Adjust Your Set*, when, instead of sticking around for another series of a semi-anarchic kids' comedy show on ITV, my fellow cast members Michael Palin, Terry Jones and Eric Idle went off to form *Monty Python's Flying Circus*. (What were they thinking of? And, more importantly, why didn't they take me? The latter was a question which, I can't deny, festered away inside me for quite a while.) But no worries, because ITV were offering me and Denise Coffey (who had also been left behind by Palin and co.) the chance to make our names in another show for children, in which a pair of plucky detectives would solve mysteries ably assisted by a gigantic Old English sheepdog. It was a lacklustre idea, in truth, but my head was turned sufficiently by the prospect of a starring role to ignore the fact that I would be playing second fiddle to a mutt who was most famous for having done a paint commercial for Dulux. Fundamentally what the producers were looking for was a vehicle for the dog – and I don't mean an estate car, which would have been most people's solution. The scripts were poor, though I wasn't experienced enough to know it – and the show duly flopped, more floppily than a floppy English sheepdog at his floppiest. Only the dog came out of it with any credit, in fact, and he didn't come out of it with much. Deep down, I think I realised that there was more to me than this stuff, and that there was work somewhere out there which might be a better match for my capabilities. But I was seduced by the thought of a prominent role on television and making my name – as who wouldn't be? Television would get you known. This much you thought you knew. And once television had got you known, the calls would surely start to come, until eventually the finger of Hollywood would graciously beckon and you would be made a star. This much you thought you knew, and you were wrong.

So that was a chastening experience, and a valuable one in the long run. It caused me to set a few things in the right order: put the quality of the work first, and be very sceptical about all the rest of it. Plus it taught me to avoid shows with Old English sheepdogs in them, a rule which I have managed to abide by ever since.

But no amount of grounding and perspective could have

entirely prepared me for the impact that *Only Fools and Horses* would have. It reached people in ways I had never anticipated and to depths that I am still being surprised by. Even now I am still being made aware of what Del and the show mean to people. They still come up to me to report the laughs it has given them, the escape it has provided them with, the release it has offered during bad times. There were two occasions when people got in touch with me and asked if I would tape a message, in the voice of Del, to play to somebody in a coma in the hope that it might get through to them, help bring them back, because this person had loved the show so much and . . . well, you would try anything, wouldn't you? I put forty-five seconds of my best Del on a cassette tape and sent it off with my sincerest wishes. 'Del Boy, here. Listen – it's no good you lying there. I need somebody to help me carry the suitcase . . .' Did it work? Well, in one case, apparently so. In the other one, maybe not – I really don't know. I'm not mentioning this in order to big up the restorative powers of Del. I'm relating it to try and convey how much this work of silliness came to mean to people. I had no idea about any of this stuff at the time – in the rehearsal room, on the set, on location. None of us did. We were just . . . making a comedy programme. The distance between the show as we regarded it while we were making it and the show as it was eventually perceived, out there in people's sitting rooms, was something that all of us would struggle to measure in the ensuing years.

# CHAPTER TWELVE

## *A date with royalty*

Fame, one quickly realises, leads to so many openings. Supermarkets, fairs, craft shows, film festivals . . . you would possibly be startled to know how many things I've been asked to open since I became famous. Fetes, bazaars, car boot sales . . . 'And if you could come dressed as Del . . .' Really? Wouldn't it be just as good if you hired a lookalike? Some people convert this spin-off work very successfully into an arm of their business. Ronnie Corbett had it down. If people wanted him to pitch up and show his face at something, he would tell them, 'I'll give you an hour,' and charge accordingly. He would arrive, and an hour later he would leave. The ground rules were in place and everybody knew where they stood. Very professional. But it's not really for me.

Fame also means invitations. Film premieres, theatre openings, charity bashes, awards dinners . . . If I had ever wanted to measure my life in lengths of red carpet and

subsist on an exclusive diet of free vol-au-vents, then after
*Only Fools*, I probably could have started doing so. But,
again, it had never really been an ambition. Plus I don't
especially like vol-au-vents.

Sometimes, though, invitations would come which you
simply couldn't refuse. Such as on that fateful morning
when I found myself tremulously holding a thick and lus-
trously embossed card inviting me and my wife Gill to
Highgrove to dine with Prince Charles. Dinner with Prince
Charles! I mean, realistically, how many times in your life?
Unless you're Camilla, of course. But I'm not Camilla, and
I'm under absolutely no illusions about that.

This was in 2001, and you can well imagine the levels of
excitement and anxiety occasioned in your author's kitchen by the arrival of the postman that day. My wife Gill
and I immediately had so many questions to ponder – not
least of all, why? Why would Prince Charles and Camilla
Parker Bowles (as she then still was) invite us to dinner? I
suppose I was, at this point, an Officer of the Order of the
British Empire, or OBE as we more gently refer to it, and
had been so since 1993. But I wasn't aware that being an
OBE came with any princely dining rights. Indeed, if Prince
Charles had to dine privately with everyone who was made
an OBE, he would practically never get up from the table.
So maybe Charles and Camilla were *Only Fools* fans. That
wasn't completely out of the question. Charles famously
like the Goons, didn't he? It was one of the things that he

and I had in common – and it seemed we'd be finding out very soon what the other things were.

While the big 'why?' question hung in the air, tantalisingly unanswered, we fell to discussing other pressing aspects of the rare evening that now lay ahead of us, most particularly: how big was this dinner going to be? How many people would be there? We very quickly dismissed the notion that it would just be a cosy foursome. That seemed just too implausible. Even if Charles and Camilla loved *Only Fools* a lot, there would have to be some others there, surely. But on what scale? Six people? Twelve? I hadn't seen *Downton Abbey*, because at this point it hadn't been made. But I had seen *Upstairs Downstairs*, which was sort of the same thing, and I could easily envisage one of those very long, polished tables, all silver cutlery and white china and candles – seating, what? Twenty people, maybe? It couldn't be any more than that, surely, because a larger number would constitute a party rather than a dinner, and the invitation was very clear that we were being asked to come to dinner.

It was also clear about the dress code: black tie. So that was me sorted. No need to trouble Issey Miyake on my account, or even Mr Marks and Mr Spencer. I would just get the old DJ out, as usual. For Gill, and for Gill alone, lay in store the fraught and draining task of selecting an outfit suitable for an evening of intimate dining and breeze-shooting with the future king and his consort. I did what I felt

was the best thing I possibly could do to help in the circumstances: I mustered all the knowledge that I possess of
occasion-appropriate fashion choices for women, and left
her to it.

The great day grew near amid rising intrigue and excitement, and, of course, mounting nervousness on our part.
Our entire family (in particular my sister, June, and Gill's
mum, Burley, whose real name is Shirley, though I call her
Burley because it rhymes) had been on tenterhooks about
this night of royal intimacy since pretty much the day the
invitation arrived – to the point where it was a mild surprise, in fact, not to find a small delegation lining the route
with flags to wave us on our way when we eventually
departed, soon after lunch on that cherished summer Saturday. Highgrove being a fair way from our house, we had
booked a room in a hotel nearby. So we headed there first
and checked in, so that we could change into our finery
before setting off again to cover the remaining six miles.
Naturally, we left in what I had carefully calculated to be
very good time for the 7 p.m. arrival (for an 8 p.m. dinner)
stipulated on the invitation. Let's face it: when you get
invited to break bread with the future monarch, you don't
want to pitch up late and have to come barging through the
door shouting apologies.

Imagine our delight, then, when, about a minute into
this last leg of the journey, the traffic in front of us slowed
to a standstill. It was unbelievable. By what ghastly joke on

the part of the cruel gods would we find ourselves stuck in a jam on this of all days, and at this of all times? As we sat there in the barely moving queue, with panic slowly beginning to rise, I briefly considered veering out onto the other side of the road, putting my boot down and overtaking everybody – honking my horn and flashing my lights in the hope of being mistaken for a doctor on call. But I realised that doing so would almost certainly result in either death or arrest, neither of which would get us to our dinner any quicker. Instead I resigned myself to sitting and fuming, hiccuping forwards at a speed which I estimated through my fury to be about fourteen yards per hour.

The traffic we were locked in with included a couple of coaches, stuffed with people. There must have been some kind of big event in the area that we hadn't reckoned on. My bet was that it was showjumping, which was very big around those parts. What was both maddening and baffling was that we didn't seem to be getting free of it. Surely at some point the traffic would have to unclog and release us. But no. Every time we needed to turn, so, apparently, did the traffic ahead of us and behind. We reached what was the last turning for Highgrove and we still didn't seem to have lost a single car along the way. 'Where are they all going?' I asked Gill.

We soon found out. The trail of traffic led through the gates of the Highgrove estate, where we were guided by stewards into a giant field set aside for car parking, beyond which a massive marquee was visible, looming on the horizon like a canvas Taj Mahal.

Guess who's coming to dinner. Everybody. Or certainly the entire contents of our traffic jam were, including coach parties. In our grassy space on the rapidly filling field, I switched off the ignition and as the car fell silent Gill and I exchanged a look of mutual humiliation. Our tête-à-tête supper appointment at Prince Charles's country residence was a stonking great gala dinner for four hundred, held in honour (we discovered in due course) of the Spanish tile firm Porcelanosa. I don't know how we hadn't gleaned this in advance. I can only tell you that we genuinely hadn't.

Biting down a mixture of disappointment and mild relief (me) and a mixture of disappointment and further disappointment (Gill), we allowed ourselves to be guided through the throng to a kind of dedicated VIP reception area, whereupon we discovered that also among our exclusive number that night were Alan Titchmarsh, the gardener and television presenter, Richard Whiteley, the host of *Countdown*, Carol Vorderman, also from *Countdown*, and the radio presenter Sarah Kennedy. Had Alan, Richard and the rest of this little gang also arrived in the expectation of something a little smaller? I suspect not, though I felt it prudent in the circumstances not to ask. Instead, we drank and exchanged chit-chat. I liked Richard Whiteley a lot – a funny, jolly man, and sadly no longer with us. All of us in the VIP conclave were gathered up at one point and taken outside for a tour of Highgrove's new Islamic-style garden, which was rather lovely and put my own Buckinghamshire-style effort somewhat in the shade. Then we returned to our VIP area and did some more drinking and some more exchanging of chit-chat.

Time was clearly wearing on by this stage, yet supper hadn't been served and nor was there any sign of the royal party, which seemed odd. Thinking about it, our tour of the garden had seemed rather artificially protracted, too. I think we ended up making about three circuits of it. I felt I could have played a key role on the panel for *Gardeners' World* by that point. Eventually, though, an explanatory message was brought to our gathering: 'Do bear with us. There's a slight delay. The Prince fell from his horse during a game of polo this afternoon and has been taken to hospital, so we're just waiting to hear what the outcome is.'

This didn't sound promising. Sure enough, a short while later, our messenger returned. 'The Prince needs to be at the hospital for a while longer, so he won't be able to join us this evening.'

'Ah, well. That's polo,' I said, trying to sound both upbeat and knowledgeable, but somehow failing on both counts. This was unquestionably a blow – not least for the original dreams of Gill and myself, who had seen the prospect of an intimate dinner with Prince Charles shrink quite rapidly to become the prospect of a very un-intimate dinner without him. Apparently, though, Camilla was on her way from the hospital to join us, along with Prince William and Prince

Harry who had agreed to step into the breach and make speeches in their father's absence. Sure enough, a lot of ker-fuffle near the entrance to the marquee soon confirmed the arrival among us of the royal party. I was straining to look along with everybody else when a member of the royal household tapped me on the shoulder. 'Would you join Camilla for dinner? She needs an escort.'

'Nah, you're all right,' I replied. 'I'll stay here with Alan Titchmarsh.'

OK, not really. I left Gill with Mr Titchmarsh and permitted myself to be withdrawn from the security of showbiz corner and thrust without prior warning into the role of Camilla's consort for the evening. In which job, I should say, I was the exact definition of a fish out of water, though I did my best not to gasp or thrash around on the floor, which I realised would be frowned upon, as well as undignified.

So, our intimate dinner with Prince Charles now found my wife on a table with the presenter of *Ground Force*, and me, a couple of hundred yards away, seated to the left of the future Duchess of Cornwall. Which I suppose, in a round-about way, for the duration of the meal at least, made me first in line for the throne, unless that's not the way it works. Whatever, I'm not going to pretend that being asked to fill this vacant seat wasn't an intimidating proposition in a number of ways. (The seat at the dinner, I mean; not the throne.) But I was at least fortunate enough to have picked up on my journey through life some of the etiquette you need on such occasions. For instance, there's a way of conducting conversation at these formal dinners which is designed to ensure that everyone always has someone to talk to and nobody gets left out. The rule is this: during the first course, you talk to the person on your left, and then during the second course, you politely disengage and turn and talk to the person on your right. And then, when the dessert comes out, you're free to stand on the table. Actually, I may have got it wrong about the dessert course.

You know what, I may have got it wrong about the other courses, too. Because, now I come to think about it, if you're talking to the person on your left, and the person on your right is talking to the person on *their* left, as per the rules, then the person on your right is basically talking to your back, and you are talking to the back of the person to the left of you, because they have turned left to talk to the back of the person next to them, and nobody round the table has got anybody to talk to. Ditto when the beef and potatoes arrive and you all turn right.

Look, I don't know. It's something like that. Google it.

Anyway, I can only report that the evening passed both pleasantly and smoothly and without me using the fish knife for the meat course or tipping the gravy into my lap, both of which might plausibly have been a concern, going in. Indeed, the only further incident of any real moment occurred after the dinner when, in the wake of Prince

William's formal speech of thanks, I found an agitated Richard Whiteley crouching at my elbow.

'David,' he hissed, 'I think we ought to reply.'

'What?'

'I think one of us ought to stand up and make a speech in return.'

'Is that a good idea?'

'I just think it would be the right thing to do. We have to reply on behalf of the guests.'

Now, I may not know an awful lot about dining in high society, and I may be unable to tell the difference on sight between an invitation to an intimate get-together with royalty and a ticket to a stonking great gala dinner and Islamic-style garden opening featuring Alan Titchmarsh and a cast of thousands. But I do know that, at an event at Highgrove hosted by Prince William and Prince Harry in the unfortunate absence through polo-related injuries of their father, standing up unbidden, rapping on the nearest wine glass and peeling off a few remarks – perhaps lobbing in the one about the Englishman, the Scotsman and the parakeet – is definitely not something the etiquette manuals advise you to get involved in. Trust me on this. You don't even need to google it.

Was this abrupt and off-piste plan, and the firmness of Richard's attachment to it, fuelled in any way by the consumption of fine wines in unwise quantities? Was he off-piste in more ways than one? All must necessarily be speculation on this matter. Let me merely state that, shortly after this hissed conversation, somebody of an official nature discreetly intervened between Richard and the microphone and a social gaffe on the scale of the Grand Canyon was narrowly averted.

Or maybe I'm wrong. Maybe Richard would have given the performance of his life and had them all in the aisles, and people would still be talking about that speech to this day. Either way, it didn't happen. The following morning Gill and I checked out of our hotel and returned to Buckinghamshire to give our family members, waiting agog for news from royalty's front line, a necessarily sheepish debrief.

Obviously, I'll stand in for the heir to the throne whenever I am called upon to do so. But to be honest, I'm more comfortable when things are closer to home and smaller. Not so long ago, I was asked if I would attend the Remembrance Sunday service at the war memorial in the village near us, and if I would read the Ode of Remembrance from the poem 'For the Fallen' by Laurence Binyon, who is not to be confused in any way with Laurence Llewelyn-Bowen. It was a call for my services that I was proud to heed. No cause for crush barriers, stewards in orange jackets and a police presence on that particular morning, and no need to set aside a field in which to park the buses. My – if I may say – rather poignant rendition of 'At the going down of the sun and in the morning' was thoughtfully received by a crowd which generous estimates later put at half a dozen.

# CHAPTER THIRTEEN

## *A farewell to Del*

I was always worried about getting trapped by a character – about falling into a role and then not being able to climb back out again. I don't mean in the sense of the old expression about the wind changing and your face staying that way. I mean in the sense of getting typecast – of coming to be associated with one role so tightly that nobody would ever be able to think of me as anything else. As *Only Fools and Horses* assumed its unanticipated position of dominance on the national skyline and printed itself so indelibly in people's minds, I think all of us in the cast grappled with some anxiety about the possibility of that.

The fear was that getting typecast would turn the jollity and larks of being an actor into a bit of a grind. Wasn't the whole point of the game that you got to be lots of different people? That certainly seemed to me to be where the fun lay, and I had always done my best, in as much as I could, to protect that aspect of things. Back in the mid-sixties, when still young, lithe and callow, I was offered a regular role on the legendary (though not always for the best reasons) ITV soap opera *Crossroads*. I had been playing (and with considerable panache, I don't doubt, though I can't check back because these scenes are tragically lost to the misty dustbins of time) the part of Bernie Kilroy, who once, in a plot twist not unusual for that trusty teatime drama, appeared to come back from the dead, thereby putting the frighteners right up Noele Gordon, the show's major star. The producers wanted to convert Bernie into a permanent character – presumably so he could start coming back from the dead and putting the frighteners up Noele Gordon on a regular basis, and I was asked to sign a contract that would no doubt have tied me to the ATV Studios in Birmingham for a good while. Now, I know, with *Crossroads* the jokes come easily: the cardboard sets, the implausible storylines, the soap that would not wash, the place where actors go to die, he didn't know whether to shoot the scene or shoot the cast, etc., etc. Yet I need to point out that this would have been steady and handsomely remunerated work – and Lord knows, I didn't have anything else to go to at the time, and certainly no track record or reputation to fall back on. Indeed, my CV at that time largely consisted of a handful of repertory theatre roles, mostly in Bromley, and a non-speaking part in a commercial for a bookmakers. That I was being considered for any kind of telly work at all at that stage was a pretty remarkable change of fortune. I steeled myself, though, stared bravely into the wind, and turned the job down. It was kind of them to ask, but I thought I perceived in this generous opportunity the eerie shape of a potential trap. Given the nature of soap operas, I could see myself being the same character, for five episodes a week, month after month, possibly year after year. I saw one door opening – and every other door and window slamming shut and locking itself forever more. Steady and regular employment had its obvious attractions, but it wasn't, at the end of the day, the dream.

Now, people feel differently, of course. Sue Nicholls, a lovely person, was in *Crossroads* at the same time as me, and she has been playing Audrey in *Coronation Street* since 1979 and wouldn't have it any other way. Bill Roache has been Ken Barlow in *Corrie* for so long he's even in the *Guinness Book of Records* for it. Some people love that single-role life and embrace it. But I couldn't have done so. It was also why I eventually – years later, after the bruises went away – grew to be relieved that fate's fickle finger winkled me out of the role of Corporal Jones in *Dad's Army*. A landmark part, obviously, in a landmark television show – but a role, in retrospect, that might have completely stymied me as far as doing anything else was concerned.

As the eighties wore on, and *Only Fools* continued to bowl forward and snowball, my growing worry was that Del Boy was going to do precisely that to me – turn into a trap that I couldn't escape. A great man once said (was it

197

Laurence Llewelyn-Bowen?): 'Celebrity is a mask that eats into the face.' And, I would add, you probably can't get a good cream for that. Either way, it made me anxious to think that Derek Trotter might end up having a similar effect with regard to my own features. He was such a bulky presence in the life of the nation, I was concerned that people would no longer be able to see past his face to mine – assuming I even had a face that wasn't Del's any more, which, what with people shouting 'Oi, Del Boy!' across the street all the time, I was often obliged to wonder about. And that, dear reader, as faithless as it may seem, was why, in 1987, with series five in the can and some time on my hands, I leapt at the chance to audition for the part of Skullion.

This was in a Channel 4 adaptation of *Porterhouse Blue*, the comic novel by Tom Sharpe about shenanigans in a fictional Cambridge University college. I loved the book, which is properly funny, and I loved the adaptation, which was by Malcolm Bradbury. In particular, I loved the central character of James Skullion, the long-serving head porter at Porterhouse College, a former Royal Marine now imperiously performing the role of gatekeeper at a corrupt and elitist university establishment through which the future great and powerful pass. Skullion goes into a furious rearguard action when the ancient traditions of the college come under threat from a new Master (Sir Godber Evans, played superbly in the Channel 4 version by Ian

Richardson) and the disreputable forces of modernisation, bringing such unacceptable developments as condom machines, a self-service canteen and (would you believe it?) female students. It was a ripe and rich set-up and I was desperate to be a part of it.

Not much linking Skullion and Del Boy, you will have observed – and that, I'm sure, was a considerable part of my attraction to the role. But with the amount of heat coming off *Only Fools* at this particular moment in history, my worry was that, when it came to casting, the producers would look at me and only see Del – who wouldn't, let's face it, be your natural or instinctive candidate for a job in charge of security and general oversight at an Oxbridge college. Indeed, frankly, knowing what you knew, you wouldn't even employ him to clean the chandeliers. But those initial perceptions weren't now in my control, of course. The game had changed forever in that regard. It wasn't about doubting my ability to inhabit another character; I knew I could do that. It was about whether other people would let me.

To be perfectly frank, if someone involved in the production of *Porterhouse Blue* hadn't been old enough to recall some of my work in the theatre, I don't think I would have got through the door to audition in the first place. Even with that little leg-up, I still had it all to do. At the audition, after a bit of a chat, I was asked if I would mind stepping outside and putting on Skullion's costume. I don't think I had ever been asked to get dressed up for an audition before.

Normally you would read something, or you might be asked to do a bit of acting, but you would do so in the clothes in which you had come in off the street. Dressing for the part – that hadn't happened to me. At the time I didn't think much about it; I just got on with it, donned the costume – the bowler hat, the pinstriped trousers, the crisp white shirt, black tie and black jacket – went back in and read. But reflecting on it now, I wonder if I was being asked to jump an extra hurdle here – if the producers needed to put me into costume so they could get Del out of their heads.

Whatever, I must have convinced them because I got the part in that blackly funny, beautifully shot drama. Great opening titles, too: choral music over pictures of doors and columns. Skullion's moustache – another handy distancing device from Del – was the actor's own. I was also able to bring in a trick my elder brother, Arthur, had taught me, back in Lodge Lane in Finchley, after his national service in the army: the 'spit and polish' method for cleaning your boots. It was the received way to get that proper, parade-ground shine on your footwear, and I'm delighted to pass it on to you here, ahead of your next parade. You stick a layer of polish on the boot first, using your finger or your cloth; then you spit on the boot; then you apply a second layer of polish (finger or cloth, again) on top of the spit and start buffing it, repeating the process, polish on spit, until the combination of the spit and the polish builds like varnish and comes up like glass. Wonderful. Skullion, as an ex-military man, would surely have known this, and the spit-and-polish method gave me some good extra business when he was cleaning his shoes at one point.

I'm not saying the boot-polishing scene clinched it, but without wishing to push my mantelpiece in your face, dear reader, I won the 1988 BAFTA for Best Actor for that performance as Skullion, on a shortlist which included Kenneth Branagh for his role in *Fortunes of War* and whose name I had confidently expected to see come out of the envelope. (Worry not: I think his career recovered.) Obviously, I was delighted – not least because of the timing, right when *Only Fools* was taking up so much of the oxygen around me. Again, I'm going to run the risk of sounding ungrateful about dear old Del and everything he brought me, and clearly I'm not. But I'm sure the scamp has cost me a few roles in my time, and I was just so pleased and relieved to discover, through Skullion, that other things, and other characters, were still possible for me.

As I understand it, a second series set in Porterhouse College was written, titled *Porterhouse Black*, which took the Skullion story on further. It was all ready to go, apparently. But then, in a tiresome development which happens a fair bit in broadcasting – and in business in the real world, too, I'm sure – there was a change of department head, somewhere higher up in the food chain, and the new man needed things to be new, as new men will or else there's no point in being the new man, and the project was dropped. I was bitterly disappointed about that. People seemed to have liked the first one, I had loved doing it, and I would have taken another crack at Skullion at the drop of a bowler hat.

Of course, it would have been unrealistic to expect one four-part television drama to break me out of the Del Boy mould entirely. I merely had to hope that Skullion had at least chipped that mould a bit, and that a few people in the casting business might have noticed and found themselves wondering, 'Well, if he can grow his own moustache and wear a bowler hat, what else might this man be capable of?' Beyond that, I knew Del was still out there, ready to reimpose himself at the time of his choosing, and I had to get used to the fact that he always would be, no matter what I did. Point in case: more than a decade after *Porterhouse Blue*, in 1999, I played Captain Frank Beck in a television drama called *All the King's Men*, about a volunteer force that Beck had formed during World War I, made up exclusively of fellow members of the royal staff at Sandringham, the Norfolk estate of King George V. This unit went off to fight at Gallipoli in 1915 and came unstuck. By this time, I had played Pop Larkin in *The Darling Buds of May* and Jack Frost in *A Touch of Frost*, both of which I'll come on to talk about in a bit. But here, with Frank Beck, for the first time in my career – excluding the odd radio impression of Harold Wilson or whoever – I found myself facing up to the responsibility of portraying not an entirely fictional creation, dreamed up by a scriptwriter, but a representation of someone who had actually lived, and moreover a man of profound integrity who had acted heroically and died in a noble cause. I felt a lot of pressure not to mess up, and I read as much as I could about the period as research.

Filming went well, the piece seemed to come across OK, and a while after it went out, I got a card from Frank Beck's great-nephew, saying how much he had enjoyed the film and how he felt that I had treated the character of Beck with dignity and respect. So that was nice to hear. However, he went on to say that when my name was first mentioned in connection with the part, it had sent more than a few ripples of consternation through the family. 'David Jason?' I could imagine them saying – and it was possible for me to picture their eyes widening in alarm to the width of dinner plates. 'What, you mean . . . Del Boy?' The ghost of Derek Trotter had loomed yet again. But I could see where their concern was coming from. A wheeler-dealer Gallipoli hero, anyone? A nightmarish vision must have risen in the Beck family's minds of a dramatic reconstruction in which their loved and revered relative would be seen stomping around Sandringham in leopard-print underpants and saying 'Luvvly jubbly' and 'cushty' every five minutes.

Born to linger – that's Del. People found it hard to let him go – and so did those of us who were responsible for him, in fact. Nobody expects these things to go on forever, and after series seven of *Only Fools*, which finished broadcasting at the start of 1991, the show seemed to have reached a natural enough end. John Sullivan was now writing other things, including *Dear John*, about a bloke whose wife has left him, and a comedy about cab drivers called *Roger, Roger*; the cast was doing its best to move on to other pastures. Yet, even if the energy wasn't there for another series, the appetite clearly remained for more Trotter-related stories, so the BBC suggested a compromise position in which the team reassembled every year for a one-off special to be broadcast at Christmas. So we did that for three years, until 1993. But that didn't seem to diminish the aforementioned public appetite, so we then did the 1996 trilogy, in which 'Time on Our Hands' made the family millionaires and brought the story to a tidy conclusion. Still no apparent sating of the appetite, though. Five years after that, the call came again: what about some more annual one-offs? So there were three further Christmas Specials after that – 'If They Could See Us Now' in 2001, 'Strangers on the Shore' in 2002 and 'Sleepless in Peckham' in 2003. You could say those shows were three steps too far. Some critics in the press did say that. But more than 21 million people watched that 2001 programme, and audiences for the other two weren't exactly shabby (17.4 million and 16.3 million), not least in the context of the times. None of those additional shows was entered into lightly, without serious forethought, and self-indulgence wasn't the motivating factor. We kept thinking we could set it aside and move on, but at every stage there was still clearly this huge public desire for more which ultimately proved irresistible. People kept wanting Del to come back. Including me.

One night in 2011, seven years after we had finally set the show to rest, I was invited to a dinner in London with Gareth Gwenlan and John Sullivan. The appointed restaurant was a Chinese, I was pleased to discover, though not your usual takeaway joint. This Chinese was based in the sumptuous Dorchester Hotel on Park Lane, in the heart, as we say, of London's glamorous West End. I remember thinking, as I walked through the gilded and marbled lobby and took my seat at the expensively linen-wrapped table, that it was an unusual kind of place in which to find John, who was a down-to-earth bloke the whole time I knew him and not really the sort to have an opinion about posh restaurants. I could only assume that the BBC had chosen the location. Anyway, I ordered a number 16, a number 23 and two number 40s and we fell to talking.

The main topic of discussion was another *Only Fools and Horses* revival. John wanted to know how I felt about doing a special number, centred on Del Boy's sixtieth birthday. The idea was that Del would throw a party and all the gang would turn up, which was a neat way of getting everyone together in the same room again.

Did we dare? The stakes always appeared to be so high. Every time you did anything related to *Only Fools*, you had the sense that you were risking the programme's entire legacy. In our minds, the consequences of coming up short in some way or other weren't simply that you would come up short in some way or other; the consequences were that you would ruin everything that you had achieved up to that point. That probably wasn't true, in fact. It was almost certainly the case that people's attachment to the show was strong enough to survive the blow of a one-off revival that, for whatever reason, didn't quite come off. Nevertheless, the feeling that there were grave repercussions hanging on any move you made in this area always lingered dauntingly.

My feeling was that this sixtieth birthday ruse would depend on the writing, of course, and I was bound to be confident about the quality of that. Even so, I think John felt that I had more to lose than he did. I was going to be the face at the front of this revival attempt, and I would no doubt have to endure a fair storm of flak if it didn't come off. The thought of going out to an expectant audience and not being welcomed with open arms was a horrible one. So all of these ruminations were going to and fro across the table that night, over some rather pricey but extremely delicious sweet and sour pork with egg fried rice.

Nothing was set in stone that evening. But I came away committed in my own mind to the idea. I just thought: boom or bust, we ought to have another go. We had built a huge audience that loved the show enormously, and either you used that fact as a deterrent, to freeze you in your tracks, or you used it as a spur. That, basically, was the choice we had, and my instinct, after that meeting, was to choose the spur.

But fortune has a way of deciding things for you. Soon after this, I was getting a phone call from Gareth to say that John was in hospital with viral pneumonia. He came out and went home after a while and we thought he was mending – but no. In April of 2011, John was taken from us, at sixty-four. It was just devastating, and, of course, most of all for his wife Sharon, and their kids, Dan, Jim and Amy.

A year after John died, they put a blue plaque in his honour on the outside wall of Teddington Studios. There was an official unveiling ceremony, attended by all of John's family, me, Nick Lyndhurst and John Challis, among many others. I was asked by the family to go up on a podium and operate the velvet cord which pulled away the curtain to reveal the plaque. Everyone gathered round and at the appointed moment, after a few words in John's honour, I gave the cord a solemn tug. Whereupon the curtain came clean off the wall and almost smothered me.

I'd say you couldn't have scripted it, but John Sullivan could have – and he would have found a way to make it even funnier.

So, the sixtieth birthday reunion never happened. But I did eventually find myself back in that old Peckham tower-block flat – wandering again amid the duff wallpaper and the stacked cardboard boxes and the china tat. This was in the spring of 2017, for that UKTV documentary about *Only Fools* that I talked about near the start of this book. They rebuilt the set – a really thorough replica of it – and we filmed some sequences there. It was less bewildering than the time in the lock-up, going through the show's props, when memories were coming at me from all angles and from all different periods at once in a full-tilt sensory bombardment. This was nostalgic, too, but it was calmer – almost romantic, in an odd kind of way. I took a moment in the beaten-up armchair that Grandad and Uncle Albert used to sit in and let it all float over me for a bit.

Mixed feelings, though. Imagine if someone opened a door and there, on the other side, was a perfect recreation of your childhood bedroom – the furniture, the carpet, everything as you had it. Imagine the competing things you would be feeling as you went and stood in there and felt the atmosphere of it all over again, with all that has happened since. It was a bit like that, venturing back onto that stupid set, as artificial as it was. Reflections crowded in. Wasn't it wonderful then? And somehow weirdly innocent. Yet gone. And wouldn't it be great to be back there?

Tessa Peake-Jones came along to that rebuilt set, too, and we spent some time reminiscing. We were laughing about the sequence at the end of series seven, in 'Three Men, a Woman and a Baby', where Raquel gives birth to Damien. None of us apart from John Sullivan had any experience of childbirth at that point in our lives (Tessa went on, after

Damien, to have a son and a daughter), but the midwives in the maternity department at West Middlesex Hospital, where we were filming, kindly organised a screening of a video of a real birth to get us in the mood. It was the full, hard-core action with no gory details spared. This was very shortly after breakfast, too – but, then, of course, babies aren't fussy about what time they arrive, and midwives aren't fussy about what time they show videos. Anyway, who knew childbirth was like that? (Answer: us, after watching that film.)

Fun to recall those times and those laughs and those scenes. But I don't go back and watch the show these days. Sometimes I might stumble across it when I'm flicking through the channels and I might pause for a while and watch a bit, just to remind myself what it was like, and that I was there. But I never watch for long. It's too painful, looking at that young bloke on the telly – the bloke I still think of myself as being, really, inside my head, until I look in the mirror and remember that I'm not. How bitter-sweet to see yourself as you once were. It's one thing in a photograph, but moving images on the television are so completely realised, somehow, and I find their impact is far heavier. It's a version of yourself that's gone, but television makes it alive. That's a very difficult bridge to cross in my mind.

Still, as Shakespeare so famously wrote: what a piece of work is Del. Or he may have said 'man'. Same thing, though.

For me, Del Boy remains inescapable. He is never off the screen, and he's in everybody's head. I have been guilty, I know, from time to time, of resenting the extent of his hold upon me. But we can be impatient even with our best friends from time to time, and they're still our best friends. Anyway, it's bigger than me – well beyond my power to change, even if I really wanted to do so. Roger Lloyd Pack said it well: 'A good sitcom gets into the DNA of our culture in a way that other things don't.' It's true. If you are in a successful sitcom, this is how you will be remembered, and you had better get used to it. Never mind other roles: between now and the end of my allotted portion on this earth, I could find a cure for the common cold, bring lasting peace to the Middle East and be instrumental in launching the first manned mission to Mars, and the headline upon my demise would still be 'DEL BOY CONKS'. In a funny way, that only makes me love him more.

# CHAPTER FOURTEEN

## *Batman, Bond and Pop Larkin:*
## *the eternal connection*

I am behind the wheel of a yellow 1926 Rolls-Royce Park Ward Landaulette, easing my way nervously down a narrow and twisty country lane in Kent. Ahead of me, a camera car films my lurchy progress. To the rear of me, perched on the leather seats, and obliged to lurch, sit Pam Ferris and Philip Franks – Ma Larkin and Charley from *The Darling Buds of May*. I am doing my best not to think about the possibility that this might end badly, with several thousand pounds' worth of rare automobile on its roof in a field. Car-crash television, in a very literal sense, is what we're trying to avoid here.

I've driven cars that were simpler to operate, put it that way. In this antique family charabanc, which is somehow both achingly straightforward and devilishly complicated at the same time, the gear lever and the handbrake are on the driver's right-hand side, which is always going to make you feel a bit like you're patting your head and rubbing your chest at the same time. And that's never advisable while driving. None of your fancy synchro-mesh gearboxes here, either: it's got a primitive 'crash box', to use the ominous technical term, so I'm having to rediscover the long-neglected art of double-declutching – stamping twice on the clutch, tugging experimentally at the gearshift, catching the engine on the accelerator and eventually, somewhere in the middle of all that, if I'm extremely lucky, finding a gear. The steering wheel offers at least six inches of dead slack before the wheels turn, which they then do in an incredible hurry, meaning that pointing the car around a corner is like trying to thread a needle, which is never easy, and certainly not while you're driving a classic Rolls-Royce. And definitely not while you're driving a classic Rolls-Royce down a narrow and twisty country road in Kent with cameras fixed on you.

This vehicle isn't exactly small, either – three rows of seats and a bonnet the approximate length of Cornwall. Landaulette? Launderette, more like. Not to mention the fact that it's rare and precious, and therefore not something you especially want to be the wally to put a dent in, or worse. I am attempting to seem relaxed and perfectly in control for the benefit of the eventual footage, though it's not easy with gritted teeth and gritted other bits, nor with low-hanging branches and bits of Kent's loveliest hedgerow going 'thwap' against the bodywork and making ominous scratching noises. Nor with Pam Ferris and Philip Franks mockingly chipping in over my shoulder every now and again with unscripted and not especially helpful comments such as 'Mind the foliage, won't you?' and 'I think that'll be second gear you're looking for, no?' and 'Keep trying – I'm sure it must be in there somewhere.'

Is the car insured? Am I insured? Is the rest of the world insured? I'm just an actor here. I simply have to trust that someone somewhere has done the necessary paperwork and act on regardless.

The plan, carefully hatched and drilled, is that we will motor in convoy, us and the camera car, along this quiet stretch of road until its conclusion, where we will reach a T-junction. At that point the camera car will swing aside to the right and I will bring this remarkable and highly photogenic machine to a halt. Then I will use the space at the junction to turn around, the camera car will slip ahead again and we will all head back along the road, God and oncoming traffic permitting, to Buss Farm, home of the Larkins, our centre of operations.

So, after a preliminary passage of kangaroo-jumping, which I offer to my passengers as a kind of overture before the full five-act musical of bad driving that lies ahead, we set off slowly down the lane. Somehow I contrive to hold the car more or less on the tarmac – which is quite a remarkable outcome, really, given the narrowness and the twistiness and the eccentricities of the steering and the

213

complications with the gears and the mockery of my fellow actors. Even with all these things in play, I still manage to keep myself from taking this Rolls-Royce up a bank and posting it expensively through a hedge. Applause if you will.

In due course, though, the T-junction comes into view, the camera crew swings aside, as planned, and I apply the brakes in order to come to a halt. At this exact moment, barely anything happens. Which is mildly alarming. It's not that working the brake lever is having almost no effect at all. It's just that it's having ... almost no effect at all. Now, it's not like we're going particularly fast, but we do need to halt at some point – and preferably before our road meets another road. Weeping quietly inside and offering prayers to all available deities, I plunge my foot down and hold it to the floor, to the point where I am practically standing up. Meanwhile, in an act which owes everything to instinct and almost nothing to physical science, I haul backwards on the steering wheel like it was a lever in a railway signal box. I then maintain that clenched position as this beautiful piece of antique engineering glides slowly across the blessedly empty road and finally agrees to come to a stop a few inches from the hedgerow opposite.

I'll tell you something that's got better since 1926: car brakes.

Still, at least I haven't crunched it. However, I am now basically blocking the road – both lanes of it. I therefore commence the hunt for the reverse gear, a voyage of

214

exploration which becomes an epic saga in its own right, about which an entirely separate feature-length production could have been made that day in Kent had the financing been available. In the early stages of this process, the traffic which was fortunately absent a few moments ago inevitably shows up and necessarily stops – a lorry to one side of me, a car to the rear. It is here that I discover one of the advantages of blocking the road completely in a rare Rolls-Royce from the 1920s: you are afforded patience by your fellow road-users to a degree that probably wouldn't be matched if you were blocking the road completely in, say, a white panel van or a red Porsche. Nobody even hoots.

But inside the stationary Rolls, the hunt for a gear continues and, partly on account of the physical effort, but also perhaps as a result of the embarrassment, I am now wearing a light but durable coat of sweat. Absorbed as I necessarily am by my labours with the gearstick, it is a short while before I notice that a figure has appeared beside me at the window. It's the lorry driver, who has got down from his cab – to see, I immediately assume, if he can play any useful part in the ongoing search for the relevant gear. And why not? Many hands make light work, and all that. But no: that's not why he's there. I offer him a weak smile and he, in return, offers me a small piece of paper and a biro and asks if I would mind signing an autograph. I have to reckon that this is not because he has suddenly become an admirer of my driving. Anyhow, I take his pen and paper, but I've got nothing to lean on, so I basically end up tearing a hole in the page with the point of the biro in the rough shape of my name. I sheepishly hand this ruined scrap back to the driver who makes a heroic effort to look grateful and returns to his lorry. I then go back to looking everywhere in the cab, including under the seats, for reverse.

Reader, what can I tell you? At some point later that afternoon, and with traffic presumably by that point backed up at least as far as the M20 at Ashford, I found it. The car abruptly shuddered and began to ease backwards – to the accompaniment of a cheer and a light smattering of possibly satirical applause from the two actors in the rear. Furthermore, having executed what was possibly the world's worst three-point turn, I got the Landaulette pointing down the twisty lane again and piloted it uncertainly back the way it had come. Let the record show that the ribbing from the two passengers behind me did not noticeably become more merciful during this stage of the journey. Nor was there any diminishment in my own personal sense that I would imminently crash into a tree. Turning eventually into the gateway at Buss Farm, and making sure to brake well before the barn, I experienced the sense of deliverance one feels when the third wheel of the aircraft finally touches down securely on the runway after a particularly torrid flight.

Well, they do say you should never go back. I hadn't driven Pop Larkin's Rolls since we filmed the original show twenty-six years earlier, in 1991, so I was bound to be a bit rusty. This was May 2017. We were shooting a sequence about *The Darling Buds of May* for a television documentary about my career, based on the best-selling autobiography, *My Life*, which I may have mentioned is still . . . Anyway, this documentary was, in a sense, the film of the book and here I was, accordingly, on another journey back into my past – looking for the reverse gear, in the much broader sense. I seem to have been doing quite a lot of that kind of thing recently, what with the *Only Fools* documentary, this book . . . God forbid that I am now officially in my anecdotage.

Anyway, it was the first time I had been back to Buss Farm and it was both moving and reassuring to discover how unchanged the place was. The little lane is as it was, the farmhouse is still there, and the oast house and the idyllic surrounding location are seemingly untouched. It looked just like it did in 1991 – which is to say it looked just like it did in 1957, the unspoiled English garden of H. E. Bates's books. Of course, all the rubbishy junk props that were strewn around the farm to make it look lived-in are gone, and the lawns and borders are all properly tended now. Much to my astonishment, Buss Farm has become a themed B&B, offering a *Darling Buds*-style stay in the country for anyone who wants it – and a quarter of a century after the show was broadcast, people evidently still do want it. While we were there for the documentary, the owner was tapping away at her computer nearly the whole time. 'You're busy,' I said. She said, 'Yes, and it's all down to the show. Without you lot, we wouldn't have a business.' So that was nice to know. True, she didn't come across with any of the folding stuff, offer me a wink and attempt to wedge it in my top pocket. But I was more than happy to think I had played an inadvertently entrepreneurial role in a thriving hotel venture – which I can't really pretend was the plan when I signed up to be Pop Larkin. It's extraordinary, though, how the show has endured. *Darling Buds* was hugely popular at the time, and right from the get-go. The first episode went out on an April Sunday evening, offering a story in which a visiting tax inspector falls for the Larkins' beautiful daughter and the rural life and ends up abandoning the Inland Revenue and joining the family instead. To the shock of all of us, it generated 19 million viewers, knocking *Coronation Street* off the top of the weekly audience chart. *Darling Buds* has not been constantly repeated in the way that *Only Fools* has, though. It's not been kept in the public eye or placed where it could reach out to new audiences who didn't see it at the time. Yet it had such a strong effect on the people who saw it in the first place that it seems to have remained in their minds ever since.

Amazing to reflect that the programme was popular and emblematic enough to warrant the issuing of collectors' die-cast models of the Rolls-Royce that Pop drove, issued in *Darling Buds of May*-branded cardboard boxes. The

Batmobile, James Bond's Aston Martin and Pop Larkin's Roller: it's a strong thread. Actually, now that I think about it, there were die-cast models of the Trotters' yellow Reliant Regal, too, so that's two shows I've been involved in that have spawned collectible model cars. Is that some kind of record? I'm claiming it anyway. My legacy is set in enamel. My place in the history of Corgi Toys is secure.

I have to say, the actual Landaulette looked box-fresh at that later meeting. It had been to the restorers since we had it on the show and the bloke responsible for the work had done a lovely job, taking it right back to its original spec, inside and out. The engine had been reconditioned and when you switched it on, it ran like an old grandfather clock. The yellow coachwork and the black mudguards were impeccable – even after I had finished with them. The restorer of motorbikes in me was both humbled and agog. That said, no amount of attention to historic detail could make the Landaulette any easier to get in and out of. Hauling your legs over the side, clinging onto the door jamb . . . not dignified. Even when we made the show, my impression was that the only people who could climb into that car with any degree of comfort or style were gymnasts. A quarter of a century later, and with my days of excellence on the parallel bars sadly behind me, that impression only solidified. As for getting out, it still seemed to be the case that the only method was to swing your legs up and out, point them vaguely in the direction of the running board, ease your backside out of the chair and then very carefully fall on the ground.

Bruises aside, we had a grand old reunion that day, me, Pam and Philip. For all of us, the show had been something unique in our careers, a special time, and its impact and effect on people had been so much greater than anything we had envisaged while making it. We had hoped that Catherine Zeta-Jones would come and reminisce with us. *Darling Buds* was, of course, Catherine's breakout show. They auditioned three hundred actresses for the part of Mariette, the Larkins' daughter, and still didn't find one that they were happy with. Then somebody saw Catherine performing in the musical *42nd Street* at the Drury Lane Theatre in London and asked her to try out. The rest is history, much of it written in the tabloid papers, who caught one sight of Catherine playing the coquettish but innocent Larkin daughter on the small screen, and swarmed all over her – and, by extension, all over our location shoots. I had seen the press gather when *Only Fools* was filming, but this was on another level. Like she said, 'With one hour of television, my life changed.' What amazed and impressed me was the level-headedness with which she dealt with it all. She was only twenty-two at that point and some would have freaked, but the whole ridiculous carnival seemed to amuse her more than anything else. The show got her noticed in America, she moved to LA, began starring in movies, met and married Michael Douglas . . . just the usual chain of events that gets triggered by appearing in an ITV family drama serial set in rural Kent in the 1950s.

Catherine couldn't come to Buss Farm that day, but she suggested I fly out to America and film a chat with her there. That sounded great to me: we'd get the interview done in her New York apartment, and then, no doubt, she and Michael would want to take me out to dinner with Matt Damon and Jeff Bridges, because they would most likely happen to be in town, too; and at some point in the evening somebody would say, 'Hey, Dave, what are you busy with right now? Because it just so happens I've got a script which I know would be perfect for you . . .' Then I woke up and remembered that this was British television, and the budget to fly me and a film crew across the Atlantic for a short interview sequence was unlikely to be forthcoming. True enough, a compromise position was arrived at. We would film an interview with Catherine in her New York apartment . . . but from Buss Farm, via a satellite link. My dinner with Matt, Jeff and the gang would have to wait.

Transatlantic teleconferencing, though: it was hard to think of anything less Larkin-like. Still, there we all sat, on a sofa in Kent – me, Pam and Philip – and there, on a giant screen, live from New York, still setting up and not able to hear us at this point, was Catherine. She looked fantastic, it goes without saying. In due course, the operator pushed in the plug, or the 20p piece dropped in the meter, or however it works, and we were in business. Pam said she Skypes

221

her sister in Australia all the time, so she felt pretty comfortable with it, but I have never Skyped Pam's sister in my life, so the scenario took some getting used to for me. There was a slight time delay, so we talked over each other a bit. At one point you heard one of her kids walk into the room – on their way to school it seemed – and she explained that she was just giving an interview about *Darling Buds* and you could hear the kid, off-screen, react as kids will; kind of, 'Oh God, Mom – must you?' It was great to talk to her again and see how unchanged she was: still natural, still grounded.

Nobody else had been cast at the point at which I agreed to do *Darling Buds*, and though it would be nice to say that I always knew it would fly and signed on the dotted line without hesitation, the truth was I had my doubts about whether there was enough drama in it. As it happened, atmosphere would carry it, as much as anything else. In the meantime, the nature of the project really appealed to me: a family-orientated, Sunday-evening show was something that I had fancied being a part of for some time, and because that particular style of entertainment already seemed to be on the wane, perhaps I needed to get in quick or lose my chance. My only stipulation for Yorkshire Television was that it had to be shot on film rather than video. *Porterhouse Blue* had been shot on film and I had come to appreciate fully the distinction in terms of richness and depth. When they agreed to use film on *Darling Buds*, I was on board. I just felt that film stock would give it heart as well as romance, and make all the difference.

After that, it was about building the character in the usual ways. I remember going into the meeting with the wardrobe designer and saying that I saw Pop Larkin in a pork-pie hat and a waistcoat. And the designer said, 'Yes, absolutely – a moleskin waistcoat.' I said, 'Moles? I'm not sure I fancy wearing moles . . .' She said, 'It's a material that people in the country would wear.' So a moleskin waistcoat it was. We pulled out trousers with turn-ups, big boots and a pair of old-fashioned blue overalls for when he was work-ing. We had to have copies of everything on stand-by because there was always the chance, given the setting, that something would end up getting accidentally covered in paint, or oil, or pig manure, which would have derailed the shoot if another set of clothes hadn't been available to change into.

As for Pop's body language, in many ways, I quickly real-ised, he needed to have an absence of body language about him. There wasn't that restless, twitchy, questing physical energy that was going on with Del. On the contrary, you needed a contentedness to pervade Pop's body – relaxed, shoulders down. This was a married man, in love with his wife and with life in general. He could afford to be much more still and loose-limbed than Del.

Something else that I threw into the melting pot early on: I've been quite a practical person in my life, having been an electrician and being a bit of a fixer-upper and a mender. So I'm used to working with tools and lifting stuff around and that, too, becomes a form of body language. I thought if I could feed some of that into my portrayal of Pop, it might make him come alive a touch more. So if he had to move a crate around, I asked that it should be a full crate, and if he had to feed the pigs, I made sure the bucket of slops was as full as it should be, rather than empty, which a lot of actors would have preferred. Just as you can always spot an actor pretending to drink from an empty cup, so you can also spot an actor picking up an empty suitcase. It tips up at one end because there's no weight to hold it flat. Same kind of thing goes for a bucket. You need some weight in there. Then your whole body shape changes to compensate in the act of carrying it, and then it looks real, because it is.

One thing Pop did share with Del, though, was a habit of eating heartily and openly. There were never half measures with him: if Ma put haddock down in front of him, it would be a whole haddock. If it was turkey, it would be a whole turkey leg. Everything he ate was the full monty. The amount of ham sandwiches we got through on that show beggars belief. Anton, our stage manager, would be behind the scenes during rehearsals, slicing up this plump white bread, slathering it with butter and stuffing slices of ham inside it. So delicious. I put on a lot of weight during the making of those three series. But that was Pop. He really enjoyed his food and he tucked in properly, without manners or graces, speaking with his mouth full, elbows on the table – the relaxed man, at home with his family.

Doing *Darling Buds* was a whole new kind of experience for me. This was the first time I had gone into a show with my reputation preceding me. The success of *Only Fools* meant I was boxing at a different weight now, whether I liked it or not. I knew that I was right for the part of Pop Larkin; at the same time, I also knew that Yorkshire Television were hoping I would bring along with me some of the audience who had watched *Only Fools* – that I had a value for them in that purely mathematical, bums-on-seats sense. It was definitely not something I had had to think about before, and, even though it was quite an empowering thought, it brought another layer of pressure. Plus there was my own determination to prove that I wasn't just a one-hit wonder; that I could successfully adopt another character that would be accepted by people and that would help me slightly slacken the powerful grasp of Del Boy. In the context of all this, I found myself being handled incredibly thoughtfully by Yorkshire Television. Perhaps a little too thoughtfully, sometimes. After the second series of *Darling Buds*, Vernon Lawrence, who was Head of Yorkshire Television, took me out for dinner. Back in the day, Vernon had been a sound engineer on *The Goon Show*, and anyone who could claim a connection with that piece of genius was good enough for me. Halfway through this meal, he suddenly got up from the table, came round to my side and, much to my consternation, plunged to his knee and took my hand, in the traditional manner of the love-struck suitor who is about to propose. This rather kindled the interest of the restaurant's other diners. 'I want you to tell me that you will do another series of *Darling Buds*,' Vernon shouted. It was ridiculous and funny, but also, I can't deny, flattering. Now this was all new to me: one-to-one contact with the head honchos, ceaseless access to and feedback from the people who were making the decisions. At the BBC I had felt very much like a hired hand – like it was my privilege to work there, which it unquestionably was. Here, though, I was given a contract to lock me in place, for the first time in my career, and I felt properly wanted. Moreover, with Vernon and David Reynolds, Deputy Controller of Entertainment at Yorkshire Television at that time, I realised that I could get things done. They were a phone call away. Got a problem? Solved. It was so unlike the BBC's set-up where you frequently seemed to be dealing with committees within committees and were constantly required to submit paperwork in triplicate and then wait around for a couple of months before anything moved.

We made two six-episode series, along with two Christmas specials, and then ran out of material. H. E. Bates, alas, was in no position to provide us with new stuff, having passed away in 1974, so writers were commissioned to supply scripts for the third series from scratch. There were a few conniptions at the time about whether this was the right thing to do, or whether the show would lose its spirit without the 'truth' of the books underpinning it. Personally, I didn't think it made a great deal of difference and I would have been happy to carry on for at least another series after that, given how much people were enjoying the show and how much we were enjoying making it. If it had been up to me, we would have sailed happily onwards.

Quite apart from anything else, we were making my mother happy. She loved that show. Of all the things I did, *Darling Buds* was her absolute favourite. It spoke to her, as it spoke to so many people, of a time she could remember very well, a simpler period when what you didn't have, you didn't miss, and when you were happy with your lot. It was carefree, sunny and escapist – a vision of bucolic bliss. OK, the interiors weren't shot in Kent at all, but up at Yorkshire Television. (All credit to the lighting director, Peter Jackson, for blending them so that nobody would know. Jackson was an artist who would not be rushed in his subtle adjustments of the lighting rig, and I can still hear now his slightly nasal voice saying, in a manner which brooked no dispute, 'I'll tell you when I'm ready.') And, OK, the strawberry-picking scene in episode one was filmed outside the strawberry season, so the field had to be planted up beforehand with greenhouse-grown strawberries imported from Holland. But nobody said this wasn't television, did they? It was easy on the eye, it was easy on the ear – classic Sunday-evening viewing in the old style, with the signature tune acting as a wonderful, gentle siren to call you through from the kitchen or down from upstairs. I sometimes think that telly could do with a bit more of that today – a family drama, designed to make people feel good. That kind of show seems to have gone, by and large. All that *Darling Buds* was really saying was, 'Aren't we lucky? Isn't it a lovely world we live in?' That message would be a tough sell for television now-adays. There appears to be more scope given to things that are angry and aggressive, loud, harsh. I understand that, but it saddens me a bit, too.

Hark at me, though – sounding nostalgic about a piece of nostalgia. And nostalgia, as the saying goes, isn't what it used to be. Strange old business, though, and a strange old place I found myself in at the start of the 1990s, as I now realise, looking back. Having spent the best part of a decade doing everything in my powers to cement Del Boy in people's memories, I then started working as hard as I could to try and make people forget him.

# CHAPTER FIFTEEN

## *My life on the beat*

I would love to tell you that, after Pop Larkin, I breezed suavely into the part of Detective Inspector Jack Frost in *A Touch of Frost*, pausing only to change my soiled blue overalls for a raincoat and a trilby, and that the rest was television history. The truth is, though, in the winter of 1992, as the transmission date for the first ever episode of that series neared, I was nervous as a kitten. I was pacing about at home, staring fretfully out of windows, and narrowly resisting the urge to chew on the furniture. I have it on the authority of my wife, Gill, that she had never seen me so much a-jitter in the run-up to a broadcast.

I had felt very confident about it while we were making it. The stories and the scripts were good. The cast was excellent: Bruce Alexander as Superintendent Norman Mullett, John Lyons as DS George Toolan, and my dear elder brother Arthur White as PC Ernie Trigg. We had certainly had a good time shooting it. Yet, as the day of broadcast got closer,

I found myself surfing a rising wave of anxiety. Among the many things making that wave was a growing sense of responsibility towards the people at Yorkshire Television, whom I had persuaded that playing a detective in a serious drama serial was the way forward for me. But would I similarly persuade an audience? Would people believe in me, barging about in a police station in my freshly grown moustache? Or had I embarrassingly overreached myself? Such things can leave an actor feeling decidedly squeaky around the nether regions – and not least when it's fairly clear that several million people will be tuning in to find out how you got on.

Inadvertently or otherwise, you create expectations about yourself and the stuff I had done on television had been overwhelmingly comic in intent rather than serious. By this time, of course, I had put Pop Larkin between myself and Del Boy in people's minds and had perhaps revealed a bit of flexibility. Then again, the gap between those two characters, though clear, was not vast. You could say that, in terms of format, going from *Only Fools* to *Darling Buds* was a shift from comedy to comedy drama but, as I've already explained, in my opinion *Only Fools* was never really a sitcom and was always a comedy drama itself, so, in that sense, it was barely even a sidestep. Also, for all the differences in demeanour, Pop and Del were, at root, a pair of lovable rogues who shared, along with a love of a laugh, a liberal attitude to taxation issues. As Pop so perfectly put it, 'Tax,

Mr Charlton? Tax? I wish I had the money to pay tax.' Though technically criminal, that foible hardly put them at the scene of grim murders, vanished prostitutes and unexplained bodies in rivers. Anyway, Del continued to sit heavily in the scales, as he always would. Accordingly, the question nagging away in my mind, as I stomped about at home in that period, was: 'Would you buy a brand-new TV detective off this man?' Or would the audience watch me arrive at my first crime scene and be waiting for me to draw a deep breath, widen my eyes and say, 'Châteauneuf du Pape, Rodney!'

In the opening episode of *Only Fools*, you may recall, Del took a load of dodgy combination-lock briefcases off Trigger's hands. In the opening episode of *Frost*, there's a dodgy briefcase, too, but it's found with half a pair of handcuffs still attached to it – handcuffs which match the other half already found mysteriously dangling on the wrist of a dead body. The distinction between those two uses of the briefcase as a dramatic device seemed to me to summarise fairly neatly the nature of the leap I was trying to make here. From Del Boy to Frost: in my own mind, I was essentially launching myself across a canyon and I would either land on the other side or end up as a distant puff of dust on the rocks below, like Wile E. Coyote.

The root of all this was a meeting at Yorkshire Television in 1992 when I had been asked the question, 'So, David, what do you want to do next?' It was the first time in my

231

career that anyone had ever asked me that, and it was quite a shock. Normally, at those kinds of meetings, people had summoned me because they had a particular job in mind for me. The idea that there was now some kind of blank slate onto which I could chalk my own feverish desires seemed implausible to me. What did I want to do next? Blimey. If ever a question brought home to me the privileged position that I had somehow come to occupy, it was that one. And because the very question had surprised me, I was right on the verge of replying 'Dunno, really' – which would probably not have sounded all that impressive or forward-looking of me. But fortunately I recovered my self-possession enough to mention playing a detective in a detective series, an ambition which had grown in me the more of those things that I watched and enjoyed on the television myself.

Now, whether my interlocutors at Yorkshire Television were also tempted to say 'Châteauneuf du Pape!' in response to this presumptuous suggestion, I couldn't tell you. I only know that they resisted the urge at the time. After I had left the room, they may have said all sorts of things. But they pushed ahead with the idea. A jocular Peckham barrow boy as a meditative TV sleuth? Many would have baulked at the notion. But I can only imagine that it smoothed the path for me not inconsiderably that John Thaw had so successfully come from *The Sweeney* to play Inspector Morse. He had made the transition from the gruff Flying Squad merchant who was always lumping wrong 'uns over the bonnet of a Ford Cortina, to a thoughtful (even over-thoughtful), classical-music-loving Jaguar driver in the Oxfordshire countryside. Once you saw him as Morse, the gruff, London dust-up merchant quickly slipped into the past and John himself got a massive shove up the ladder of actorly credibility. None of this was ever put into those exact words, but I don't doubt that John's success with Morse diminished the leap of faith that Yorkshire needed to take in my case.

Whatever, Yorkshire went to Excelsior, the production company that had done *Darling Buds*, and told them I was looking for a detective series, and the people at Excelsior did some research and sent me what they found – four books, including *A Touch of Frost* by R. D. Wingfield. So that was my holiday reading sorted for that Easter. Every-thing they had sent me would probably have worked to some extent, but it was Wingfield's book that hooked me. That was where I met Detective Inspector William Edward 'Jack' Frost, who seemed to have a real pile of trouble on his plate at the time, including a serial killer on the loose, a possibly suspicious road accident involving the son of a Member of Parliament and a burglary in a strip club. The man got more work than Ant and Dec. I was totally drawn in by what I was reading. The plotting was woven together so cleverly that you were actually racing to turn the page while the story was gradually revealing itself. That level of enthralment is also what good narrative television is about, if you can get it right. I could see a future for Frost on the screen.

Richard Harris was chosen to take the first shot at adapting the books for television. I had been in a couple of Richard's plays – *Albert and Virginia*, and *Partners*, which was the one where I used to get into a nightly fight with a tiger rug. Richard had also worked on the scripts for *The Darling Buds of May*. In our first meeting, Richard pointed out the great truth about detective series which is that, essentially, there are no new plots – not now, not after all this time. The variable is the detective. That's where you make the difference. The success or failure of the show would come down in the end to what Frost was like. So I set my mind to constructing him.

My first concern was to lighten him considerably from the Frost in the books, where he is quite a dark creation. There's a deeply troubled hinterland looming behind the detective there, and a hardened, embittered attitude to other people. But, without losing all the aspects of that edge, I wanted to make him more day-to-day, more accessible and above all more sympathetic. I wanted viewers to be able to feel some warmth for him and relate to him, because this is television after all, and that's where my strength seems to lie. On the page, Frost is a heavy smoker but I had only just quit smoking myself and was reluctant to go back to it. So the on-screen Frost became a reluctant quitter – someone who

Del Boy and Rodney's adventures in Monaco is the only show from the twenty-first century in the top 12 most watched programmes in British television history. Cheers to that! – 'If They Could See Us Now', Christmas special, 2001.

*The Darling Buds of May* had such a strong effect on the people who saw it that it seems to have remained in their minds ever since.

Pop Larkin's yellow Rolls Royce – both achingly straightforward and devilishly complicated at the same time.

Always one for realism, no empty wheelbarrow for this actor.

For all of us, *The Darling Buds of May* had been something unique in our careers, a special time.

A *Touch of Frost* was the start of a whole new chapter for me – forty-two episodes which kept me busy and in demand over eighteen years. I was even an executive producer. What a turn-up: proper employment at last.

A TOUCH OF FROST
'IF DOGS RUN FREE'
DIR: PAUL HARRISON          DOP: ROBIN VIDGEON BSC
ROLL #        SLATE        TAKE
36B          944          7 P/U
DATE: 7th JULY 2009
DAY        EXT
PROVISION
B

Ronnie Barker: my hero and mentor.

'We're lucky, aren't we? We're getting paid to make ourselves laugh.' Lucky indeed. Beyond lucky.

Back then, when Ronnie wrote me this note, *Open All Hours* without him would have seemed implausible.

**7.30 Open All Hours**. Granville goes all out to impress a local beauty and improve his lowly status. Comedy starring David Jason. (R) (T)

*You agent is getting a bit above himself*

*Ronnie B.*

I never suspected that Granville would serve me so loyally all this time, though I suppose Arkwright, in his own curmudgeonly way, was always suggesting it would be thus.

9.5 million watched 'Beckham in Peckham'. Not too shabby, Dave. Not too shabby, my son.

A rare red-carpet moment of me with
my daughter Sophie and my wife Gill.

Left to face the flashbulbs alone at the
National Film Awards 2017.

has given up the fags but still hankers after them, a feature which was usefully human and gave us some nice bits and pieces for Frost in scenes where he was around other smokers. Indeed, there was probably more to be had out of Frost as an ex-smoker than there would have been if he had just been puffing away the whole time.

Then there was his bearing. Did I mention anywhere in this book that I'm not particularly tall? I think I may have done. I'm certainly not tall enough to have made it into the police force, for which you needed to be 5ft 7, which lofty benchmark I would have fallen half an inch short of, had the fancy taken me to become a copper back in the day. It's Scotland Yard's loss, I'm sure. Anyway, this marginal shortcoming could have presented me with an issue of plausibility, playing Frost. That's why his body shape is extremely upright, almost every time you see him. Frost draws himself up to his full height and carries himself like a tall person, even though he isn't one. I also went to an extra effort to make him physically imposing where I could. In any interior scene, I would try to be sure he took up the dominant position in the room, which is normally to be found around the fireplace. The hearth will tend to be a room's focal point, so the minute Frost enters a room, likely as not, that's where you'll see him heading.

Frost's moustache is part of the attempt to add authority, too. I remember from knocking about in my youth how the very young policemen, who didn't wish to appear so, would grow a moustache in order to suggest some unearned seniority. For some reason, a bit of growth under the nose adds a little extra weight and presence, so I decided Frost had played that game, and I grew him a tache. He needed an authoritative tone of voice, too – a sharpness, a crispness, a decisive edge. It was never in the script, but I used to put in something my father used to say to us as kids: 'Chop-chop! Come on – chop-chop!' It's pidgin Chinese, apparently – brought back to Britain by sailors. It goes very well with a clap of the hands, and my father was very fond of it. It was also a good, crisp phrase for Frost – commanding but not hectoring. Once you've got a few little keys like that, the rest of the character opens up and grows. As for wardrobe, Frost was very easy to dress: jackets and ties, the clothes of someone whose work requires him to look respectable but who doesn't really care that much or have the money to spoil himself. Plus he's a widower, so you get a faint, melancholy overtone from the clothes of the fact that there is nobody in his life who is looking out for him in that area. He basically wore the same hat and raincoat for eighteen years. But then, people do.

God bless Yorkshire Television, meanwhile, who, whether because they were concerned about the ghost of Del Boy scuppering things or for other reasons, went to a lot of effort to invest this project with seriousness. I was delighted that Peter Jackson, the lighting director who had done such great work on *The Darling Buds of May*, was back on board for *Frost*. The director of the crucial first episode was the late, great Don Leaver, who had worked on *Prime Suspect* but also, still more impressively, on the legendary sixties show *The Avengers*, which was radically experimental in the way it was shot. Don developed the *Frost* style and other directors took it on from there. I really enjoyed working with Don; perhaps a little less so with Herbie Wise, the Austrian-born director who was another ambitious appointment to the series, being famous for directing the landmark Robert Graves adaptation, *I, Claudius*. Herbie was very much a solo artist. He worked at home on the script and built every shot beforehand. Then he would come to the set and shoot it, very rigidly in accordance with his pre-formed plans – which plans tended to be very smart, I have to say, and right on the money. But Don Leaver had been a much more fluid operator and Herbie's approach – essentially, 'you say the lines and I'll film you doing so' – took some getting used to. So did his habit of talking to you indirectly, through his cameraman or his first assistant, rather than coming to you in person. There was also one slightly unfortunate moment when we were setting up an interior shot of me going through a doorway and Herbie made the following formal announcement: 'We will shoot this side of the doorway and Mr Morse will come through, and then we will pick up Mr Morse on the other side.' Oops, wrong detective. Still, seen one, seen 'em all, I guess.

We took the decision to lead off with a properly dark

story in a properly dark episode, called 'Care and Protection'. It featured thirty-year-old human remains, gunfire and the disappearance of a prostitute's daughter. Well, if we were going to put Del Boy right out of people's minds, and say, emphatically, 'This ain't cheery Peckham, everybody,' we needed to do it properly. In due course, then, after those weeks of gradually ratcheting worry, I sat down and watched A *Touch of Frost* go out. In a funny way, it felt a bit like a first night in the theatre – the same rush of high anxiety and mild giddiness. Obviously, I had already seen the finished show – had, indeed, made notes on edited versions of it along the way. I certainly knew how it ended. Nevertheless, you're sitting there at home and watching it and knowing that potentially millions of other people are doing the same, and that's quite a feeling. In order to pass muster, the character on the screen has got to convince me that he's himself and not me. If there are any moments at all when I think I can see me, it's not doing its job. On this occasion, as the story unfolded, to my enormous relief, I didn't see me peeping out at all. To my even greater relief, I didn't see Del peeping out, either.

That was the start of a whole new chapter for me – forty-two episodes of serious drama which kept me busy and in demand over the next eighteen years. Happy times. The show's producer David Reynolds and I would head off to the Fawsley Hall Hotel in Daventry, which was no hardship, and spend a couple of days with our finest toothcombs out, going over the scripts. Was the story too linear? Were we pointing too obviously at the criminal right from the start? What could we shuffle around to change that? How can we take the audience further down the wrong road so that the surprise and pleasure when the truth is revealed is that much greater? I discovered there was as much fun and interest to be had in stitching a red herring into a plotline as there was in finding an extra joke between the lines of a sitcom script. Drama at this point seemed to be budgeted at roughly three times the budget for comedy, which caused my eyebrows to rise, I must admit. But because David was in control of the money and knew what it would cost to add things, we could have proper, reasonable discussions about production values. Does Frost have a scene with the pathologist here? Or does he simply have a line: 'What did the pathologist say?' What works best on the screen? What better assists the pacing? Eventually, all our gathered thoughts would go back to the writer in the form of notes – and would be grabbed with both hands, mostly. It was a really rewarding position to be in, to feel that my experience in putting bits of television together really did count for something and that my ideas would be taken seriously. I had a job title and everything: executive producer. What a turn-up: proper employment at last.

We were also able to retain some executive power over what went out in the *Frost* trailers, which was a growing problem back then and is an even bigger annoyance for me nowadays. You could sense a growing desire among broad-casters to trail programmes ever more strongly and reveal more and more about their contents in advance. It was about the competition for audiences, clearly, and the basic insecurity that followed from that. The thinking seemed to be that the more you showed of what you'd got – and especially the good bits – the more people you would get on board. But, just as with leaked photographs from the sets of *Only Fools*, I was adamantly against anything that risked a spoiler and entirely on the side of doing everything you could to retain the impact and the surprise for the viewers who tuned in when the show went out. That seemed to me to be especially crucial with a narrative-driven programme like *Frost*.

We had a police consultant to guide us on procedural matters and tell us when we were straying away from reality, although we weren't necessarily sticklers for applying what he told us. On one occasion our man was observing us film-ing an interrogation scene, in the typical windowless room at the police station, with the alleged perpetrator of the crime sitting in a chair at a table and me walking about the place in shirtsleeves, asking my questions. At one point, my theatrical wanderings had carried me around the table and behind the interviewee and afterwards the police consult-ant stepped in. 'You wouldn't really do that,' he said. 'You're not allowed to go behind the suspect in an interrogation because it could be interpreted as intimidation.' I thanked him for his input, but my feeling was that if Frost couldn't go round behind a suspect and get right in his ear, then where was the life in it? Fortunately, the director agreed. There was one interrogation, I remember, where I walked behind the interrogee and leaned myself up against the wall for a while with my arms folded. Those were just things I instinctively found myself doing, otherwise the scene would be just two people round a table and, as gripping as the dialogue doubtless was, the viewers would be dropping off in droves. So we decided to let Frost go rogue on this one. If anybody was informed enough to call us on it, we'd explain that it was just another signal that Frost was a bit of a renegade, when push came to shove. The rules, as they say, are there to be broken – and certainly in television.

This being a detective series, there were, of course, many morgue scenes, and for these we would often head off to the actual working mortuary at Leeds Hospital. The corpses you saw on your screen, I hasten to add, were actors smothered in make-up, but the building and the examination rooms were the real McCoy, and we were looked after and offered guidance, when we were in there, by an extremely nice and thoughtful pair of pathologists from the autopsy unit. Now, you might possibly assume that the coincidence of a bunch of thespians and a place associated with grim and absolute seriousness could plausibly have given rise to larks aplenty in a richly black-humoured vein. You might possibly assume this even more strongly in the case of the *Frost* cast, which was more given to larking about than probably any other cast I have had the pleasure to perform childish pranks with, most of those childish pranks having as their butt the wonderful but frequently luckless Johnny Lyons. (He always gamely forgave us – and that was part of the problem.) However, I have to report that a genuine solemnity would descend on us during the filming of those morgue sequences – a truly unusual lack of levity. Which is odd, really, because I'm sure that people who actually work in morgues, and do the real things that we were pretending to do, muck about and use black humour all the time – indeed, I don't know how you would cope in that line of work without doing so. We, on the other hand, seemed to experience a brush with our own mortality in that chillingly antiseptic place that gave us all the absolute shivers and made the prospect of a prank or an off-colour remark appear entirely out of the question. When I got outside after doing those scenes, emerging into the daylight in the yard, I would feel my spirits lift and experience a palpable sense of release.

I think I can honestly say that I have never been a particularly demanding actor, in the sense of calling for special treatment and perks. Top-quality champagne in the dressing room, bowls of M&Ms with the brown ones removed – these are not the kind of starry backstage privileges that I have ever insisted upon as the condition of my participation. I mentioned earlier the state of the standard-issue motorhomes that Nick and I shared on the sets of

242

*Only Fools*, most of which, we got the impression, had been lucky to scrape through an MOT test and wouldn't have wanted to try their luck any further with a visit from the health inspectors. Yet we used them. It was the same back in 1972 when I took over from Michael Crawford as Brian Runnicles, the lead in *No Sex Please – We're British* at the Strand Theatre in London – my big arrival in the West End, the whole 'name in lights' shebang, a huge deal for me at the time after years of chipping away in the provinces. Being the star of the show meant I got the Strand's Number One dressing room. Despite the glamorous label, it was a poky, tatty room with a chipped sink and a carpet like a tramp's trousers, whose only privilege resided in being closer to the stage than any of the other dressing rooms. Mariah Carey, I'm sure, would have taken one look and insisted on a complete repaint, fresh orchids every night and a daily pedicure for her poodle. I just lumped it. But I guess that's just one of a number of things that Mariah Carey and I don't have in common.

However, I have to confess that, during the shooting of *Frost*, I finally capitalised on my leading-man status by drawing myself up to my full five foot six and a half and asking if, instead of booking me a room along with everyone else in the chosen crew hotel, the production could run to renting me a place of my own, out in the Yorkshire countryside: somewhere I could go back to and shut the door and find a bit of quiet at the end of a working day, when I was increasingly finding that I really needed the peace to descend. Lo and behold, my Barbra Streisand-like, bill-topping magnitude prevailed, my demands were met, and a hired cottage was found, with French windows and a little garden. I don't think this was extravagant, in all honesty: it was probably cheaper than a hotel room, in fact. I certainly didn't ask them to redecorate or fly in lobster from Sicily or anything.

The truth was, I had grown tired of the hotel thing. I had done an awful lot of it during the *Only Fools* and *Darling Buds* days and had developed a number of bugbears regarding such routine hotel-life irritations as slamming fire doors and noisy lift mechanisms and late-night conversations in corridors and people having fifty shades of fun on the other side of your paper-thin wall. The popularity of those two programmes hadn't made staying in hotels any easier, either. There was a tipping-point moment on a *Darling Buds* shoot one evening when I phoned downstairs and asked if I could have some room-service supper brought up. My relatively simple order seemed to unleash a long line of visits to my room, unfolding over a period of anything up to forty-five minutes. First someone arrived with the half-bottle of wine. Then he left and closed the door. Then there was another knock, and someone came in with the main course. Then he left and closed the door. Then there was another knock, and someone else came in with bread and butter. Then he left and shortly after there was another knock and somebody else came in with the dessert. Then he left there and shortly after there was yet another knock. 'Ah,' I said to myself, for I had got into the rhythm of it by now. 'That'll be someone else with the coffee.' It was, indeed, someone with the coffee. I began to suspect that the word might have got out about who was up there in that room and that people were finding an excuse to pop in for a glimpse. I also began to feel like a monkey in a cage, which was a bit disheartening, especially when you're trying to eat your supper.

So, now I had my own place. And in that cottage, what starry behaviour would unfold? What acts of rock'n'roll-style debauchery would be witnessed? Well, dear reader, what can I say? I would get in at night, close the door and cook myself a meal. I might already have peeled the potatoes before leaving for the set in the morning, so they would be ready in the saucepan for when I got back. I might also have brought along a few runner beans and tomatoes from home and I would grill a pork chop or fry up a bit of chicken or something to go with them. Does Johnny Depp do this while on location? The honest truth is, I don't know. He seems, from a distance, to do almost everything else. But I would recommend it to him, if he doesn't. Making the meal was part of the winding-down process – a little space in which to sort my brain out. To the rest of the cast, who would have been staying in a hotel together and probably gathering for a drink in the bar and a meal out (certainly something my brother Arthur and Bruce Alexander liked to get up to), this must have looked a little stand-offish. It certainly wasn't intended to appear that way. It was just something that I had realised I needed in order to get the work done – not least the script-learning. I always found learning lines to be a chore, and it wasn't get any easier with the passing of time. In fact, I look back at the quantity of words that my younger self committed to memory for a play like, say, Alan Ayckbourn's *The Norman Conquests* and I'm aghast. There's pages of the stuff and how it ever ended up between my ears I simply don't know. I'm not saying the stars of the silent-movie era had it easy, but they definitely had fewer words to learn. Anyway, in my rented cottage, I would eat my meal, have a glass of wine, learn my lines and eventually retire to bed, a happy actor.

Things lead on to other things in unpredictable ways. We were filming a scene one day in 2004 where Frost turns up at a big house following a particularly nasty burglary in which the place has been utterly trashed. Amid the chaos, all the books have been pulled off the shelves of the library and scattered on the floor. We had done the shot where I entered the room and reacted to the mayhem, and now we were shooting a sequence where I picked around for evidence in the wreckage. There was a necessary break in the middle of all this while lights and cameras were being adjusted. I was in a slightly locked-in position at that moment, on a chair surrounded by mounds of junk, and I was asked, 'Do you want to get out?' But I thought it might make things easier from a continuity point of view if I sat where I was until we started up again. So I said, 'No, I'll stay put.' So there I sat, waiting among the debris while the crew went about their business, not thinking about much, when I happened to glance down at my feet and notice the title on one of the books that were littered around me: *Ghostboat*. That rather intrigued me, so I reached down, carefully picked it up without disturbing the others around it, and turned to page one. It started with a present-day scene in the middle of the sea where the captain of a trawler is minding his own business when suddenly, right in front of him, a Second World War submarine breaks the surface. I thought, 'Blimey, I'm interested in this.' I realised that if I put this book back among the junk on the floor, I would never find it again. So I slipped the paperback into my jacket pocket and moved a couple of other books to cover the gap on the floor where it had been.

Now, let me make absolutely clear at this point that I am not in any way attempting, in the telling of this story, to condone the theft of props by actors during film-set shoots because that way, surely, only chaos lies. If cast members were to start permitting themselves, willy-nilly, to half-inch the scenery, then no programmes would ever get made. Or only very bare-looking programmes. However, the undeniable truth is, on this one-off (I swear) occasion, I walked off with that book at the end of the day and read on greedily into the night. I was completely gripped. It was by George E.

Simpson and Neal R. Burger, who were writers I had never come across, and it was about this British submarine that had disappeared without trace in the Baltic, only to re-emerge forty years later in the middle of the Cold War, but with no crew on board. I loved that set-up, and the very next day I rang David Reynolds and said, 'I think I've got something for us here.'

David was as enthused as I was. We talked it over and eventually decided that we could do it as an extended filmed drama, three hours divided into two ninety-minute parts – really push the boat out or, at any rate, dredge the submarine up. After that, David and I were about a year and a half putting the project together. We got Guy Burt to adapt it for the screen and Stuart Orme to direct it, and *Ghostboat* went out on ITV over two consecutive nights in April 2006. I played Jack Hardy, the sole surviving submarine crew member who had been picked up in the sea by a German boat but has no recollection of what happened to the sub or his fellow submariners and returns to the salvaged craft to help with the investigation. Quite apart from anything else, the part enabled me to outdo Frost by going beyond the moustache and growing a full seafaring beard. But overall the role was another shuffle in another direction for me, and one that I'm really proud of. We went to Malta to film the exteriors, which was no hardship. Still more excitingly, though, we filmed the interiors at Cinecittà in Rome, the great Italian film studio – birthplace to

Fellini's *La Dolce Vita* and Zeffirelli's *Romeo and Juliet* and a bit of a step-up in general from the Leeds Studios on Kirkstall Road. They had a mocked-up submarine there, left over from an American movie, which we helped ourselves to. Those were some of the most exciting weeks of my working life, driving onto the Cinecittà lot at six in the morning, heading to make-up, working for twelve hours . . . it was completely thrilling, just like in the movies. At night I would head back to a little one-bedroom Italian apartment that had been rented for me at the top of an old thirties block, where I had access to the roof, with a chair and a small table and a low wall that I could put my feet up on, and I would sit there in the warm air with a glass of wine and the next day's script and look out across the rooftops of Rome, all orange-lit, and I would think to myself, this is the dream, the absolute dream. Work doesn't often supply an experience like that and when it does you have to grasp it and savour it.

The motto of this story: check carefully under your feet because you never know what you might be standing on.

It was also while working on *Frost* that I received a letter asking if I would consider going on display in wax. No, not a *Crossroads* revival: an invitation to model for Madame Tussauds. Now, that's not a summons one treats lightly. When you think of the people who have been selected for that honour before you: Henry VIII, Freddie Mercury, Dr Crippen . . . The list is endless. So, I told them they could definitely count me in. It's quite a process, though. They come and photograph you first of all, and then you head up to London to their studio, getting met at a side door behind the famous museum on Marylebone Road, and going up to a room which had strong echoes of the morgue in *Frost*, if I'm being honest: random arms and legs and stray bits of body all over the place. Not that there were stray bits of body all over the place in the Leeds morgue, obviously, but you know what I mean. In this slightly macabre workshop, they perform a bewildering number of measurements: height, waist, head, chest, inside leg, silly mid-off. Then they do skin tone and go after the colour of your eyes very carefully. I went back for a second session a few weeks later, when they were doing the hair. A woman was sitting there with my head on her desk – an arresting sight for me when I walked in the room – apparently pushing each strand in, one by one. I asked her if the whole business drove her mad, but she said she found it quite rewarding, and the head on the desk didn't seem to be complaining.

Eventually I was ready to be unveiled. They put on a little ceremony at the museum and the covers came off, and there I was. It was like standing in front of a three-dimensional mirror – altogether spooky. My daughter, who was quite little at the time, certainly found it so. She was terrified and wouldn't go anywhere near it. I got a slightly more positive reaction from my sister, June, when I took her in to see it a short while after. Madame Tussauds make it clear that you are always welcome to go in and visit yourself, and they even allow you VIP after-hours access to yourself. So I was able to pop in quietly with June one evening, which was quite fun. The place is such an institution and both of us were tickled to think I had risen to the point where I was judged to rub waxy shoulders with Henry, Freddie, Dr Crippen and the lads. I believe I stayed on display in London for two or three years, after which they moved me to one of their other premises in Blackpool. At that stage, I lost touch with myself. Where am I now? I wonder. Answers on a candlestick. I've probably been melted down to help make Donald Trump.

As for Frost, he eventually retired from full-time work on the force in November 2008. I was sixty-eight by then, practising a good decade after the police would normally have asked for my badge, so once again the magic of theatre had won out over the rule book. I consider myself very fortunate to live in a world in which that can sometimes be the way. Even the old Jack might have had a few more cases in him: not long ago there was talk of a revival in which the old boy, having retired to the Isle of Wight, was helping his daughter run a private detective agency. It never got developed in the end, but I would have been more than up for it. Crime-solving gets to be a habit. Once a copper, always a copper.

# CHAPTER SIXTEEN

## *The truth about me and Golden Balls*

M y part in the soaring career of David Beckham? It's a small but – I like to think – significant one. I taught him everything he knows about falling over sideways.

It was early 2014. *Only Fools* had been off the air for eleven years; John Sullivan had departed this earth three years ago, taking with him the chances of any further plot developments in this particular area. Or so I had assumed. Yet the call had come through: would I do a short sketch for Sport Relief? John's sons, Jim and Dan, had written a new script, which included some previously unused material written by their father. What they had come up with was a ten-minute skit intended to star me as Derek Trotter, Nick Lyndhurst as Rodney, and the former captain of the England football team as the former captain of the England football team. They had given the sketch the name 'Beckham in Peckham'.

Generally speaking, I was inclined to shy away from

things proposing to revive *Only Fools*. My thinking was that
it was over, sad as that may be, and so the best thing to do
was to walk on and keep walking. But in this case, I was of
a mind to say yes, even before I had read the script. The
involvement of John's sons seemed to me to hand the project the official stamp of authority that it needed. Also, you
don't say no if you can possibly help it to Richard Curtis's
Comic Relief charity operation, of which Sport Relief was
an offshoot. This wouldn't be the first time I had pitched in
as Del Boy on behalf of that extraordinary fund-raising
machine. John Sullivan had scripted a special sketch for
the 1997 Red Nose Day telethon, with Del, Rodney and
Uncle Albert around the breakfast table and with Del
announcing a plan to sign up Damien, his son, for a modelling agency. Del was also in one of the very earliest Red
Nose Day shows, in the late eighties, part of a roster of live
action in which various stunts and bits of action were going
off in different locations around the country. The scheme
that time was to back a van into a square in the centre of
Manchester and then have Del grab a pile of junk out of the
back of it (mostly old VHS videos, as I recall) and try and
flog these items to some predictably startled passers-by. So
off I went to Manchester, ready to do my bit. The Red Nose
Day productions are very slick nowadays but back then they
were a little more random, as live television shows taking
place in multiple locations tend to be. I knew I wasn't too
high up the pecking order because we had a skeleton

crew – the bare minimum of technicians – and no director had been appointed to the site. Instead, there was just an assistant in a pair of headphones who was liaising with the main production staff in London. Still, you want to do your bit, however small.

We reached the appointed moment in the evening, I got the signal from the assistant and I was away. 'Now, gather round, ladies and gentlemen. I've got such a deal for you today – such a deal I've got. I'm not here to be laughed at, charfed at or generally mucked around. I'm here to sell my wares. They're guaranteed to cure hard-core, soft-core and pimples on the tongue . . .'

This nonsense was patter I had thrown together way back in my youth, while messing about around London with my mate Bob Bevil, later my partner in the electrical business. When we weren't singing stupid songs in made-up Italian, or riding around on my motorbike and honking the horn and waving wildly in order to fool complete strangers into waving back at us as if we were someone they knew (hours of fun, kids), we'd be throwing market trader banter at each other, just for the sheer silliness of it. There was one time when Bob and I had a job in the East End, working near Petticoat Lane, and we happened on this bloke selling dresses on the street, who had his patter down tight. 'Listen, girls, step up – this is the bargain of the year here. You've all heard of Christian Dior? Well, I'm Moishe Dior . . .' We imitated him forever afterwards and all those years later, while filming the marketplace scenes for *Only Fools*, I would use this patter, when the cameras were running, to kick a scene off, just to get everyone, the cast and the extras, loosened up before we got into the written dialogue.

So, out this stuff now pours for the benefit of the passing public of Manchester and for the watching Red Nose Day millions. 'You'd pay for these, wouldn't you, lady, down at Littlewoods? Well, I'm Bigwoods, me. No! Put your money away! I don't want your five pounds. I don't want your four pounds, neither. I don't even want your three pounds, darling. One pound fifty, that's what I'm selling 'em for here. Or five for a fiver! You won't find cheaper. I'm practically robbing myself, girl . . .'

An intrigued crowd was beginning to gather and I was just getting into my stride and about to turn it up a notch when I heard the assistant shout, 'Thank you, David. We're out.'

'We're out?'

'Yes, they've gone to Newcastle.'

'Oh.' I tried not to look hurt. 'Well, are they coming back?'

'No, that's it. Thanks, David.'

I'd been on screen for about a minute. I must have had at least six minutes of that stuff, ready to roll. But that's market trading for you, I guess. And live television. I quietly helped pack the goods back into the van and went home.

'Beckham in Peckham' was a more stable proposition and

accordingly it was with a glad and willing heart that I reported one morning to Wimbledon Film Studios, a nice little unit in which I've had cause to work a number of times over the years, and which has an indoor soundstage but also an outdoor backlot with a street set on it – a little slice of Hollywood in south-west London. Or certainly a little slice of Peckham, very plausibly.

Nick was already there when I arrived. I hadn't seen him for quite a while, so this was a bit of a reunion for us and we embraced each other accordingly. Our paths had gone in different directions since the show ended, which was always likely. You move on to the next thing. I had reached out to him a couple of times, suggesting get-togethers, but nothing had come back and it hadn't happened. I didn't push it, either. For one thing, I knew he was busy with work. For another thing, I am always anxious that, for Nick, I represent, to a certain extent, the downside of his career in acting. Think about it: I'm the bloke who took the terms 'plonker' and 'wally' – not to mention the terms 'twonk', 'div', 'pranny' and 'dipstick' – and wedged them into the English language, almost exclusively by shouting them at Nick Lyndhurst on national television. Obviously, I, as Derek Trotter, was shouting them at Nick, as Rodney Trotter, while reading off a script in the limited and fictional context of a comedy series, but that's by the by. As an unwelcome consequence of these exchanges, Nick has lived with people shouting 'plonker' and 'wally' at him in the street ever since – and meaning it in the nicest possible way, of course. But you can see how having strangers greet you on sight in this manner would quickly lose its novelty value and begin to grate.

My version of this, by contrast, is people coming up and saying, 'Hey, Del Boy – where's Rodney?' That, too, I have to admit, has lost a certain amount of its novelty value down the years, but it's undoubtedly less alarming to hear, out of the blue, than a crisp 'You plonker!'

Anyway, it was great to see him. It's that brotherly relationship again: you can exist apart from each other for a spell, but when you do come together, you're still brothers. Nick had been playing Shakespeare in the West End; he'd had the part of Trinculo in *The Tempest*. Very impressive. Of course, when he left the theatre at the end of the evening, people would be round the stage door with pictures from *Only Fools* for him to sign. John Challis went through the same thing. He took a role at one point on a London stage, in a dark and serious play by Ira Levin called *Veronica's Room*. Levin is most famous for having written *Rosemary's Baby*, and *Veronica's Room* is a melodrama which is all about murder and insanity and the treacherous nature of people's memories and very much not about second-hand car salesmen in south London. Further emphasising the distance, John's role required him to adopt an American accent. Completely in character, he walked out onto the stage and spoke his first line, only to hear a woman whisper loudly in the front row: 'That's him, that's Boycie!' It was hard to give the show the slip, no matter what you did. It followed us all wherever we went – and it was going to do so, we realised, for the rest of our lives. I think all of us had to go through a process of reconciling ourselves to that, and Nick, who was by a long way the youngest among us, may have had it the hardest.

To say that the atmosphere in that Wimbledon studio was abuzz in anticipation of the arrival of David Beckham would be a gross understatement. You could have powered a pair of arc lights off the excitement and general jitteriness in advance of his appearance that morning, not least among those of a female persuasion. In this context, I might observe that the suspiciously swollen gathering of essential assistants that day included my wife, Gill, and also Nick's wife, Lucy, both of whom had worked in the business and who, after all this time, wouldn't always need or want to be by our sides at a film shoot, but who had nevertheless, quite by coincidence and entirely independently of one another, chosen to accompany their partners to this one. I wonder why that was.

I had encountered David Beckham once before this, but only fleetingly. That was at the *Sun* Military Awards, a couple of years previously. At some point during that evening, a figure immediately recognisable to me had appeared out of nowhere at my table and politely and modestly asked if he and his son could have a quick photograph with me, because they were such fans of *Only Fools*. To which, obviously, I had replied, 'Listen, mate – can't you see I'm trying to eat my dinner here?'

OK, I hadn't said that. For one thing, I think dinner was finished. For another, I was more than a little flattered, if I can be perfectly honest about it, and had willingly and even excitedly posed for the photograph, and then felt warmly touched by the incident for the rest of the night. It was certainly something to impress my daughter with and, Lord knows, one clings to those as time goes by.

Now here was Mr Beckham again, accompanied by his PA, walking into the backroom where I was sitting in a chair having make-up done. We shook hands, him smiling with that rather wonderful combination of warmth and shyness that he has. He was thirty-eight at the time – a little bit of a charmer, you would have to say, and a man of considerable sex appeal. Has anyone else noticed that about him? Somebody should get on to it. Good-looking boy like that – I reckon there's a rich seam of commercial opportunities to be tapped into there, with the right people in place. Anyway, it occurred to me that his physical allure would have been there even if you had stripped away the extra layer of pulsing magnetism that was placed around him by global fame. Watching this man advance perfectly humbly across a room and noting how women wilted to either side of him like corn in a hot wind, I found myself reflecting on how things had been for me in that area, back in the day.

And what I found myself concluding was that things had been very different. Frankly, as a callow but willing youth on the north London dance-hall scene, and as an international man of jet-set pleasure in waiting, I had to work my socks off to attract the attentions of the desired sex, as a direct consequence, I suppose, of being both short and not especially shaped like David Beckham. The idea that female attention could have been yours by some kind of automatic physical right, upon mere entry into a room, without you putting in a serious shift of chatting, smarming, joking, larking, fooling, pranking, wheedling, begging, etc., would have been mind-blowing to me. Fame changes the game, it's true, in terms of the impact you have on a room, but I'm not sure Becks would have known such struggles, even had celebrity never launched him into the stratosphere.

We chatted for a while. He hadn't been blowing smoke, back at that Military Awards do, when he said he was a fan of *Only Fools*. He obviously really loved it. He was an east London boy, of course, so there was plenty about the show which chimed with him. He had watched it with his parents, and now he watched it with his kids. Getting to appear in a scene from it was apparently the fulfilment of a long-standing dream. It was extremely sweet, in the circumstances, how nervous he was. He told us that he hadn't got a lot of sleep the night before because he had been so worried about getting his part right. He had taken his lines to bed with him in order to keep running over them, and had eventually fallen asleep with the script on top of him. I could sense the women in the room thinking, 'Lucky script.'

I don't know about a lucky script, but it was certainly a pretty good one, and faithful enough to the show. The skit opens with Del trying to flog a load of David Beckham underpants at the market, with Rodney modelling the garment, absurdly, over his trousers, and cursing Del, as ever, for making him do the donkey work and look ridiculous. Scepticism greets the news that this batch of underwear has been individually signed across the backside by Golden Balls himself, and, indeed, as Rodney fumingly turns to show the crowd his rear view, the autograph in pen does look like any old piece of scribble. However, Del does his best to reassure any potential buyers that he has a personal connection with Becks which has enabled him to land these prized garments. 'It was me what arranged a bouncy castle for his son Brookside's birthday party,' Del explains. This manifestly bogus claim couldn't cause the crowd to disperse any faster had it been a water cannon, and they remain unimpressed even by Del's desperate announcement to their retreating backs of a sudden price crash ('£4.50 each or two for £9'). Del and Rodney thereafter adjourn to the cafe to have a cup of tea and a rethink.

What followed was the main scene – Del and Rodney together at the table in the cafe, discussing the problems of selling Beckham-branded underwear, with the camera only eventually drawing out to disclose to the pair that they're sitting next to the man himself. Beckham had some dialogue to produce in a very short space of time and it goes without saying that he was a long way outside his comfort zone. He would get halfway through a line and then dry and he would be covered in embarrassment and full of apologies – as if Nick and I cared. That stuff is par for the course and happens to the best of us. You can have a script entirely nailed – DLP, or 'dead line perfect' as we say in the trade. But then you're in the studio, the director shouts 'Action!' and the camera rolls and the room falls horribly silent in anticipation, and the pressure causes a kangaroo to be let loose in the upper paddock of your mind. Been there, done that, a thousand times.

Anyway, the specific effect of this pressure on Becks was that he got quieter and quieter – and he hadn't started out all that loud to begin with. After a couple of botched takes, he was practically whispering. Me and Nick told him not to worry about it. It was just a lump of tape, after all. We could do it line by line, if necessary – patch it together that way. I also told him a couple of stories about times when I had completely dried, and I confessed to him that sometimes, if I was struggling, I would have a line written for me on a board and held up to the side of the camera. Those tales seemed to put him at his ease and he relaxed into it. The volume returned to his voice and he got it done – and in some style, I would say.

There's some good stuff in that sketch, not least the line

of Rodney's, 'Asking Trigger for help is like asking Ozzy Osbourne to look after your bats.' Then there's the nice exchange where Becks, having established that Rodney has a GCE in art, asks him who his favourite artist is. 'I'd probably have to say Matisse,' says Rodney. 'Because I don't think anyone could get near the way he could convey intensity using pure colour, you know? I mean, Matisse did for colour what Picasso did for form. How about you?' To which Beckham replies, 'I love Tony Hart. That Morph cracks me up.'

Becks then gives Rodders some modelling tips, instructing him to 'glide' and 'oscillate'. That leads us back out into the marketplace, where, thus encouraged, Del and Rodney have another go at selling the pants, while Becks watches on from a distance. And this was where we did the sideways fall.

Apparently it was what Becks was bursting, above all, to do: to recreate the drop through the bar flap from the 'Yuppy Love' episode. He said he thought it was about the funniest thing he had ever seen. He's not alone in feeling that way, clearly. Time and again, the bar-flap fall features in polls and lists of the great sitcom moments. Asked to nominate one scene from a British television comedy that made them laugh above all others, a large number of people will tend to plump unswervingly for that time when Del leaned on the bar next to Trigger, discussing what attracts women to men, then stood upright to acknowledge the seeming attentions of a girl on the other side of the room, only for a passing member of the bar staff to lift the flap behind him so that Del, returning to his position, drops through the gap like a felled tree. The definitive *Only Fools and Horses* comedy moment? You would probably have to put it in the top three, along with the dropped chandelier and the Batman and Robin sequence, and if, come the final reckoning before the great panel of comedy judges in the sky, my stand-out contribution to the field of light entertainment should turn out to be this solitary pratfall, then so be it, because I'm quietly rather fond of it too.

Let my further bequest be a willingness to pass on the secrets of that fall to any members of a future generation wishing to duplicate it. Especially if they're as determined to get it absolutely right as David Beckham was. I had to give him top marks for that – he didn't want this to be a half-hearted fall. He wanted the full effect and he was prepared to do whatever it took to achieve it.

Top tip number one: it's all about the eyeline. This much I was able to explain to him. The direction in which you're looking at the start of the fall should be the direction in which you continue to look while falling. Alas, this is going to involve you in an almighty scrap with your natural instincts, which are going to be screaming at you to turn your eyes in the direction of the fall, for the very good reason that bodies are generally pretty keen to find out where they're going, especially when they're falling over. If your eyes go, your head goes with them, your arm comes out and your knee turns reflexively to break the fall – and all of that happens in a split second, in accordance with the human being's prime desire to protect his or her head.

Now, I'm not saying that a fall conducted in accordance with natural human instincts isn't funny. Del Boy could have started to drop through that gap where the bar flap used to be, and he could have turned and put his arms out to save himself, and it would still have got a laugh. Indeed, when John wrote the scene, he suggested that Del should begin to fall through the flap but catch himself and hold himself up. It was more like a stumble than a fall in John's original vision for it. That, too, would have been funny.

But what I *am* saying (nay, insisting) is that a fall conducted in accordance with natural human instincts, though funny, isn't anywhere near as funny as a fall conducted without them. My suggestion to John was that Del should go down like a plank of wood because . . . well, because that's just funnier. And the reason I knew it was funnier was because I had spent a large portion of my earlier life as an actor in the theatre putting this particular theory on falling over to the test.

I refer here to my distinguished years, during the sixties and seventies, as a theatrical performer in the genre known as farce. You will perhaps, dear reader, have witnessed a theatrical farce at some point in your life, or at least be familiar with the basic features of the genre. These could be said to include leading male characters whom the plot will eventually separate from their trousers, leading female characters whom the plot will eventually separate from several layers of their outer clothing, constant and often complex comings and goings through manifold doors, unexpected visits, frequently from wives or, if not, a vicar, or sometimes both, and a sequence in which at least one character ends up hiding in a wardrobe (trousers optional).

However, amid all of this, the essential item on the set of any farce is a sofa, commonly placed at the very centre of the stage. Indeed, one of the best ways in which to ascertain whether the play you are watching is a farce or not is to ask yourself, 'Does it have a sofa in it?' Actual trades description statutes, I'm sure, insist that a play cannot be labelled as a farce unless a sofa is on the stage for at least 80 per cent of its duration, and should you ever attend a play purporting to be a farce and discover, upon the lifting of the curtain, that there is no sofa present, you should depart the theatre immediately and commence legal proceedings against the producers on the grounds of false pretences.

*Darling Mr London*, *A Bedfull of Foreigners*, *Chase Me*, *Comrade*, *Honeymoon Bedlam*, *Look*, *No Hans* . . . reader, I appeared in them all and am ready to attest that a sofa was the key item of furniture and the centre of the principle action in almost every case. Sometimes it was a particularly ingenious sofa. In *Darling Mr London*, for example, it was a sofa bed that was designed to return from its expanded bed state to its compressed sofa state while I was still in it – indeed, when I had just dived on top of it in search of a hiding place. From the auditorium the sofa appeared to have swallowed me – as indeed, with my participation in unlocking certain bolts and throwing certain parts of the structure back over myself, it had.

Mostly, though, you would find yourself working with a standard, non-collapsing sofa and, as such, in the interests of spicing things up a little bit, you developed a few tricks or bits of incidental business (not strictly speaking scripted) which brought the sofa into play. For instance, during a conversation you might walk idly round to the side of the sofa and then, without looking at it, you might stretch out your hand and lean to one side to support yourself meditatively on one corner of it. Whereupon it was readily apparent that if your hand slightly missed the sofa and had to clutch at it in order to hold you up, you would earn a laugh from the audience. What was even more apparent, however, was that if, during that seemingly innocent gesture, your hand missed the sofa altogether, causing you to fall sideways behind it and thus disappear completely from view . . . well, the laughter you earned from the audience was exponentially greater. Furthermore, if, during that fall, you continued to hold the gaze of the person with whom you were supposed to be having the conversation, then the laughter increased in volume yet again. This much I had established through long and dedicated practice and by steady honing in front of live audiences, all over the country, night after night. As absurd as it may seem, when John Sullivan put the script for the pub scene with Trigger in front of me, I had in effect been preparing for that moment for about twenty years.

All of this I gladly imparted to David Beckham. Keep looking where you were looking and hold the body stiff. Only break the fall right at the last minute, by which time you will be out of shot. Here's the good news: you've got a crash mat to fall onto. Knowing that you at least have a soft landing ahead of you helps the mental process considerably. Beckham is an athlete, of course, so I was working with a good student. He picked it up really fast – and it worked.

While he was looking on at Del and Rodney from across the market, we had him leaning against a metal trolley. Then he crouches down to sign an autograph on a football for a little boy and the trolley gets pushed away, so when he stands up again and goes casually to resume his position, there is nothing there for him to lean against. It was very nicely set up, I thought, with the words that Beckham whispers to the little boy about keeping hush and not drawing everybody's attention to him forming a neat parallel with Del's line to Trigger in the original: 'Play it nice and cool, son – nice and cool, you know what I mean?'

Unfortunately there was no time after all this for Becks to teach me how to bend a free kick. Maybe some time in the future. But the finished item, when it was broadcast, got

9.5 million viewers, the peak viewing figure for the night. Not too shabby, Dave. Not too shabby, my son.

However, I'm not saying I took this personally, but the year following these efforts, for the 2015 Comic Relief fund-raising effort, they used a Del Boy statue. They stood a life-size model of Del outside Whitemead House in Bristol, whose exterior had so selflessly played the part of Mandela House in the series, and encouraged people to go and put money in it. It was quite a technologically fancy statue, it has to be said. You could tap a contactless credit card on one of its pockets and automatically donate a quid or two. Even so. Replaced by a statue! I ask you. Is there any greater ignominy for an actor – least of all for the one who taught David Beckham to fall over?

# CHAPTER SEVENTEEN

## *Back on the shop floor*

In the early 1980s, when I had been appearing as Granville opposite Ronnie Barker's grumpy corner-shop owner Arkwright, in the sitcom *Open All Hours*, Ronnie sent me a clipping from a newspaper's television listings, stuck to a white card. The clipping read:

7.30 *Open All Hours*. Granville goes all out to impress a local beauty and improve his lowly status. Comedy starring David Jason (R).

Underneath, the actual star of the show had written, 'Your agent is getting above himself. Ronnie B.' A slip of the subeditor's keyboard, I assure you. Back then, the notion of *Open All Hours* without Ronnie Barker, my hero and mentor, firmly in charge of it would have seemed implausible to me.

Time will always surprise you, though. Some thirty years later, in 2013, I was invited to have lunch in London with Mark Freeland, who was then the BBC's Controller of

Comedy Production and who wanted to talk to me about the possibility of getting me back on the BBC in some way. Again, I'm aware that it's possible to sound rather casual, or even blasé, about these summonses to the meal table by the great and good to break bread and listen to enquiries about my general availability. But as someone who spent so many years grabbing any work that came within the vicinity of his outstretched fingertips in order to keep his career ticking over, I can't overstress how remarkable and unlikely this position of privilege still feels to me. Quite apart from anything else, there's free food on offer: I mean, what's not to like?

Anyway, in the course of my conversation with Mr Freeland, I mentioned something that I had found myself thinking about a lot in recent years: whatever happened to Granville? Freeland asked me what I meant. I said, 'Well, you know – what became of him? He was stuck in that corner shop, working for his greedy old uncle, wearing that terrible tank top, longing to break out of his little dead-end world, but never making it . . . Did he escape? Did he find love? Or is he still there?'

'Who was the writer on *Open All Hours*?' Freeland asked. I said, 'Roy Clarke.'

Freeland said, 'Is he still with us?' Which was a terrible question to hear, of course. But what can you do? This is where we are.

I said, 'He was with us the last time I looked.' (Roy was

eighty-three at this point, and in robust good health, where he blessedly remains. I should point out that, relative to Roy, your author is a complete and utter spring chicken – a full decade younger than him.)

I could see Freeland was intrigued by this idea regarding Granville and he promised to go away and have some further conversations about it. Sure enough, he got back to me a while later and, without committing firmly to anything, suggested that it might be a good idea if I got together with Roy Clarke and took the notion a bit further. So I rang Roy and, because it's simply not done in the business to talk about these things with your stomach empty (it's considered rude, in fact), we arranged a lunch meeting in L'Etoile on Charlotte Street.

I was in the restaurant when Roy arrived. I hadn't seen him to talk to properly for about thirty years, but when he walked in the room (he had come down on the train from his home in Yorkshire), it was as though no time whatsoever had passed in the interim. He was the same tall, surprisingly quiet but extremely funny man (the author, most famously, of *Last of the Summer Wine*) that I had first encountered working with Ronnie B in the seventies. He even had the same satchel.

He was also, it emerged, quietly excited about the thought of revisiting Granville. As we talked over lunch, this rather lovely idea emerged that Granville had sort of become Arkwright, by a process of osmosis. To an extent,

Arkwright – his attitude, his manner, his way of life, and above all his penny-pinching shopkeeper's meanness – would have been imprinted on Granville over the years, simply by their proximity to one another and by Arkwright's dominance over him. Moreover, when he died, Arkwright might perfectly plausibly have left Granville the shop in his will – a possibility that Arkwright had alluded to frequently in the original series, where it always tended to sound more like a threat than anything else – but only on the condition that Granville kept the place open and continued to run it. In that way, Arkwright would reach out to trap Granville even from beyond the grave. There would be no reason why Nurse Gladys Emmanuel, the object of Arkwright's fruitless lust all those years ago, couldn't still be living in the house opposite the shop, assuming that Lynda Baron was up for playing the part; and no reason why Mavis and Mrs Featherstone, the reliably riotous shop customers, shouldn't still live in the vicinity either, if the same could be said for Maggie Ollerenshaw and Stephanie Cole. Beyond that would lie the opportunity to bring in a range of new cus-tomers and passers-by, capitalising on the excellence of the corner shop as a sitcom setting, where fresh life is only ever a clang of the opening door away.

But what about Arkwright's shop itself? We talked a lot about that, during our lunch. Had it changed at all? Had it modernised? Might it have become more like a mini-supermarket in a service station? These thoughts were temptingly comical, but we kept coming back to the fun that was inherent in the original set-up – this tiny corner shop, years out of date, preserved in aspic and yet somehow clinging on. It's not like you don't see them any more. Around this time, I found myself driving home through Kilburn in north London late one night and noticing these still-lit, seemingly never-closing shops, with their thrusts out onto the pavement, their soot-coloured fruit and dirty peaches offered up to the street, their windows pasted with flyers and handwritten cards – little London Arkwrights, still out there. It confirmed for me that we should definitely keep the shop as it was.

*Still Open All Hours* was pretty much born out of those two lunches. The plan was to bring the show back once, for a Christmas special in 2013, but I think we all knew that, if it played strongly enough and hit home with people, there might be more in it. Gareth Edwards was hired to produce the programme, and Dewi Humphreys, who had worked on *The Vicar of Dibley* and on John Sullivan's *Only Fools* prequel, *Rock & Chips*, was appointed to direct it, and almost before I knew it, I was heading, along with Lynda, Maggie and Stephanie, back to Balby, near Doncaster in South Yorkshire where, from the mid-1970s onwards, we had shot the show's exteriors. The original Arkwright's was actually a hairdresser's named Beautique (do you see what they did there?) in a street called Lister Avenue which Syd Lotterby, the producer of the original *Open All Hours*, had scouted.

Syd tells a story about how, having secured permission from the owners of Beautique to borrow their salon for a while, he then nipped across the road to see if he could nail down a house to use for Nurse Gladys Emmanuel's dwelling place which needed to be opposite. Syd was wearing a rather spivvy sheepskin coat which he was particularly partial to at the time, and he'd knocked and rung at about five doors along that terraced row before somebody finally answered. Naturally, Syd asked where everybody else was. The bloke pointed out that, dressed like that, they all thought he was the rent collector.

It seemed too much to hope that the shop and the street would still be there for us to use again. But they were, almost exactly as we had left them. The running of Beautique had passed from mother to daughter and once more they agreed to put their business on hold and let the BBC's set designers convert their premises into a corner shop. Driving from the production base up to Lister Avenue that first morning, in the autumn of 2013, and getting out of the car and standing on that street again and being welcomed back so warmly by the local residents, some of whom had been children the first time and now brought their own children . . . well, it was just the most extraordinary experience. It was like I had been shot backwards in a time machine, and it made me feel joyful and sad and also bewildered, all at once, because so much time had gone, and I didn't quite know where, and because nothing had really changed and yet so much clearly had. Trying to process all of that was really pretty difficult, I have to say. There was a line of Arkwright's from the very first episode of the first series which was running around in my head and which seemed now to carry so much extra weight. That was the story in which Arkwright was trying to get rid of a batch of tins without labels, holding them up to his ear at one point and shaking them to try and determine their contents ('M-Mulligatawny and Leek . . . Beefy Chunks in Gravy . . .'). It was also the episode in which he said: 'Listen, Granville, just remember that, as my nephew, all of these old tins will be yours, you know, when I'm gone.'

Now I was back on that same street, in that same space, and Ronnie *was* gone, but so much was unaltered and the ghosts and echoes of those days were everywhere. My mind was ceaselessly travelling back. I was pulling on a brown shopkeeper's coat, like Ronnie wore, and recalling a picture Ronnie had of his father in a coat exactly like that, which must, in some way, have been an inspiration for Arkwright. I was remembering shooting the breeze in the cast hotel in Balby with Ronnie and Lynda and Syd Lotterby and Syd's trusty assistant, Judy. I was remembering Ronnie getting recognised a lot, because he was a giant TV star at that time. But I was remembering how much Ronnie defied and redrew my expectation of people who were giant TV stars – that they had to be somehow far above us and unreadable, when, like him, they could just be so rooted and thoroughly pleasant. I was remembering the time an *Open All Hours* shoot coincided with my birthday and Ronnie – resisting the urge to ignore the occasion all day, as I did with Nick Lyndhurst that time – took the whole lot of us out to a Chinese restaurant in Doncaster and presented me with a model of Granville's famous shop delivery bike. I was remembering how much I learned about rhythm and timing from my interactions with Ronnie on this show and the extent to which it had stood in, belatedly, for a formal dramatic education for me. I was remembering how I chafed sometimes at the role of Granville because I was desperate to star in something and I was already in my forties and nothing seemed to be in sight, and how Ronnie said to me, 'Don't worry – it will happen for you eventually.' I was remembering how great I used to feel when Ronnie told people that *Open All Hours* was his favourite of the sitcoms he worked on, even more than *Porridge*, because of the fun he'd had with me in the making of it. I was remembering that emblematic moment for me when Ronnie and I had invented some bit of business which had caused the pair of us to crack up completely, and then Ronnie had looked at me and said, 'We're lucky, aren't we? We're getting paid to make ourselves laugh.' Lucky indeed. Beyond lucky.

For the new show, we hung a framed photo of Ronnie as Arkwright in the backroom of the shop for Granville to commune with at various points in the episode, and I found it a difficult thing, being confronted so clearly by his presence and, at the same time, his absence. Even harder, though, was taking on the role of the show's traditional closing monologue, with Granville out there in the street as Arkwright used to be, putting things away at closing time, in the dying light, recapping the events of the day in a voice-over that always seemed to me to have just a tiny flavour of a bedtime prayer about it. Too much symbolism there for me.

Sometimes Granville would mimic Arkwright. 'I was t-t-t-trained by the m-m-m-master,' he would say, as he operated the famously vicious till (worked by an invisible assistant, in fact, yanking hard on a piece of string to bring the tray clattering shut at the appointed moment). I was indeed trained by the master. Roy Clarke hadn't written Arkwright with a stammer, by the way. That was Ronnie's idea, and some people thought he shouldn't have acted on it – that he was making comedy from affliction. Personally, when Ronnie played Arkwright, I could hear no mockery in it. Mockery wasn't Ronnie's thing in any case; he was a far warmer comic than that, and I know for a fact that there were people with stammers who told Ronnie that they felt he was representing them in some way, standing with them rather than against them. Stammering just seemed to intrigue him, like a million other aspects of life. After Ronnie died in 2005, Joy, his wife, who had been going through his things, sent me a clipping she had found that Ronnie had obviously seen in a magazine and decided he needed to keep. It was an advert for 'Fur-Felt Hats'. Ronnie had written in the margin, 'Stammering advert.'

Clearly the thing to do, up there in Doncaster, was to redeem the melancholy and make a show that Ronnie would have approved of. It was certainly fun to go back and be Granville again – or rather to be Granville as he might have become. To see Lynda, Maggie and Stephanie recapture and adapt their old roles so adroitly was an inspiration, too. We were getting the band together again, but there was no pressure on us to force the clock back and be the people we used to be; we could unashamedly and even proudly be the age that we all were and there was something very liberating about that. Roy Clarke had also created a new shop boy, Leroy, played with great ease and natural charm by James Baxter, who had done a couple of years before this on *Emmerdale* but for whom this was a first big comedy role. So, in a sense, the baton had been handed on and if I could end up being even a fraction of the influence on James that Ronnie B was on me, then I would feel I had contributed something.

It struck me on the set one day, when I was fixing a 'Farm Fresh Eggs' sticker to a box of eggs that were clean out of the factory: Granville is a kind of Yorkshire Del Boy – a chancer, being wildly inventive to try and sell something. 'Farm Fresh Eggs' are basically 'Peckham Spring Water' in another form. Certainly, just as the Trotters' junk-filled flat was fertile ground for incidental bits of comic business, so the shop yields opportunities aplenty to try and find the extra laugh. One day, for instance, I was doing a scene with James by the sweet rack and it suddenly occurred to me, in the middle of our dialogue, to take a packet down, open it up, pop a sweet in my mouth, reseal the packet and replace the sweets on the rack. It just seemed like a very Granville-via-Arkwright thing to do. I also knew it would get a laugh from the studio audience, which it duly did. Unfortunately, it also got one from James, who corpsed, which in turn set me off, so we had to go again. Still, the routine with the sweets stayed in.

For all that we might have nurtured some fond hopes for its future, I don't think any of us was expecting *Still Open All Hours* to take off the way that it did. I certainly understood that it was an old-fashioned piece in so many ways – muted, melancholy, given to the pleasures of innuendo, the kind of sitcom that doesn't really get made any more. Yet the first inkling that we were involved in something people wanted to see was the fact that there were 360 seats available for the studio shoot of the initial Christmas special, which took place at the BBC unit in Manchester, and there were 28,000 applications for them. Maybe we should have done it in a football stadium. When that show went out on Boxing Day, it was watched by 12.23 million, which was the biggest audience for any programme on any channel that Christmas season, and the largest audience for a comedy show on British television since 2007. A month

281

later, to nobody's particular surprise, the BBC commissioned a six-episode series, and then two more after that. Each of those series has generated audiences around the seven or eight million mark, by which I am apt sometimes to feel a little disappointed, as the veteran of the *Only Fools* 20-million-plus days, but which cannot be deemed in any way shabby at this particular point in the twenty-first century. So, to my delight, it turns out that there still is an audience for this kind of television. And on it goes. At the time of writing, in the summer of 2017, I am getting ready to shoot *Still Open All Hours* series four. I never suspected the boy Granville would come back to serve me so royally all this time later, though I suppose Arkwright, in his own curmudgeonly way, was always suggesting it would be thus.

Incidentally, I should mention that when we wrapped the 2016 series, the cast and crew gathered, as ever, for a few farewell drinks and, in a moving ceremony, I was called forward to be presented with a special Golden Sausage award for my unstinting work in supplying innuendo throughout the making of the series. Well, you know what Groucho Marx used to say: love flies out the door when money comes innuendo. The trophy was, as described, a golden banger, mounted, as it were, on a plinth by those fine craftsmen in the BBC props workshop, who really do know how to make a sausage stiff, and, as I made clear in my necessarily moved and bashful acceptance speech, I shall treasure it always. 'It will remind me,' I said, staunching a tear in the corner of my eye, 'of days gone by.'

And it will. Yet, at the same time, it's a pointer to the future. Another series awaits and another occasion dawns for competitive innuendo. Do I have another Golden Sausage in me? I can't wait to find out.

# CHAPTER EIGHTEEN

## *And the award goes to . . .*

Never mind the Golden Sausage. In late March 2017, I was asked to attend the National Film Awards in London with Nick Lyndhurst, so that the pair of us could be honoured with a Lifetime Achievement Award by the UK National Film Academy in recognition of our work together in *Only Fools and Horses* – our 'contribution to drama' as the Academy's citation put it.

Proof once more: it's the show that never goes away. At that point, getting on for thirty-six years had passed since the first episode of *Only Fools* was screened; twenty-six years had passed since the filming of the last series proper; and getting on for fourteen years had passed since the final *Only Fools* Christmas special had gone out. Yet still people want to return to the show, to remember it, to celebrate it, to vote for it in polls designed to rank the best British comedies of all time, to hand it awards.

What a piece of luck to land up at the centre of a

television programme which really came across to people, in the way that *Only Fools* clearly did – and then kept coming across to them, long after it had finished. What fortune to have been involved in something that keeps finding new audiences, across generations. What a thing to have been part of a show that seems to have lodged itself so firmly in the pages of television's short but colourful history book – or, if you prefer, in the pages of television's short but historical colouring book. I was forty-one years of age when I first came across Derek Trotter. Now here I was, more than a third of a century later, at seventy-seven, and he was still showing no signs of letting me go.

Still, having read this far, you will be well aware what my first question should have been, when the invitation to this event was initially relayed to me. 'Is the ceremony taking place in Afghanistan, or in any other, similar war zone where combat gear will be obligatory and where rebel torpedoes are even a remote possibility?' But it only goes to show how quickly the toughest lessons are often forgotten. Or perhaps it shows how rapidly the spirit of human optimism and the desire to greet fresh challenges rise to conquer even the most intimidating memories of the past. You decide. Either way, as it happened, 'Is the ceremony taking place in Afghanistan, or in any other, similar war zone where combat gear will be obligatory and where rebel torpedoes are even a remote possibility?' was only my second question. (To which the answer, incidentally, was, 'No, it's at the Porchester Hall in London.'

I must say, I couldn't quite picture that venue at this point, but I knew enough about it to realise that it was nowhere near Camp Bastion, so all clear on that front. Stand down the Hercules.)

In fact, in all seriousness, my first question on this occasion was, 'Is Nick doing it?' I hadn't seen Nick for a couple of years – not since we'd been hanging out with David Beckham that day back in 2014, doing the *Only Fools* sketch for Sport Relief. Would Nick be likely to say yes to receiving this Lifetime Achievement Award? I very much doubted it. I was sure that he would have felt flattered to be asked, as I was. But I know that Nick shares with me a certain amount of reluctance to delve back into the *Only Fools* days. It's not that we aren't fiercely proud of what we did on that show. It's not that a giant trove of happy memories isn't to be found back there. It's not like we wouldn't defend the work, or rush to the work's assistance if it was ever in trouble and needed our help.

However, for both of us, I know, to revisit that work these days is to open ourselves up to a fair old amount of melancholy, in among the warm recollections. How could it not be so, when so many members of the tight family that we formed when we made those programmes are no longer with us? As well as John Sullivan, the genius who wrote the show and who was the greatest writer I ever knew, who died in 2011, and the properly clever Roger Lloyd Pack, who died in 2014, dear old Buster Merryfield – our

287

Uncle Albert – died in 1999. Kenneth MacDonald, that sweet, kind man, who was Mike, the landlord of the Nag's Head, died of a heart attack while on holiday with his family in America in 2001, at the unfairly premature age of fifty. Plus, of course, we lost the magnificent Lennard Pearce, who played Grandad, merely twenty-three episodes into the show. People talk about the so-called 'curse of *Dad's Army*' – which is to say the seemingly unusually heightened mortality rate among the cast of that great show – but surely the less noticed 'curse of *Only Fools*' runs it a close second. Nick actually once said to me: 'The only time we see each other these days is when another one drops off the perch.'

So, a reluctance to rake over the old coals might dissuade Nick from taking the National Film Academy up on their offer. It was certainly in my mind to decline the invitation on those grounds. Then you had to factor in the nature of the award on offer. Again, without wanting to sound ungrateful, your Lifetime Achievement Award has a reputation as a bit of a gold watch. I don't mean the kind of gold watch the Trotters might have sold; I mean a proper one that actually works – but nevertheless a gold watch offered after a whip-round by the workforce upon your retirement, a fond send-off as you head away on horseback into the sunset, or, more likely, back home on the bus to tend the garden. It might not be meant that way, but you can't help suspecting that it is. Thanks for everything you did and goodnight.

Enjoy the restful years ahead – because you've deserved them, no, really, you have. Oh, and please switch the lights off on your way out. Nobody, after all, ever refers to them as a Lifetime So Far Achievement Award. There's an air of finality lingering over the concept, and even as you stood there on the night, proudly holding the trophy, you would be bound to wonder at some level: is this really, metaphorically speaking, some vouchers towards a lawnmower?

Yet, at the same time, I'm not sure that actors really *do* retirement – or not of their own volition and not while their faculties are by and large intact. They certainly don't like to think about retirement too much. I may be wrong, but I don't think there's an actor alive who, despite any amount of evidence they've been shown to the contrary, doesn't think that there will be another part, eventually, somewhere round the corner. That's certainly the frame of mind that I seem to have about it – and so far, in terms of more or less retaining my faculties, and in terms of there being another part, I've been lucky enough to be right. [*Author at this point reaches forward to touch all available wooden surfaces.*] But my point is, for actors, things that raise the subject of retirement are generally to be tiptoed away from.

All in all, and considering everything, I wasn't banking on Nick saying yes to being at the National Film Awards 2017. And, call me a coward, but if Nick wasn't going, then I wasn't going either. Safety in numbers, and all that.

Here's the thing, though: the invitation did seem rather

impressive. To be honest, the National Film Awards weren't something I had been aware of until this point. Organised by the UK National Film Academy, and apparently voted for by the public via the Academy's website, these prizes were only in their third year, so they were, relatively speaking, in the context of the more seasoned industry gong ceremonies, brand new. Clearly they weren't to be confused with the National Television Awards which I did know about and, indeed, had attended around half a dozen times, as both a recipient and a hander-out. Clearly, also, they were to be confused even less with the British Academy of Film and Television Awards, or BAFTAs, which are the big boys in our line of work. (Reader, as I believe I have already mentioned, I have a couple of those on the mantelpiece, as well. Four of them, in fact. I know this because I just went round my office here at home and did a bit of totting up, and yes, there's four BAFTAs in total. Incidentally, I also, on the way round, counted two Royal Television Society awards. Which is nice. Oh, and eight National Television awards, too. Plus, of course, the three British Comedy awards. And then, if my calculations don't deceive me, there were three Sony TRIC awards. Not to mention two *Radio Times* awards, five *TV Times* awards and two *TV Quick* awards. Oh, and I suppose we should include the OBE. Yeah, and the knighthood. Not that one should dwell on these things, of course. Far better not to mention it. Wouldn't want to be thought of as the sort of person who, in an idle moment, went round the room counting up his awards and making a list of them. Not for a minute. Really not my style. But just completing the calculations here ... that's, what, twenty-nine pieces of silverware in total? Thirty-one, of course, if you lob in the OBE and the knighthood. Not that I'm counting. Really, I'm not.)

However, there was one thing about these National Film Awards – something that couldn't be denied – which, OK, definitely tweaked my interest: they had the word 'film' in them.

Now, I've got to admit – and I speak here as someone for whom Hollywood, for reasons that remain utterly unfathomable to me, still hasn't come a-calling – that as I stared at this invitation, there was a certain compelling aura hanging about that word 'film', especially when seen in tandem with that word 'national', and not least when annexed to those words 'awards ceremony'. Furthermore, consider, if you will, the high-class calibre of the people who, according to the publicity literature accompanying the invitation to the National Film Awards, would be joining us in the Porchester Hall (wherever that was) on this night of a thousand stars, this £200-a-seat (nominees dine free, though) gala dinner. Julie Andrews! Joan Collins! Ewan McGregor! Hugh Grant! Catherine Zeta-Jones, my old accomplice from *The Darling Buds of May*! I mean, say what you like, but that's not the cast of *Geordie Shore* is it? No disrespect to the cast of *Geordie Shore*.

Moreover, to climb on a stage, and stand in front of these genuine, bona fide legends of British film and receive an honour . . . well, it didn't sound like the kind of thing at which a humble TV actor should necessarily be turning up his nose, irrespective of whether or not he had previously heard of the National Film Awards or the Porchester Hall. Strictly speaking, Nick's and my work on *Only Fools* wasn't a film industry achievement. It was a television industry achievement. That, in itself, was a bit puzzling. But if the film industry was reaching out to embrace us and pull us close, who were we to spurn its welcoming bosom?

Something akin to this train of thought may also have passed through the mind of my former co-star. Maybe Nick, too, saw the word 'film' and thought, 'Hmm, that sounds a cut above.' At any rate, the feelers were put out, my people spoke to his people, and the word came back: Nick, it turned out, was in. Therefore, the maths was simple: so was I.

But first, picture if you will the growing anticipation in the Jason household as the month of March 2017 wears on and this night of nights approaches. Picture your author's mounting excitement as he dusts off his dinner jacket, selects his starchiest shirt, de-fluffs his bow tie and, with eyes of childlike wonder, gazes dreamily into the middle distance while his imagination tremblingly contemplates the evening of Cinderella-like joy that awaits him among the perfumed glitterati of British entertainment.

Actually, can I be honest? Within a couple of days of

saying yes, the prospect had started to lose its lustre. Does that sound churlish? Apologies if it does, but I can't deny it. Nothing to do with the National Film Awards per se, I should swiftly add. It's the same every time: I sign up for these things and then almost immediately regret it. The initially magnetic attractions (an award! big stars in the room! a chance to see Nick! free dinner!) lose their charge and I instead begin to get agitated and somewhat rueful. The thought of what lies ahead starts to haunt me and prey on my mind. I cast my thoughts forward to the way it's likely to play out: the exposure, the attention, the high possibility of some kind of red-carpet scenario in which I am going to have to stand in front of a wall of press photographers, grinning like a berk . . . in short, the whole 'celebrity' thing.

I know there are people who love this aspect of the business and find it exciting and pleasurable and carry it off with aplomb – and Lord knows, I wish I was one of them. I also know there are people for whom this sort of thing is the dream – people for whom standing in front of a battery of Fleet Street's finest snappers, all of them shouting 'Over here! Oi! This way!' represents the promised land. And for those people, the way I feel about it must seem extremely odd.

The fact is, though, I find it all a bit daunting. It's the palaver *around* these events. Maybe if you could just go there one night, on the quiet, and somebody could slip you the award, in a brief but moving private ceremony, and you

293

could shake hands and go home again with the profound satisfaction of a job well done – maybe then I'd be more comfortable with it. But it's the crowds of people, the shouting, the jostle, the camera flashes, the sense of being on show. It's not really what I signed up for. I find it embarrassing. It puts me way outside my comfort zone and, even after all these years, I don't really know how to handle it.

Psychiatrists: help yourselves. But whether you, dear reader, are a qualified mental health professional or not, you're probably saying: 'Hang on a minute. How can the thought of a few moments of attention give someone like you, in particular, an attack of the jitters? You're an actor: you've spent your entire working life *seeking* attention.'

And you're absolutely correct, of course. As an actor, I have indeed sought attention for a living. But the difference is (if I could just try to work this through a bit here), I am acting when I get it. I have make-up on, I am wearing a costume, I am working from a script. I am playing characters. I'm not just standing there being myself. Standing there being myself is what I seem to have the problem with. Outside of a role, removed from the protection of the make-up, the costume, the script, attention just makes me feel awkward and exposed. Embarrassed. Possibly even a little bit fraudulent. 'It's not me you're interested in,' I feel like saying. 'I'm not why you're here. It's those other people – the characters. And I'm not them. Not really.'

Anyway, however we analyse it, that's where I found

myself as the pages of life's deluxe desktop diary turned inexorably to the appointed date of the National Film Awards of 2017. It's bizarre, really. If you had told a version of my younger self – perhaps the teenage one that was lying on the freezing concrete floor of Popes Garage in Finchley, repairing cars while a wind direct from Lapland whipped through the foot-tall gap under the doors and cut a frosty path up the legs of his oily overalls – that one day he would be getting invited to receive an award at a glittery dinner among the greats of British film, he would have laughed his oily overalls off at the suggestion. If you had then told him that he would be feeling mostly glum about it . . . well, I think that version of my younger self would have assumed you were entirely bonkers and would have put his oily overalls back on and returned to fixing the car. I can't lie, though. That's where we are, and these things don't always end up being quite the way that one envisages them from the outside.

Of course, there's one reliable and widely deployed solution to the problem of nerves ahead of public attention: alcohol. Medical science came out in favour of this one a long time ago. Research has demonstrated that, if applied thickly enough, a layer of alcohol can dramatically reduce and even eliminate many of the symptoms of painfully inflamed award-ceremony-itis. Dear reader, it does me no credit but I certainly can't pretend I haven't applied alcohol to the affected area at awards ceremonies in the past.

It's the chief reason why that historic evening in 1984 on which *Only Fools* won its first ever award is so permanently not emblazoned on my memory.

The prize in question was a Sony Television and Radio Industries Club award, or TRIC, handed over on an evening of lounge-suited pomp and circumstance at the Shepherd's Bush Hilton. What an occasion that was – the unforgettable night on which our show, which was just beginning to enter its real prime, received the boost of its first official endorsement from the industry. If only I could remember the first thing about it. Actually, I can remember the *first* thing about it; it's the things that came later, after the first thing, that I struggle with – the second, third and fourth things. (Don't bother going back to the tapes, by the way: the ceremony wasn't televised, which is probably just as well.) I do recall the presence at our table that night of Nick, John Sullivan and Ray Butt, the producer and director of the first five series of *Only Fools*. I do recall a certain amount of boys-together giddiness taking hold, from the off. I do recall thinking, 'Ooh, look – a free bottle of wine,' and then, subsequently, 'Ooh, look – another free bottle of wine.' I even more or less recall scrambling onto the stage with the others to receive our award in a mood of high amazement.

And then there was almost certainly some more free wine, followed by some more free wine, after which I just about retain an image of the four of us – me, Nick, John,

Ray – departing the venue and heading off in a taxi into the London night. My memory vaguely insists that there was a somewhat ungainly kerfuffle on the pavement at that moment, as three of us contrived to stuff Ray Butt through the taxi's door, Ray being by that point afloat on a considerable sea of gin and tonics and therefore having some temporary difficulties aiming himself in the right direction. However, beyond the clunk that then announced the slamming of the taxi door, my memory has nothing whatsoever to offer, squeeze it as I may.

That was thirty years ago, though. I was a far younger man, with a far younger liver – and, clearly, a far younger man who was led astray in his innocence by a group of equally far younger reprobates (viz. Messrs Sullivan, Lyndhurst and Butt) under whose influence that far younger man had unfortunately, if only briefly, fallen. Or that's my version of it, anyway.

But the truth is, that, while by no means averse to the odd glass, I've never been all that inclined to use alcohol as a support system – and certainly not for performing, where it wouldn't work for me at all. In a similar vein, deliberately and with forethought, using alcohol as a crutch for an awards ceremony wouldn't have seemed quite right, either. The conscientious part of me couldn't help feeling that turning up at the door of the National Film Awards in a state of advanced refreshment would be somewhat unprofessional, not to mention rude, and certainly unfair to the people who had been kind enough to invite me. It would also hardly constitute conduct becoming a knight of the realm, like what I am. That's quite apart from the fact that I was intending to go to this ceremony in the company of my wife and our sixteen-year-old daughter, Sophie (her first time at this kind of event), and having to be carried out of the car and into the venue by my dearest spouse and off-spring, one at each end . . . well, it wouldn't be a particularly good look, would it?

Mind you, I can well understand why people decide to put a few lightly spiced drinks between themselves and the reality of those occasions, because there's a truly strange atmosphere at awards ceremonies. The set-up doesn't auto-matically make for a comfortable room. It follows logically that for every winner in each category there's at least three or four losers, plus all of the people who came in support of those three or four losers, so just think of the amount of dis-appointment and resentment and thwarted ambition throbbing hotly around those ballrooms at any particular moment. It's a wonder the wallpaper stays up.

Trust me here, because this is an area I know about from deep and lasting personal experience. During the *Only Fools* years, I was nominated for Best Light Entertainment Per-formance at the BAFTAs four times before I eventually won it. Four times I went along to the glamorous West End of London in my best bib and tucker, four times I had to sit there under the chandeliers and quell my beating heart during the agony of the envelope-opening, and four times I had to compose my 'so happy for the winner and not at all disappointed for myself' expression. Four times! I started to feel like Charlie Brown trying to swing his leg at Lucy's football, only for her to whip it away every time and him to end up flat on his back staring at the clouds.

That said, let's be fair, I lost out to some quality names in those years. In 1986, the winner was Victoria Wood. No shame in coming second in a laughing competition with Victoria Wood, God rest her lovely soul. In 1987, my fellow nominees were Julie Walters, Victoria Wood and Nick Lyndhurst, and we all lost to Nigel Hawthorne for *Yes, Prime Minister*. Again, no great reason to feel the sting of ingratitude there. In 1989 I lost to Victoria Wood again, and in 1990 I lost to the incredibly funny Rowan Atkinson for his role in *Blackadder*, in a year when Barry Humphries was nominated for playing Dame Edna Everage, who is a creation of comic genius. When, to my enormous relief (and especially to the enormous relief of my facial muscles which seemed to have been frozen into an attitude of selfless delight for half my flipping life at this point), I finally won the damn thing in 1991, I had to see off Rowan Atkinson, Dawn French and Nick. Say what you like, those were pretty tough times in which to be trying to go home with a Light Entertainment BAFTA.

What was it Bing Crosby used to say? 'A singer like Frank Sinatra comes along only once in a lifetime. So why did he have to come along in mine?' At the BAFTAs in the 1980s, I was left feeling something very similar. 'Comic actors like Victoria Wood, Nigel Hawthorne, Rowan Atkinson and Barry Humphries come along only once in a lifetime. So why did they all have to choose *my* lifetime?'

Anyway, having ruled out buckets of alcohol as a potential remedy for my bout of foreboding in the long and increasingly anxious days leading up to the National Film Awards of 2017, I just had to live with it. It was, accordingly, a troubled me who joined his wife and daughter in the car which took us from our house in Buckinghamshire to London on the appointed night. Gill and Sophie were resplendent in their finest finery, and I was wearing, as per the invitation, black tie, albeit with, at my wife's suggestion, a rather jaunty and even possibly 'fashion-forward' chequered bow tie, added to the outfit in the hope that it would make me look cheerful and at ease, at least from the chin down.

Thus attired, we arrive at the Porchester Hall, which turns out to be an art deco building on a street corner in Bayswater. Porchester Hall is, of course, just a typing error away from being the Dorchester Hotel, where they stage the BAFTAs. But it's a considerable distance across the typewriter from the O2 Arena, which is where the National Television Awards are staged. Peering uneasily out of the car window, I suddenly have a dim memory of doing some filming somewhere around here, back in nineteen hundred and frozen to death. What the filming was for, though, I can't recall. Was it, possibly, that advertisement for Tetley tea bags where I had to jump into a giant teacup and get bombarded by enormous polystyrene sugar lumps, nearly having my head sliced off my shoulders in the process? Ah, happy days.

What I can see now, though, is a thick crush of people on the pavement, a traffic jam in the vicinity of the front doors. Some of the people in the crush are clearly dressed for the party and trying to get into the venue; other people in the crush are clearly watching the people who are dressed for the party trying to get into the venue, and there seems to be no obvious separation between the two. My anxiety levels rise a little.

We can't get the car near the entrance, on account of the other cars busily discharging their human cargo, and we can't really get out of the car where we are, on account of the crush of people on the pavement. So the driver carries on, travels round the block and makes another pass at it, like a plane trying to perform a tricky landing on a remote airfield in thick fog. This time he manages to find some clean air and a break in the weather and drops in behind another couple of cars, and after some nudging and noodling, we get ourselves up against the kerb, with only the width of the pavement separating us from the entrance and the sanctuary of the venue.

Nevertheless, the width of that pavement still contains

an entire forest of waiting people. The word is out, clearly, on Nick's and my attendance, because lots of these people seem to have photographs of the pair of us dressed as Batman and Robin, and, even before we open the doors, they are already pushing these pictures up against the closed windows of the car for autographs.

Actually, on closer inspection, some of these people appear to be holding whole portfolios of photographs covering every era of the show, suggesting that they are either a) *Only Fools* fans of an especially avid kind, or b) canny entrepreneurs with thriving online businesses selling signed memorabilia, which, it has to be said, you get a lot of these days. Well, good luck to them, either way, I guess. Whatever their backgrounds and purposes, though, I feel I have, alas, no option at this particular moment but to ease open the car door as far as it will go, haul myself upright as far as *I* will go, put my head down as low as *it* will go, and press my way through the lot of them. The fear flowing through my somewhat over-sensitised mind informs me that otherwise, if I stop to sign even one of these brandished pictures, I'll be swamped, trodden flat and subsequently scraped off the pavement by a road cleaner the following Tuesday.

So, using the skills I acquired in twenty quietly impressive years as a club rugby player, I lower my shoulder, crouch slightly to adjust my centre of gravity, and power my way forward through the scrum, lithely fending off pictures of myself in a Batman costume as I go. Actually, I have never played rugby in my life. But it seems to work anyway. Gill, just in front of me, who has also never played rugby, adopts much the same tactics and the two of us arrive, breathless but otherwise intact, inside the door.

It's a great relief – although, almost immediately, as we stand there gathering ourselves, we are both simultaneously gripped by the eerie feeling you get when it creeps over you that you might have forgotten something, but you can't quite put your finger on what it is. What could it be? Did we leave something behind?

Ah, yes! Our daughter!

Sophie, obliged to fight a solo rearguard action, has got bogged down somewhere behind us and is still out there in the rugby match on the pavement. So now I have to go back out through the door, reverse-push my way through the scrum (many of the members of which look slightly surprised to be playing me at rugby again so soon), grab a hold of Sophie, turn round, plough back towards the door again and pull her inside.

So far the evening is shaping up splendidly. You will have heard the expression 'making an entrance'. I think what I just pulled off, on arrival at the fabled Porchester Hall, is what is known as 'making an entrance of yourself'.

Anyway, all three of us are in now, and taking a moment to catch our breath – although my immediate impression is that the lobby of the venue isn't noticeably less crowded than the pavement outside. I can't see any faces I recognise at this point – no obvious sign of Julie Andrews or Joan Collins or Hugh Grant or any of the other promised luminaries. Maybe they've been smuggled in through the back door. But the place is rammed to bursting with people attired in lounge suits and in sparkly frocks, and the lobby is alight with a deafening roar of excited conversation and an equally deafening roar of clashing perfumes and aftershaves. There are many daringly backless dresses, and a number of daringly frontless dresses, too, as well as a couple of dresses which, being both backless, frontless and, to all intents and purposes, sideless, seem to be held aloft by nothing more than spit and positive thinking. Impressive. Many of the men, I notice, are accessorising their black-tie outfits with belts with formidable buckles – big silver ornaments, the size of babies' heads. Is that a thing now? In terms of boundary-pushing sartorial bravery, my chequered bow tie suddenly feels like a somewhat timid gesture.

Anyway, we hover inside the door for a short while, and bewilderment is beginning to settle upon me quite thickly when somebody official-looking fastens onto us, kindly informs me that I'll need to sign in, and points me in the direction of a queue leading to a desk. We then duly stand in this queue until it's our turn to be in front of the young woman seated behind the desk among boxes and sheets of paper and envelopes.

She looks up at me with a smile and says, 'Your name?'

'It's Jason,' I say.

'And your surname?' she says.

'No, that is the surname,' I say. 'Jason. David Jason.'

'OK,' she says. Her eyes are travelling down the lists in front of her. 'And are you a guest or an award nominee?'

Do you suppose it's like this for Nicole Kidman at the Oscars? I very much hope so, but I have my doubts.

'I think I'm supposed to be receiving an award,' I say.

The woman at the desk consults the sheets of names in front of her, running her finger down the page before whipping over to the sheet below, and a few moments pass. I begin to wonder whether I've got the wrong night, which would be a touch awkward. Or the wrong awards ceremony, which would be even more awkward. Maybe it's not my Lifetime they want to honour tonight, but somebody else's Lifetime. Maybe there's been an unfortunate game of Chinese whispers somewhere along the line of communication and they're expecting another David altogether – David Tennant, maybe. Or David Schwimmer from *Friends*. Or David Beckham. Sir David Frost, of course, would have been an easy mistake to make, if you think about it for a moment, except that he's been dead for four years at this point. Still, news doesn't always travel fast, and, however else you want to look at it, four years after they passed would certainly be a tactful time to give someone a Lifetime Achievement Award . . .

But no. The receptionist now seems to have found a reference to me in the paperwork. 'Ah, yes,' she says. She then draws a line in blue biro across the page and dips her hand into the box beside her.

'Would you mind putting this on?'

She holds out a bright yellow wristband made of reinforced paper. Printed on it in black ink is the legend 'National Film Awards 2017 – VIP'. I'm tempted to say, 'But it's yellow – it's going to clash fearfully with my outfit.' Decorum prevails, however, and I say nothing and strap the sticky band round my wrist.

So, wearing a chequered bow tie and, now, a yellow reinforced paper label that formally declares me to be a Very Important Person, I depart the queue with Gill and Sophie, who are similarly tagged, and am pointed in the direction of a broad and tall flight of carpeted steps up which people are herding in large numbers in the direction of the main hall.

As we make our slow progress up the stairs, I cast my eyes around again. Still no sign of Julie, Joan, Hugh, etc. Maybe they're planning a fashionably late arrival. Or perhaps they couldn't wait and were first through the door. Either way, I'm not seeing many faces I know. Or any, actually. But that's OK. Everyone seems very cheerful and my anxieties are beginning to settle. It's going to be all right, isn't it? We've survived the scrum at the entrance, and we're clearly well on the way to the safety of our table. Moreover, blessing of blessings, at least there wasn't one of those red-carpet-style, grin-like-a-berk, photo-opportunity things.

At which point, I cast my eyes ahead of us and notice a platform area set aside at the top of the stairs. It's the red-carpet-style, grin-like-a-berk, photo-opportunity thing.

Well, there's not a lot I can do about it now, is there? This crowded staircase is to all intents and purposes a conveyor belt at the end of which the Very Important Persons (the yellow-tagged ones) are getting siphoned off to pose for pictures in front of a hoarding covered with the names of the evening's sponsors.

I could rip off my yellow tag, of course, and hope to pass through incognito. But no: even if I wanted to give it a try, these wristbands stick fast and it's going to take a pair of kitchen scissors to slice through it, which, foolishly, none of us thought to bring. Or maybe when we get to the top, I could make a break for it – wait my moment, get my head down and bolt, hopefully reaching the other side undetected before the searchlight from the guards' watchtower catches me. Not that there's a searchlight or a guards' watchtower. But you know what I mean.

Again, though – no. There's a girl in a black suit with an earpiece and a clipboard who is busily coordinating this photo operation, diverting people as they reach the top of the stairs, and when we get alongside her she spots my tag before I can run, and moves in. She seems to want all three of us to line up in front of the hoarding for a family shot, but Sophie, brilliantly, does the runner that I had planned to do, and gets herself out of snapping range before anyone can stop her. Nice work. I can only look on admiringly. So that just leaves me and Gill to be ushered queasily in front of the phalanx of photographers. Yet, after a couple of shots, Gill, too, who is no more a fan of this situation than I am, goes rogue and slips away, and I'm left on my own – deserted by my own battalion. You find out who your comrades are at these times.

So, after a spell of awkward smiling to order ('This way, David'; 'Over here, can you, David?') which probably only lasts about twenty seconds, at most, but seems to me to go on for the best part of a week, the girl with the clipboard gently guides me away from the hoarding and further down the platform to where a small group of journalists is gathered behind a rope, clutching notebooks and voice recorders, and apparently keen to hear from me. I'm not sure I've got much to contribute to the rolling international news agenda at this particular juncture, and this wouldn't be the most relaxed or natural set of circumstances at the best of times in which to attempt to have a conversation with a bunch of strangers, but I do my best.

'Excited about tonight?' Yes, I say: very excited. 'What does it mean to you?' Well, I say, obviously it means a lot – it's very nice. 'Will there be any more *Only Fools and Horses?*' No, unfortunately not – because we lost John Sullivan, you see, so there's no writer.

These questions are OK. I'm coping here.

Then somebody asks, 'What do you think about Brexit?'

Reader, I didn't have to go to Afghanistan and hook up with the British Army's Counter IED Task Force to be able to recognise a minefield when one is placed in front of me. And that question, in the context of a snatched interview with the papers at an awards ceremony, is a corking great minefield. Seriously, it wouldn't matter which way I went with it, or how diplomatically I expressed myself. For instance, I could say: 'Well, views differ, obviously, but perhaps there does need to be some kind of tighter control on immigration somewhere down the line.'

Cue likely headline: 'DEL BOY SAYS, "GET 'EM OUT." '

Or I could go completely the other way: 'Well, the results of the UK's referendum on EU membership are in and need to be respected, but I only hope we don't regret walking away from an alliance which has brought sixty years of peace to a previously fractured continent.'

Cue likely headline: 'DEL BOY: ENEMY OF THE PEOPLE.'

As for making a joke – trying to brush the question aside with some little quip or other – forget it. Jokes, you quickly realise, don't translate in these circumstances. They have a horrible habit of turning serious on you, in the cold light of print. It may be that Ronan Keating wrote the manual on impromptu press interviews, when he famously sang: 'You say it best / When you say nothing at all.'

Anyway, I keep it together. I don't go there. Stepping

carefully around this well-laid Brexit-shaped trap, I bumble out something along the lines of, 'Ah, well, we're not really here to talk about that, are we? We're here for a party.'

See the swerve I pulled off there? Admire the work of a master.

Having thereby more or less uncontroversially dispensed with my duties to the world's media, and breathing an enormous sigh of relief, I rejoin Gill and Sophie, raising an eyebrow to convey that their abandonment of me in my hour of need has been duly noted in the record book. Then, at last, we enter the hall.

It's a massive room, set for dinner, with countless large, round tables covering the floor and with a big, gold-painted stage at one end. Again, we don't quite know where to go, but somebody guides us, leading us through the throng and between the chair-backs – and there, already at the table and rising out of their seats to say hello, are Nick and his wife, Lucy. What a joy. I'm so happy to see them. Nick's son, Archie, is there, too – sixteen, the same age as Sophie. The last time I saw Archie he came up to my waist: now, I come up to his. I know, I know: it's what happens if you feed them. Yet how has this boy become a man? Where did this lump of time go?

Nick and I fall easily into each other's company again and our families settle in and the entertainment begins. The set-up is absolutely the familiar one: a string of awards, each with their own special presenter, clips of all the nominees shown on the big screen, then an envelope-opening and a handover and an acceptance speech. The clip packages are pumped out through the PA system at stunning volume – loud enough, I would estimate, to make a charging rhino think again and turn back. But it keeps you on your toes, I guess. *A Street Cat Named Bob* gets Best British Film. There's an award for a crowd-funded movie and overall there seems to be a lot of innovative UK film-making going on, which is a good thing.

Alas, though, you would be quite a long time listing the people who unfortunately could not be with us tonight – including, it turns out, the big stars whose names glittered so prominently on the promotional material. Julie Andrews? Not in the building, apparently. Joan Collins? Somewhere else entirely, it now emerges. Hugh Grant? Otherwise engaged. Catherine Zeta-Jones, whom I really would have loved to bump into? Not around, sadly. Ewan McGregor? Has belatedly discovered a pressing need to stay at home and wash his hair, it seems. Ricky Gervais, bless him, sends a filmed 'thank you' for his Best Comedy prize for the movie *David Brent: Life on the Road*. Only Simon Pegg, who wins the Global Contribution to Motion Picture Award, seems to have made it in time for dinner.

No matter. Nick and I are having a very nice time. The award for Best Drama is sponsored by Blind Pig Cider and, although it does us no credit whatsoever, this detail catches Nick and me at the wrong moment and we lose it for a

while. Much to our further surprise, the half-time entertainment is a troupe of belly dancers. Now, I consider myself
a fairly well-travelled person, whose work has taken him as
far afield as Singapore, Hong Kong, Kuala Lumpur, and
even to Billingham near Middlesbrough. But, in all those
horizon-expanding voyages, this is the first time that I have
witnessed belly dancing in the flesh, done full-on, in all its
remarkable suppleness, and as the performance unfolds, in
every sense, in front of us, in quite spectacular style, I find
myself most intrigued – purely from a professional and
technical standpoint, as a fellow stage performer, you understand. It may be that Nick is as impressed professionally as
I am, but I wouldn't know for sure because he, too, is trying
very hard to appear politely uninterested.

At around 9.50 in the evening, soon after the dessert (an
extremely rich and indeed practically explosive chocolate
bombe, unlikely to be forming part of anybody's calorie-
controlled diet any time soon), Nick and I get our big
moment. Some kind words are said about the lasting effect
and influence of *Only Fools*. They show some clips on the
big screen. The bar-flap sequence is in there, obviously, and
it gets a laugh, as it always seems to. Batman and Robin also
ride again – me and Nick emerging through the mist like a
pair of idiots – and there's laughter for that, too. We
are summoned to the stage separately – me first. Fighting
down the lingering aftermath of the chocolate bombe, I
head up the slightly rickety wooden stairs, step over a

couple of trailing cables and emerge into the lights, where the head of the Malta Tourism Authority, who are the award's sponsor, hands me a tall glass vase with a star at the top and my name on the base. I improvise a few words of thanks, and – really movingly, for me – everybody in the room is on their feet and there's a lot of warmth coming off people which I know isn't just the wine or even the chocolate bombe. I don't, after all, despite my premature fears, feel like anyone is trying to retire me or subtly nudge me in the direction of the garden. On the contrary, I feel buoyed up – ready to accept a major movie project if anybody in the room wants to offer me one. Say what you like about the surrounding faff, but standing on a stage while a roomful of people applauds you for some stupid larking around you did in front of a television camera several thousand years ago is a flattering situation to find yourself in.

I'm then taken backstage to have some more photographs done – though this time the pictures are of me holding the award, which is a bit easier and more purposeful than the earlier situation, with me simply standing there holding myself, as it were. However, these duties mean that when Nick goes up for his award, I'm still out of the room and miss it. Apparently he had prepared a speech, though, which is more than I had. Black mark for me; shown up again. Still, I'm sure Nick covered everything. [*Author clears throat; moves on to next paragraph.*]

By the time I head back across the floor to the table, a

musical interlude is under way, featuring a twenty-voice choir, amplified at a volume which is almost sufficient to chip the plaster off the ceiling. The level of the sound has two consequences. Firstly, when I am taken aside, along the way, by a producer who wants to press a business card into my hand (and who tells me, above the music, that he thinks he has a project in development that is just right for me), he has to lean in so close to introduce himself that I can feel his lips against my ear. Very intimate – as intimate as I have ever been, I can confidently say, with a film producer at an awards ceremony. Secondly, as I pass in front of the stage in order to reach our table, I end up jamming the flat of my hand against my head to protect my eardrum from the PA system which, I belatedly realise, might have looked a bit rude to the singers in question. So let me just be clear: the choir was great. It was only the volume of it.

Soon we will skip the after-party and head to our respective homes, going out the back door this time, to avoid the fuss at the front of the venue – although, actually, when we stick our heads out of the door and look up the side street for our cars, a crowd of autograph hunters appears out of nowhere and forms a thick knot, having got wise to the plan somehow. As Nick and I stand and sign pictures of ourselves from 1983 and other eras, there it is – that question again, the question that both of us get asked pretty much every time we raise our heads in public: 'Will there be any more *Only Fools and Horses?*'

It is, at least, an easy one to answer. There would be more episodes of *Only Fools and Horses* if there was anyone alive who could write them. But there isn't, and nor will there be for as long as John Sullivan is no longer with us. John was one of the greatest scriptwriters I have ever had the pleasure to know – and, among other things, he was a supreme improviser, an utterly brilliant solver of problems that arose along the way. He was always open to any of my thoughts and ideas, which made the process doubly rewarding, but this turns out to be a problem there is no getting around. Making a further contribution since his sad departure has thus far proved beyond even John Sullivan's wildly abundant gifts. I guess everybody meets their limits in the end.

So, no. No, there won't be any more *Only Fools and Horses*. Yet *Only Fools and Horses* carries on – unstoppable, it would appear. And Nick and I each have a 2017 National Film Award to prove it.

# POST-SCRIPT

As I prepare to lay down my clammy pen, the film producer who so warmly caressed my earlobes when I crossed the room on my way back to the table that night at the Porchester Hall has yet to call for a second date. Trust me, though, I'll be waiting by the phone. Indeed, be assured that all plausible job offers will receive due consideration. Of course, you have to be reasonable. My days of diving into a sofa are probably over – though I reckon I could still drop sideways through a bar-flap if called upon to do so. One thing I do know, is that retirement doesn't yet seem to feature in the game-plan. Indeed, if I could be shot back right now through time's misty envelope to my humble beginnings, would I do it all again? As Rowan & Martin used to say, you bet your sweet bippy I would. The whole journey. Point me at it. The paths taken, the paths untaken, the rough, the smooth, and all stations in between. The love of the job is still in there, firing away – the same idiotic determination to succeed. Indeed, I've got this feeling that, even as they're easing my coffin lid into place, if I were to hear a phone ring, I know I'd pop up and say, 'If that's my agent, tell them I'll do it.' I don't seem to be able to stop. Why should that be? No idea. But a very wise man once said it better than I can:

> 'Where it all comes from is a mystery
> Like the changing of the seasons
> And the tides of the sea
> But here's the one that's driving me berserk:
> Why do only fools and horses work?'

What more can I say?

# PHOTOGRAPHIC ACKNOWLEDGEMENTS

In order of appearance:

## First Plate Section

Pages 1-3 © Mirrorpix
Page 4:
- Top © BBC
- Middle © Mirrorpix
- Bottom © BBC
Page 6:
- Top © MirrorPix
- Bottom © BBC
Page 7 © Mirrorpix
Page 8
- Top © Rex/Shutterstock
- Middle and Bottom © Mirrorpix

## Second Plate Section

Page 1:
- Top © BBC
- Bottom © Mirrorpix

Page 2 © Rex/Shutterstock

Page 3:
- Top © Mirrorpix
- Bottom © Rex/Shutterstock

Page 4 © Rex/Shutterstock

Page 5:
- Top © Rex/Shutterstock
- Bottom © Dave Bennett/Getty Images

Page 6:
- Top © BBC

Page 7 © Rex/Shutterstock

Page 8:
- Top © Desmond O'Neill Features Ltd.
- Bottom © Rex/Shutterstock

All other photographs are author's own.

# INDEX

acting: building characters, 69–85, 88–94, 223–5, 234–6; pratfalls, 264–70; with sofas, 267–9
adverts, 79–82, 301
Afghanistan, 1–12
Aghajanoff, Perry, 28–9, 32, 36
Alexander, Bruce, 229, 245
*All the King's Men*, 202–3
Allen, Billy, 59
Allen, Dave, 105
alligators, 165–7
Andrews, Julie, 291, 311
Anholt, Tony, 136
*Are You Being Served?*, 108
Atkinson, Rowan, 299–300
*The Avengers*, 237
awards: BAFTAs, 290, 298–300; DJ as presenter, 1–12; Golden Sausage, 282–3; National Film Awards, 285–315; others, 290–1

BAFTAs, 290, 298–300
Barber, Paul, 100
Barclay, Humphrey, 46

Barker, Joy, 279–80
Barker, Ronnie: character, 277–8; and food, 88; 'get well' letter to DJ, 147; getting into character, 84–5; and *Open All Hours*, 46–7, 271, 277–80; and *Porridge*, 44–5, 278; and *The Two Ronnies*, 46
Baron, Lynda, 274, 275, 280
Baxter, James, 280, 281
BBC: attitude to *Only Fools and Horses*, 104–8, 111–12; Television Rehearsal Rooms (TRR), 87, 94; working with, 226
Beckham, David, 253, 259–70
Bevil, Bob, 51–2, 255–6
*Blackadder*, 299
Bowles, Peter, 105
Branagh, Kenneth, 201
Branson, Richard, 31
Brexit, 308–10
Broadbent, Jim, 55–8, 136
bulletproof vests, 8
*The Bullion Boys*, 82–3
Burt, Guy, 248

Bush, George, Sr, 156
Butt, Ray: background, 47–8; and
    Pearce's death, 113, 114
    AND ONLY FOOLS AND HORSES: at
        awards ceremony, 296–7; casting,
        55, 59–68, 99, 118; creation, 48–9,
        51; leaves, 142; Series 3, 111–12;
        slipped disc means temporary
        withdrawal from producing, 101;
        'To Hull and Back', 136, 138–9

Cambridge Arts Theatre, 17, 18, 22
Camp Shorabak (formerly Bastion), 6,
    10–12
Carry On films, 160–1
cars, 211–16
celebrity perks, 242–3
Challis, John, 100, 102, 141–2, 207,
    258–9
character building, 69–85, 88–94,
    223–5, 234–6
Charles, Prince of Wales, 184–93
Charley's Aunt, 90
Chas & Dave, 109
Cinecittà, 248–9
Citizen Smith, 47, 109
Clarke, Roy, 65, 272–5, 279, 280
Clement, Dick, 45
cockney rhyming slang, 58, 138, 149–51
Coffey, Denise, 179
Cole, Stephanie, 274, 275, 280
Collins, Joan, 291, 311
Comic Relief, 254–6, 270; see also Sport
    Relief
Corbett, Ronnie, 62, 105, 183
Coronation Street, 197
Cotton, Bill, 106–7
Cranham, Kenneth, 99–100
Crosby, Bing, 299–300
Crossroads, 196–7

Dad's Army, 54–5, 197, 288
The Darling Buds of May: Buss Farm,
    217–18; casting, 220; overview,

211–28; Pop, 223–5, 230–1; Pop's
    car, 211–16, 218–20; Series 3,
    226–7; shooting, 222–3, 227;
    strawberry-picking scene, 227;
    viewing figures, 218
Darling Mr London, 267–8
David Brent: Life on the Road, 311
Davies, John Howard, 111–12
Davis, Lt Col. Mark, 12
The Day of the Triffids, 95–6
De Gaye, Phoebe, 70–3, 75
Dear John, 204
Depp, Johnny, 245
Do Not Adjust Your Set, 179
dolls, blow-up, 145–6, 151–5, 157–8
Dow, Tony, 142, 143, 164, 171
Dunn, Clive, 54

Edwards, Gareth, 275
Everett, Kenny, 105

farces, 178–9, 266–9
Ferris, Pam, 211, 213, 216, 220, 221–2
Fletcher, Mandie, 124–5
Foster, Richard, 154–5
Franks, Philip, 211, 213, 216, 220, 221
Freeland, Mark, 271–3
French, Dawn, 299

Galton, Ray, 42
The Generation Game, 108
Gervais, Ricky, 311
Ghostboat, 246–9
Gibb, Barry, 170–2
Gilbert, Jimmy, 49
Golden Sausage award, 282–3
Grant, Hugh, 291, 311
'grass' expression, 58
Gwenlan, Gareth, 101, 114, 164, 165,
    205, 207

Hark at Barker, 46, 61, 70
Harris, Richard, 234
Harry, Prince, 189–90

Hawthorne, Nigel, 299–300
Hazlehurst, Ronnie, 108
Hercules aircraft, 10
Highgrove, 188–93
Hinchcliffe, Gill *see* White, Gill
*The Hitchhiker's Guide to the Galaxy*, 105
Hockley, Derek, 51–2, 76
Holderness, Sue, 100, 167
Hopkins, Anthony, 158–60
Hordern, Michael, 80
Humphreys, Dewi, 275
Humphries, Barry, 299–300

*I, Claudius*, 237
Idle, Eric, 179
improvised explosive devices
    (IEDs), 2
*Iris*, 56
*It's Only Me, Whoever I Am*, 62

Jackson, Peter, 227, 236–7
Jameson, Louise, 20
Jason, David (DJ; born David White):
    and alcohol, 295–8; attractiveness to
    women, 260–1; and awards
    ceremonies, 292–300; background
    and childhood, 9, 24, 41–2, 51–5,
    62–3; early TV work, 46, 61, 70,
    179–80; fame and recognition,
    176–81; favourite sort of TV, 227–8;
    height, 9; interests, 121–2;
    lawnmower accident, 147–8; love of
    accents and voices, 79; and practical
    jokes, 122–36; in rep and farces,
    17–24, *17*, 90–3, 178–9, 266–9; and
    retirement, 289, 317–18; and stunts,
    167–70; and swearing, 146–8; and
    typecasting, 195–8; voice-over work,
    79–82; waxwork model, 249–51; *see
    also individual productions and TV
    programmes by name*
Jason, Gill *see* White, Gill
Jason, Sophie *see* White, Sophie
Jones, Terry, 179

Keating, Ronan, 309
Keith, Penelope, 105
Kennedy, Sarah, 188

La Frenais, Ian, 45
Lawrence, Vernon, 225–6
learning lines, 246
Leaver, Don, 237
Levin, Ira, 258
Lindsay, Robert, 47, 48
Lloyd Pack, Roger, 99–100, 210, 287
Lotterby, Syd, 45, 59–63, 275–6
*Lucky Feller*, 66
Lyndhurst, Archie, 310
Lyndhurst, Lucy, 259, 310
Lyndhurst, Nicholas: awards, 285–92,
    296–7, 299, 302, 310–15; and Gibb,
    172; interests, 121–2; at Lloyd Pack's
    funeral, 100; and Merryfield, 119–20;
    and *Only Fools and Horses*, 65–8, 106,
    111–12, 137, 144, 154, 157, 165; and
    Pearce's death, 113–14; and practical
    jokes, 122–32; public recognition,
    107; relationship with DJ, 121–33,
    257–9; Shakespeare roles, 258; and
    Sport Relief sketch, 253, 257–9, 263;
    and Sullivan's death, 207
Lynn, Jonathan, 19
Lyons, John, 229, 242
MacDonald, Kenneth, 288
McGregor, Ewan, 291, 311
Madame Tussauds, 249–51
Main Wilson, Dennis, 43–4
make-up, *17*, 22
market trader banter, 255–6
Meg (agent), 3–4
Merryfield, Buster, 118–20, 137, 287–8
Miami, 163–72
Mitchell, Bill, 80–1
*Monty Python's Flying Circus*, 179
Morecambe, Eric, 74–5
*Moving*, 99
Murray, Billy, 99
Murray, Patrick, 100

'nark' expression, 58
National Film Awards, 285–315
Nedwell, Robin, 59, 74–5
Nicholls, Sue, 197
Nicholson, Jack, 177–8
*No Sex Please – We're British*, 243
*The Norman Conquests*, 90–2

Ollerenshaw, Maggie, 274, 275, 280
*Only Fools and Horses*: appreciation
    society and annual convention, 28;
    awards, 285–315; BBC attitude,
    104–8, 111–12; cardboard boxes,
    37–9; cast deaths, 113–18, 287–8;
    casting, 49–68; celebrity guest actors,
    158–61, 170–2; Del Comic Relief
    statue, 270; Del's clothes, 34–5,
    69–76; Del's hair, 76–7; Del's
    physical gestures, 77–8; Del's voice,
    79–85; DJ's favourite episode, 30;
    DJ's feelings about now, 209–10,
    287–8; eating during scenes, 88–90;
    end of, 203–10; fan and paparazzi
    attention, 140–4; Grandad, 61, 65–7,
    77, 113–18; language and morality,
    145–58, 255–6; longevity, 285–6;
    memorabilia, 25–6, 29–40;
    neologisms, 149; overview, 26–40,
    49–181; rehearsals, 87–95; Rodney,
    65–8, 77; running jokes, 97; scripts,
    39–40; Series 1, 100–4; Series 2,
    108–11, 126–31; Series 3, 111–12;
    Series 4, 112, 113–18; Series 5, 112;
    Series 6, 112; Series 7, 203–4;
    shooting and practical jokes, 122–44,
    163–72; Sport and Comic Relief
    sketches, 253–70; success, 173–81;
    theme song, 108–9, 318; title, 50–1,
    108; Trigger, 96–100; UKTV
    documentary about, 26–40, 207–9;
    Uncle Albert, 118–20; viewing
    figures, 104, 110–11, 112, 173–5, 204
    EPISODES: 'Ashes to Ashes' (Trigger's
        grandfather's ashes), 35–6, 110;
'Big Brother' (first episode), 65,
    95–6; Christmas specials, 112,
    204–5; 'Danger UXD' (blow-up
    dolls), 145–6, 151–5, 157–8; 'The
    Frog's Legacy' (Christmas special,
    1987), 160; 'Heroes and Villains'
    (Batman and Robin, part of
    Christmas trilogy, 1996), 34,
    98, 142–4, 173, 312; 'It Never
    Rains . . .' (Spanish-based), 30,
    126–31; 'The Jolly Boys Outing'
    (seaside day out), 141–2; 'The
    Losing Streak', 149–51; 'May the
    Force Be With You' (Roy Slater),
    56–8; 'Miami Twice' (Christmas
    special, 1991), 30, 146, 163–72;
    'Modern Men' (part of Christmas
    trilogy, 1996), 173; 'Mother
    Nature's Son' (spring water
    Christmas special, 1992), 33–4;
    proposed Del Boy sixtieth
    birthday special, 205–7; 'A Slow
    Bus to Chingford', 102; 'The
    Russians Are Coming', 102–3;
    'Strained Relations' (Grandad's
    death), 115–18; 'Three Men, a
    Woman and a Baby' (Damien's
    birth), 32–3, 208–9; 'Time on
    Our Hands' (part of Christmas
    trilogy, 1996), 36–7, 173–5; 'To
    Hull and Back' (Holland
    Christmas special, 1985), 31–2,
    135–40; 'A Touch of Glass'
    (chandelier drop), 110; 'Yuppy
    Love' (bar-flap fall), 264–70, 312
*Open All Hours*, 46–7, 63–4, 84–5, 87,
    271, 275–80; see also *Still Open All
    Hours*
Orme, Stuart, 248
*Over the Moon*, 47–8

Palin, Michael, 179
Parker Bowles, Camilla, 184, 189–90
Peake-Jones, Tessa, 100, 117, 208–9

Pearce, Lennard, 65–7, 113–18, 122, 129–30, 288
Pegg, Simon, 311
Piggott-Smith, Tim, 82
Porchester Hall, London, 300–1
*Porridge*, 44–6, 61, 84–5, 278
*Porterhouse Blue*, 198–202
pratfalls, 264–70
'Pride of Britain' Awards, 1–12

*Radio Times*, 176
Red Nose Day, 254–6, 270
Reitel, Enn, 55
*The Relapse*, 17–24, 17
Remembrance Sunday services, 193
Reynolds, David, 226, 238–9, 248
Richardson, Ian, 198–9
*The Rivals*, 18, 66
Rix, Brian, 178
Roache, Bill, 197
*Roger, Roger*, 204
Rolls-Royce vintage cars, 211–16
Royle, Derek, 178

*Seconds Out*, 48
Shardlow, Martin, 101–2
Simpson, Alan, 42
*The Simpsons*, 156
Sims, Joan, 160–1
Sinatra, Frank, 299–300
Siner, Guy, 20
sofas, acting with, 267–9
*Some Mothers Do 'Ave 'Em*, 108
*Sorry!*, 62, 105
Speight, Johnny, 42
*Spitting Image*, 55
Sport Relief, 253–70
*Steptoe and Son*, 42
*Still Open All Hours*: creation, 271–5; Leroy, 280; location, 275–6; overview, 271–83; reception, 281; the till, 279; viewing figures, 281–2
Stocker, Chicky, 50, 76
Strand Theatre, London, 243

*A Street Cat Named Bob*, 311
Strong, Gwyneth, 117
stunts, 167–70
Sullivan, Dan, 253
Sullivan, Jim, 253
Sullivan, John: background, 41–6; blue plaque, 207; character, 64–5; *Dear John*, 204; death, 207; DJ's verdict on, 287, 315; early writing for BBC, 46–8; influences, 42; and Pearce's death, 113, 114, 115; *Roger, Roger*, 204
AND *ONLY FOOLS AND HORSES*: at awards ceremony, 296–7; bar-flap fall, 266; BBC reaction, 105; and celebrity guests, 159, 171; characters, 97–8, 116–17; creation, 46–68, 73, 76; 'Danger UXD', 145–6; DJ–Lyndhurst 'row', 125; language, 149–51; Lyndhurst's birthday cake, 131; Merryfield joke, 120; proposed Del Boy sixtieth birthday special, 205–7; publicity, 103; Red Nose Day sketches, 254; Series 2, 110; theme song, 109; title, 108; 'To Hull and Back', 136

Tate, David, 79
Thatcher, Margaret, 49
Thaw, John, 232–3
*Till Death Us Do Part*, 42
Titchmarsh, Alan, 188, 190
*To the Manor Born*, 105, 108
*The Top Secret Life of Edgar Briggs*, 64, 168–70
*A Touch of Frost*: creation, 231–4; directors, 237; DJ as executive producer, 238–9; DJ's fears about reception, 229–31; first episode, 237–8; Frost, 234–6; location shoots, 242–6; morgue scenes, 241–2; overview, 229–46, 251; and police procedure, 240–1; practical jokes, 241–2; trailers, 239–40

touring, 177–8
*Two D's and a Dog*, 179–80
*The Two Ronnies*, 46

*Veronica's Room*, 258–9
voice-overs, 79–82
Vorderman, Carol, 12, 188

Wallis, Bill, 79
Walters, Julie, 299
*The Waltons*, 156
*Week Ending*, 79
White, Arthur, 200, 229, 245
White, Gill (née Hinchcliffe): and
    Beckham, 259; on *Frost*, 229;
    Highgrove dinner, 184–90, 193; at
    National Film Awards, 298, 300,
    303, 306, 308, 310

White, Sophie: and DJ's waxwork
    model, 250; at National Film Awards,
    298, 300, 303, 306, 307–8, 310
Whiteley, Richard, 188, 191–3
wigs, 22–3, 33
Wilde, Brian, 47
William, Prince, 189–90, 191–2
Wimbledon Film Studios, 257
Wise, Ernie, 74
Wise, Herbie, 237
Wood, Victoria, 299–300
Woodhead, Chris, 155–6

*Yes, Minister*, 19, 108
*Yes, Prime Minister*, 19, 299
Yorkshire Television, 225–6

Zeta-Jones, Catherine, 220–2, 291, 311